Technical Territories

Technical Territories

Data, Subjects, and Spaces in Infrastructural Asia

Luke Munn

University of Michigan Press

Ann Arbor

Published in the United States of America by the
University of Michigan Press
Printed and bound by CPI Group (UK) Ltd, Croydon, CR0 4YY
First published July 2023

A CIP catalog record for this book is available from the British Library.

Library of Congress Control Number: 2023003049

ISBN 978-0-472-07603-1 (hardcover : alk. paper)
ISBN 978-0-472-05603-3 (paper : alk. paper)
ISBN 978-0-472-90337-5 (open access ebook)

DOI: https://doi.org/10.3998/mpub.12584902

An electronic version of this book is freely available, thanks in part to the support of libraries working with Knowledge Unlatched (KU). KU is a collaborative initiative designed to make high quality books Open Access for the public good. More information about the initiative and links to the Open Access version can be found at www.knowledgeunlatched.org.

The University of Michigan Press's open access publishing program is made possible thanks to additional funding from the University of Michigan Office of the Provost and the generous support of contributing libraries.

Cover illustration courtesy iStock.com / Sergey Lahtionov.

Contents

Digital materials related to this title can be found on the Fulcrum platform via the following citable URL: https://doi.org/10.3998/mpub.12584902

Illustrations

Figures

Tables

Acknowledgments

This research was produced as part of Data Centres and the Governance of Labour and Territory, a multiyear Discovery Project funded by the Australian Research Council. Chief Investigators on the project were Professor Brett Neilson, Professor Ned Rossiter, and Associate Professor Tanya Notley, all from the Institute of Culture & Society at Western Sydney University. I want to particularly thank Brett and Ned for taking this emerging researcher onboard, for giving me freedom to pursue different avenues, and for providing insightful feedback on early drafts. Initially focused on data center clusters in Hong Kong, Singapore, and Sydney, the project quickly expanded both physically and conceptually in interesting ways, and reiterated for me how "merely" technical forms shape the lives and livelihoods they intersect with.

Several of these chapters were adapted from earlier articles in academic journals. Chapter 2 is derived in part from "Red Territory: Assembling Infrastructural Power," published in *Territory, Politics, Governance*, October 20, 2020, copyright Regional Studies Association, available online at https://doi.org/10.1080/21622671.2020.1805353. Chapter 5 is derived in part from "Sand, Silica, Silicon: Singapore's Triple Territories," published in *Verge: Studies in Global Asias*, Spring 2021, copyright University of Minnesota Press. And chapter 6 is derived in part from "Twinned Power: Formations of Cloud-Edge Control," published in *Information, Communication, and Society*, August 20, 2020, copyright Taylor & Francis, and available online at https://doi.org/10.1080/1369118X.2020.1808043. Thanks to the editors of those journals and the anonymous reviewers for their insightful and practical feedback that strengthened that material. Thanks also to Elizabeth Demers, Haley Winkle, and all the rest of the crew at the University of Michigan Press for embracing the project and shepherding it through to completion.

Finally, the greatest thanks goes to my own family—Kimberlee, Ari, and Sol—for their care, kindness, and steadfast support, and to my extended family for their encouragement and solidarity. *He aha te mea nui o te ao*—what is the most important thing in the world? *He tāngata, he tāngata, he tāngata*—It is people, it is people, it is people.

—Luke Munn
Tāmaki Makaurau, Aotearoa New Zealand
March 2022

Part I • Technical Territory

1 • Introduction

In Singapore, a sensor ticks rapidly upward, logging the location of individuals connected to a mobile network. Such data will register the trace of the digitally savvy citizen, while excluding others subjects such as the migrant or the elderly. In doing so, it constructs a very particular understanding of national territory.

In Hong Kong, a protestor dons a gas mask, obscuring her face from cameras and the networks they are connected to. She is not only concerned about stopping the capture of this biometric data, but about preventing its transfer to the Mainland. In that territory, one both legally and operationally distinct from the island, her data could easily be weaponized against her.

Deep beneath the Pacific, an undersea cable is switched on, funneling information from one continent to another. Though miles from a state capital or a corporate headquarters, such infrastructure commands a certain territory, governing the data flows that mediate business and social life. While this technical empire is erected from cables and protocols, its operations grant a kind of authority or advantage, conferring a geopolitical edge.

Territories are being reworked. If territories were once a bounded power container, that container is now shot through with the signals and circuits of information infrastructures. Undersea cables blaze high wattage trails through the ocean, delivering media, merging markets, and stitching together zones of connectivity. Data centers act as a nexus, interconnecting partners, channeling data points into pools, and mining these massive repositories for insights. These technical operations offer new vectors for territorialization, allowing it to be extended and reshaped. The stable line of the border may persist, but it is overlaid with more flexible and fluid configurations of power.

Infrastructural empires work for those who erect them. As lives become increasingly dependent on data, power comes to those who best capture and capitalize on it. Information infrastructures lay hold of these flows, coordinating their movement, structuring them toward certain ends, and collecting their value. And yet these interventions do not take place in a peaceful void, but in a fiercely contested milieu—a territorialized world. In this antagonistic space, infrastructures carve out zones of compatibility, enclaves that run according to their standards, their values, and their visions—and not those of their rivals. Powerful public/private actors take up these capacities, further amplifying their control while marginalizing communities and undermining individuals. States grasp these affordances, eager for new tools to advance sovereign dreams and exert strategic influence. In advancing some interests at the expense of others, these "purely" technical infrastructures become both political and geopolitical.

This book explores these "technical territories." It examines how layers of infrastructure come together to create forms of spatialized power. It explores how these technical territories intersect with existing formations and spill over borders, creating strange new topologies. But, above all, it investigates how these territories touch down at the level of the individual, altering the abilities and experiences of their inhabitants. It moves from sand miners in Singapore to asylum-seekers on Christmas Island and protestors in Hong Kong, pointing to the kinds of forces wielded against lives and livelihoods. Technical territories construct new zones where subjects are assembled, rights are undermined, labor is coordinated, and capital is extracted.

Such force is effective precisely because it is often imperceptible, subtle rather than spectacular. Cables are buried from the public eye; data centers are nondescript beige boxes; technical standards are arcane and boring. This is invisibility through banality, a tactic that has seemed to work politically as well as visually. When scanning for the sources of power, these services and systems are overlooked. And yet, as the book will argue, it is here where we should focus. Contemporary power is carried out by design as much as by decree, by protocols as much as by parties. As Keller Easterling stresses, these "dynamic systems of space, information, and power generate de facto forms of polity faster than even quasi-official forms of governance can legislate them."[1] Technical structures rapidly establish wide-ranging rules at scale, while conventional state power lags behind.

In one sense, then, these technical territories peel governance away from government, fulfilling the cloud imaginary of decoupled control and collapsed distance. There is, as Stephen Kobrin argues, "an emerging geographic incongruity between the reach and domain of the territorially defined Westphalian state—as legal jurisdiction, political authority and self-governing democratic community—and the deep and dense network of transnational economic relations that constitute the early twenty-first century world economy."[2] But rather than floating in some nebulous ether, these territories remain partially bound to their political and geographical roots. These infrastructures are dug into the soil, they are grounded in corporate structures and legal frameworks, and they rest on local sociocultural norms. Indeed, technical territories exploit this tension to their benefit, drawing upon the rights that accompany a jurisdiction, for example, while simultaneously venturing beyond it.

The scenarios explored across these pages are drawn from my work on "Data Centres and the Governance of Labour and Territory," a multiyear project funded by the Australian Research Council. I worked as a research associate on this project over a two year period, examining how data center clusters in Hong Kong, Singapore, and Sydney reformatted power across Asia's geographies. My contribution focused initially on some key questions surrounding these infrastructures. Where were cables located? How did they link up with data center clusters? How did software and hardware standards influence these operations? How were these infrastructures financed and constructed? Who were their clients, and what did they use them for?

To answer these questions, I dove into the literature surrounding these objects. Rather than a "systematic" survey of journal articles per academic convention, this meant combing through the "gray literature" of corporate websites, technical specifications, financial filings, government documents, and industry presentations. An environmental permit revealed the exact contours of a new high-speed cable. A financial report disclosed a cloud company's top customers (and how much each spent). By synthesizing this material, I developed a baseline understanding of the information infrastructures at these sites: their clients and histories, architectures and affordances.

And yet if Hong Kong, Singapore, and Sydney were the sites of focus, it quickly became apparent that tracing these infrastructures would mean leaving tidy city boundaries. Cables link up with other cables; data centers hook into cloud zones that are increasingly global. Indeed, to view these elements in isolation would be to miss the point: they aim to connect places, to connect markets, to connect key nodes to form denser networks. Such technical territories are not present everywhere equally; but neither do they obey the neat lines of the nation-state. The result is that these initial sites form the backdrop to a wider story, a larger narrative that sprawls across what we might call "infrastructural Asia." The chapters here reflect this oscillation in scale, zooming in and out between local conditions and national visions, between a single cable and the distributed cloud, or between individuals and the wider industry.

Along with messy scales, another early insight was the messy interplay between materialities and imaginaries. If the gray literature above set out the technical specifications of data centers and cables, it also gestured to the broader visions surrounding these objects. Following this thread, I started to immerse myself in the voices and viewpoints of the industry. I began listening to the "#ilovedatacenters" podcast and became a regular visitor of popular industry websites like Data Center Knowledge, Data Center Dynamics, and particularly Data Center Frontier: "charting the future of data centers." The voices here highlighted the distinct visions that were both championed and contested. Hyperscale was taking over; hybrid cloud would solve your problems; edge computing would usher in new innovations. While these imaginaries were certainly based at some level on material infrastructures and technical affordances, they also moved over and ahead of them, attaining investments, organizing labor, and directing corporate plans. If data infrastructures were underpinned by low-level protocols, they were also shaped by big-picture paradigms. This book folds in this insight, striving to ground its analysis in empirical and technical detail while remaining attentive to the conceptual and political visions that attend them.

However, the main insight, as the project title of "governance of labor and territory" had anticipated, was how these "merely technical" infrastructures were always already political. Infrastructures privileged some populations and excluded others. They amplified state power while undermining the agency of individuals. They shaped labor, pooled capital, and unlocked new modes of control. Such power was not theoretical but fundamentally operational, embedded in systems and enacted at scale. Territory, as the next section will discuss, reflects a desire to foreground the political within the infrastructural, to keep these power asymmetries and social inequalities front and center.

Territory as Approach

Infrastructures, like other technological architectures, often stress their apolitical qualities. According to their promotional material and press kits, they are carrier neutral, agnostic about the clients and content they support. Indeed, the gray literature surrounding these objects is often gray in tone, a combination of highly technical specifications with boilerplate business bromides, stripped of any political tinge. Earnings are up, new spaces are coming online, the future looks bright. Both problems and their solutions are seen through a narrow technocratic lens. The focus is on efficiency and resiliency; the concerns are latency, power redundancy, and network throughput.

Territory offers a framing device that pushes back against this supposedly disinterested rhetoric. Territory is occupied space, a jurisdiction that exerts a certain force on its subjects. Territory is strategic space, one that provides an advantage to those who control it. And territory is contested space; it is never guaranteed, but must be constantly maintained against external forces. Rather than smooth and effortless, territory is spiky, highlighting the frictions and antagonisms that permeate this infrastructural power. The scenarios presented here—from political protest through to environmental violence and edge-based surveillance—follow this logic. While they certainly emerge from particular places and certain research material, they were also pursued in part because they are controversial and consequential. They aim to show the sociopolitical fallout of these technologies, their darker impacts. Such impacts are often obscured, hidden beneath layers of banal corporatism and technical rhetoric. As a framing device, territory focuses on these critical operations and important implications. It stresses the stakes of infrastructural power.

Territory, of course, has a long lineage. Stuart Elden, in his exhaustive genealogical treatise, *The Birth of Territory*, has demonstrated how the concept evolved over hundreds of years. "The idea of a territory as a bounded space under the control of a group of people, usually a state," he argues, "is therefore historically produced."[3] The divergent versions of what territory might mean have converged and calcified into the concept understood in the present. Indeed, the term has solidified to the point where it is often used without reflection or consideration. As Elden notes, in disciplines such as political theory and international relations, territory often remains assumed and uninterrogated. And yet, if Elden's genealogical work draws out the multiplicities of this concept over time, it too arrives ultimately at a stable and rather limited definition, where the state and the land both continue to play decisive roles in what constitutes a territory.

In *Territory beyond Terra*, editors Kimberley Peters, Philip Steinberg, and Elaine Stratford Kim critique this constrained vision of territory. Territory is often presupposed on fixed borders and stable terrain. Yet increasingly, observe the editors, "economic activity and political power are exercised in spaces that are neither static nor 'grounded' surficial units of land."[4] Contemporary conditions introduce distinct new modes of power; contemporary technologies usher in a novel set of conditions. But theorizations of territory have largely failed to acknowledge or include these shifts, blunting their analytical edge. "Today's political technologies of territory, which emerged in the context of continental (and specifically European) land masses," concludes the trio, "are inadequate for the spaces that increasingly are subjected to modern forms of governance."[5] While the contributions in their volume are more ecologically rather than technologically inspired, their challenge is nevertheless valuable. Framings of territory based upon historically derived norms need to be reconsidered, updated, or even supplanted by new understandings.

For *Logistical Asia* editors Brett Neilson, Ned Rossiter, and Ranabir Samaddar, a contemporary understanding of territory begins by acknowledging the key role of logistical practices in the present. Logistical regimes circulate objects, organize labor, and extract capital, producing new forms of spatial order. If such territories continue to intersect with the state in complex ways, from economic policies and border control to government initiatives, they also exhibit an array of new dynamics, where the imperatives of transnational corporations and the movements of global flows need to be accounted for. "Understanding the varieties of political order, power, and space that such installations generate means documenting how logistical practices can reconfigure territory in ways that rival and parallel the traditional territoriality of the nation-state."[6] From tracking shipping containers in Kolkata to unraveling e-waste in Hong Kong, the essays in their volume demonstrate the challenges, but also the productive insights, to be gained by grappling with these territorial forms.

While this study overlaps in many ways with such logistical concerns, we might home in even further on the computational and the infrastructural. Benjamin Bratton's sprawling volume *The Stack* interrogates the contemporary relationship between software and sovereignty, examining in particular the geopolitics of the cloud. Over several chapters, Bratton outlines the nomos of the earth as understood by political theorist Carl Schmitt. For Schmitt, the ground of politics is the literal ground—political sovereignty arises from the strict delineation of a nation's soil and the administration of activities that take place within it. Yet, as Bratton notes, the emergence of informational technologies and global platforms in the present day mean that this Schmittian understanding must be updated. "If the space of planetary-scale computation is a new kind of 'free soil,'" argues Bratton, "then that 'soil' is land, sea, and air all at once, equally tangible and ephemeral. It can be both inside the line of the Westphalian state and its internal legal optics but outside its borders and sovereignty."[7] Rather than merely erasing jurisdictional lines that were once established and assumed, such technologies introduce a new flexibility, allowing them to be amplified or undermined, intensified or obfuscated.

These technical infrastructures seek to command space, to establish dominance over a particular channel or standard, and to assert their vision over and against that of others. In that sense, it is useful to think of territorializing as a general set of techniques or practices that can be carried out by public or private actors. While states can certainly leverage these tactics, so can global telecommunication companies, investment consortiums, or even tech startups, albeit with different abilities at their disposal. David Storey refers to these as "territorial strategies" that politicize space in their "attempts to achieve particular outcomes, to exert (or resist) control."[8] Technical territories push and pull, ordering the world and jostling with others in a bid for primacy and position.

Through their operations in the world, technical systems may expand the agency of some (e.g., citizens) while restricting the movements or abilities of others (e.g., migrants). They may extend a particular corporate or national empire while gnawing away at the influence historically enjoyed by others. In these brief examples, which will be expanded in subsequent chapters, we can already get a glimpse of power shaping the subject, pressing down on a person with a distinct race, gender, identity, and nationality. Lives are contoured by territorial strategies, opened up to new possibilities or shut down and shunted in various ways. While technical territories may sprawl across the globe, their impacts are felt by peoples and communities at an everyday level. This is the reason for including "subjects" in the book's title, and one that remains a focal point, even as I attend to the complexities of database structures, cellular stations, and latency speeds. Technical territories can be both geopolitical and personal, touching down at the level of the individual.

What Lies Ahead

Part I of this book introduces technical territories. After sketching the initial concept in this introduction, chapter 2 provides an extensive example. In the last few years, Chinese technology firms such as Huawei have steadily assembled layers of informational architecture, financing new undersea cables, constructing hyperscale data facilities, and claiming thousands of technical patents. From sea to cloud and fog, the chapter explores the influence exerted at each of these layers. For many commentators, these infrastructures are the front in a new geopolitical battle, advancing the sovereign visions of Sino actors while eroding the historical influence of the West. Yet rather than a simple expansion, the chapter shows how these technical territories take strange new forms. Dialoguing with work from Louise Amoore and Saskia Sassen, the chapter discusses how these infrastructural operations both complicate and update conventional theorizations. From software to standards, technological infrastructures exert territorial influence.

Part II of the book focuses on the instrumentalization of these new capabilities—how to do things with territory. The case studies here, while disparate in content, are linked by a common theme of asymmetric power. Those with the rights, land, labor, and capital to command infrastructural operations use them to reinforce their command over social and political life. Technical territories become a means to buttress existing hegemonies while undermining the agency of already marginal groups.

Chapter 3, "Countering the Protestor," begins in Hong Kong. The special administration region has been rocked by massive protests following a proposed extradition bill. Yet, for protestors, the extradition of biometric and other identifying data to the Mainland is also a major concern. The chapter traces a notional scenario of this "data extradition" by drawing together protest accounts with existing data infrastructure in the region. A protestor's face is captured in Hong Kong, transmitted across the border as data, and processed in the Mainland, with its distinct set of legal and computational conditions. Underpinned by infrastructure, the circulation of information to another territory changes the conditions of data, opening up a potentially devastating set of new capacities that can be wielded against subjects. Far from abstract, territorial movement of data could enable its weaponization, with consequences for those individuals deemed to be dissidents.

Chapter 4, "Filtering the Migrant," shifts to Christmas Island. The island is home to the Immigration Detention Centre, where asylum-seekers are held while their applications are processed. Yet the island has recently become a hop point for both the Australia-Singapore and Indigo-West undersea cables, infrastructures aiming to connect the island with the rest of the world. For the asylum-seeker, this territory is designed to arrest their progress, to immobilize their bodies, and to exclude them from the "nation." For the already legitimate citizen, the same territory promotes the circulation of information and their inclusion within broader circuits of capital. Living side by side, the asylum-seeker and the villager nevertheless experience very different conditions. The chapter thus argues that territory is not a monolithic legal zone that treats all subjects equally, but rather a filter that enacts state values, integrating some while expelling others.

Chapter 5, "Constructing the Nation," travels northward to Singapore. For Singapore, sand has long provided the material basis for land reclamation, literally expanding the country's conventional "territory" grain by grain. However, the silica of fiber optic cable is another way that the country has attempted to enlarge its global footprint. Early on in its formation, it embraced the vision of an "intelligent island," a tiny yet hyperconnected territory that could command outsize influence on the world stage. More recently, the silicon of processors and cloud-computing have driven its dreams of becoming a "Smart Nation." In this vision, by drawing on sensors and millions of data points, subjects can be assembled and state services optimized with the running of a query. Yet who counts in this territory remains a key question. The chapter demonstrates how territories can be both powerful and pathological—in marching into a hyperconnected future, the island-nation leaves behind marginalized noncitizens and damaged environments.

Finally, part III of the book looks briefly to the future. Chapter 6 explores how, across Asia and beyond, a major shift is underway from the cloud to the so-called edge. The deluge of data produced by millions of connected devices over the next few years cannot be accommodated by the centralized cloud model, and will need to be processed closer to the source. In effect, the territory of computing—and the governance that attends it—needs to be extended into the nooks and crannies of the everyday, from neighborhoods and shopping malls down to homes and single bodies. If this territorial shift is an extension, it is also a recalibration, supplementing the data empires of the past with a distinctly different architecture. Lighter and more localized, edge territories present new ways to extract data and undercut the political agency of individuals.

Such technical territories take strange new forms and exhibit novel modes of operation. This book does unpack some general properties of these territories, showing how they differ from the inherited political orders that have come before them. Yet the aim here is not to "solve" the concept of territory with an all-encompassing theorization, but instead to work up territories as a productive problem. The study of territories "should not be deduced axiomatically from disciplinary conventions, requirements, agendas, or common sense," asserts Andrea Brighenti, but "should emerge piecemeal through engaged problematizations and critical explorations."[9] Contemporary technologies frustrate former assumptions and fracture long-held relations, forcing formations to be rejigged. My goal is to crowbar into these cracks rather than smooth them over with theory. What kind of capacities do these infrastructures offer? How are these affordances spliced into existing formations of power? And how does this territorial force manifest in the everyday lives of subjects?

From Singapore to Sydney, this book will show how spatialized power intrudes on these lives, altering labor, transforming environments, ordering practices, and shaping the experience of its inhabitants. The conditions produced within such spaces are not neutral or universal, but motivated and distinct. They assume a specific understanding of the world, advance a certain set of interests, and privilege particular values. Here, information is captured, parsed, and recirculated, rapidly and often invisibly. Such politics exerts significant force precisely because of its silent, structural qualities. It is functional, not rhetorical, procedural, not theoretical, maintaining asymmetries of power as a matter of routine. If technical operations construct worlds, they are undeniably political worlds.

In foregrounding the political stakes of these operations, this text hopes to contribute to two distinct strains of scholarship. On the one hand, it strives to "mediatize" political theories, updating conventional understandings of territory to account for contemporary technologies and their ability to create formations that govern spaces and shape the agency of subjects in significant ways. On the other hand, it seeks to "politicize" infrastructure studies and media theory, showing how, in capturing and steering data, information infrastructures are able to intensify inequalities, forging novel political conditions and new political subjects. Reasserting our agency within this political space requires understanding these operations and engaging critically with them. New conditions need new interventions. To explore how these operations engender spatial power, the next chapter turns to a case study of Huawei, tracing how it has assembled a technical territory, layer by layer.

2 • Assembling Technical Territory

In May 2019, Chinese electronics firm Huawei was blacklisted by the US government. While the corporation was multinational, the Trump administration believed it maintained close ties with Beijing, and that this undue influence would lead to backdoors, vulnerabilities, or other surveillance mechanisms being embedded into future information technologies.[1] The blacklisting triggered a flurry of activity: supply chains reworked, new manufacturers located, contracts made and lost. The event signals a growing awareness that networks and telecommunications have become key sites of contestation for security and intelligence. Infrastructures are critical and influential.

But what does it actually mean to speak of influence in this context? How might technical infrastructures exert force over subjects and spaces? And what kind of new territorial forms emerge as a result? These are the key questions this chapter pursues, investigating how technical infrastructures enact new forms of territorialization. From financing new undersea cables to constructing hyperscale data facilities and claiming thousands of 5G patents, Chinese technology firms like Huawei have steadily assembled layers of informational architecture. For many commentators, these infrastructures constitute the front lines of a new battle, where control over the production, transmission, and mediation of information confers a certain geopolitical advantage. They enact and extend a China-centered technical territory while eroding the assumed influence of the West. From software to standards, technological infrastructures exert territorial influence. However, rather than simple expansion, the territories enacted by such infrastructural operations take strange new forms. In drawing on local norms and capacities while also venturing beyond them, these forms of spatialized power complicate conventional understandings.

If the last chapter briefly introduced the concept of technical territories, this chapter paints a portrait of one "on the ground," exploring how it is constructed piece by piece. The Huawei blacklisting has seen much press.[2] Yet many of these analyses have remained at a broad and rather conventional level, couching the event in terms of the usual East/West binaries and Washington/Beijing rivalries. Rather than sweeping statements and national politics, this chapter approaches these questions by zooming into a single location in Hong Kong—Tseung Kwan O—and exploring its particular technical affordances. By examining its networks, facilities, and platforms, the chapter investigates how territorialization proceeds through infrastructural operations. Moving across the zones of sea, cloud, fog, and tide, I develop a portrait of this "technical territory" as a particular form of spatialized power and outline the kinds of influence it exerts.

The term "technical territories" points toward contemporary information technologies as an increasingly influential and political site, where activities and identities are mediated through software, platforms, and services. Yet if technical territories are certainly digital they are also highly material, comprised of copper and cabling, data centers and cell towers. If technical territories are geographical they are also topological, with their networks and operations extending far beyond their immediate facilities. And if technical territories are enacted they are also contested, with authority being challenged at operational and infrastructural levels. Technical territories contribute to theoretical conceptualizations by productively complicating them, developing a messy, media-aware portrait of spatialized power.

Territory is strategic space, providing an advantage to those who control it. As Jonathan Hillman observes, the design and construction of infrastructure "provides an avenue for setting standards, transferring technology, and collecting intelligence," while the ownership and operation of infrastructures "can be leveraged for deeper intelligence collection and to restrict or deny a competitor's access."[3] If the telegraph lines and shipping lanes of earlier periods conferred a degree of geopolitical influence, the same holds true for contemporary data infrastructures. These systems allow data to be captured, stored, and recirculated, rapidly and often invisibly. And yet far from being neutral or universal, their operations are motivated and distinct. They assume a specific understanding of the world, advance a certain set of interests, and privilege particular values. As lives become increasingly mediated through this data, the control of its production and circulation becomes a key political hinge.[4]

To a certain extent, the territorialization-via-infrastructure explored here can be understood in the broader context of China's Belt and Road Initiative or BRI. Belt and Road is a global development strategy announced by the government in 2013 and underpinned by a vast array of ambitious infrastructure projects. Digital or informational infrastructures have become a key element of this national strategy. As Hong Shen asserts, the "China-centered digital Silk Road" has "expanded its influence and control over transnational network infrastructures" and has risen to become "a critical component of BRI."[5] Financing and building out this digital network not only links China to neighbors and the world, but establishes a degree of ownership and control over the submarine, satellite, and terrestrial connections themselves. These infrastructures seek to promote financial growth in the region and simultaneously advance certain political interests in the international arena, to realize an imaginary that is both geoeconomic and geopolitical.[6] For some, these regional and global moves progress naturally from successes on the Mainland. As Nadège Rolland suggests, the transcontinental Belt "will enable China to continue to use its traditional tools of central government investment in infrastructure executed by state-owned companies, this time outside already saturated Chinese territory."[7] In this sense, infrastructure is not merely the material pipes and cables, but the implementation of a model or method that has first been tested domestically.

However, here we should stress the distinction between imaginary and infrastructure, between vision and implementation. The influence exerted by technical infrastructures may not necessarily conform to state dreams, nor can the "territory" enacted by these operations be found on a map of grand BRI schemes. In digging into the specificity of technical infrastructures, we inevitably encounter complications and negotiations. Territory is contested space; rather than given, it must be constantly maintained. The focus on force and enactment here builds on what John Agnew has termed effective sovereignty. For Agnew, territory was never a fixed and bounded space; neither was the authority over it guaranteed or presumed. Instead of de jure sovereignty, Agnew argues that "de facto sovereignty is all there is when power is seen as circulating and available rather than locked into a single centralized site such as 'the state.'"[8] Effective sovereignty places an emphasis on the practical over the theoretical; it foregrounds the material rather than the legal. Using the language of Stephen Krasner, who differentiated the "script of sovereignty" from the "rules of sovereignty,"[9] we might say that effective sovereignty cannot be assumed, but must be incessantly performed. If technological infrastructures now lie "at the heart of global governance dynamics,"[10] then how is this performance carried out? If power is circulating and available, how is it made operational?

To explore how territory is made operational, I focus on the Tseung Kwan O Industrial Estate in Hong Kong, or TKOIE. Densely connected and filled with data centers, the TKOIE has become a critical nexus for telecommunications infrastructures in the region. An analysis of this site revealed the rapid rise of Chinese-affiliated companies—Huawei in particular—both here and beyond. To follow this infrastructural empire, this chapter draws on the TKOIE while progressively expanding the scale of analysis in each section. "Sea" examines how submarine cables connected to the TKOIE extend territory and contribute to a broader geopolitics of critical infrastructures. "Cloud" investigates TKOIE's data centers to consider how cloud computing complicates traditional understandings of territory. "Fog" explores Huawei's dominance of global technical standards as a new path for influencing territory. And "Tide" demonstrates how infrastructures enable strange new territorial formations, extending in this case to Africa. These sections strive to unpack the conditions instantiated by infrastructural technologies—to connect technical operations to potential political influence.

Sea

Infrastructure begins underwater in the form of 11 submarine cables connected to Tseung Kwan O. Submarine cables are cables laid along the seabed that carry electricity between two points. Modern cables are composed of fiber optics and wrapped in layers of protective sheathing to prevent damage. Initially cables carried telegraph information, and later on telephone calls, before taking on their present role of transmitting the data communications that dominate today's signal traffic. Indeed, while satellites often predominate in the popular imagination, submarine cables continue to carry up to 99 percent of all international telecommunications.[11]

Far from being a legacy technology, then, cables are critical infrastructures. Nicole Starosielski suggests that cables matter for four reasons.[12] Cables support media, and media, in turn, drives the construction of new data infrastructures. Cables alter the speed of data circulation, or what Starosielski calls the "temporality of information exchange," enabling lower latency for some, higher lag for others. Cables "implicate users within new and unseen structures of power," facilitating new mechanisms for censorship and new intrusions on privacy. And cables "perpetuate imbalances in media production and consumption," reinforcing a digital divide between those who have access to information and services, and those who do not.

If cables span the globe, they connect some points far more than others. "Rather than extending uniformly across space," asserts Starosielski, "cables have often remained embedded in existing geographies, and their effects on media industries, user experiences, and the politics of circulation occur unevenly around the world."[13] The asymmetric geography of cables emerges from the lineage of telegraph cables, a history inextricably bound up with colonialism. Cables were often placed along well-traveled pathways that linked the ports and colonies of a particular empire. Starosielski describes this "copper cable colonialism" as a trend in which "the geography of telegraph routes in the late nineteenth century followed transportation and trade routes, many of which had been pioneered by British colonial investment and served to support existing networks of global business."[14] The paths of telegraphs closely adhered to the paths of existing trade.

Telegraph cables were seen as a way to convey critical information from the colony to the motherland. Even at this early stage, there was an awareness that ownership of this infrastructure meant obtaining a competitive edge, whether for a national corporation or a nation-state. In a chapter titled the "Imperial Telecommunications Network," Daniel Headrick observes that the submarine telegraph cable, like other inventions, was "also an instrument of power, so it is not surprising to find it intertwined with the power struggles of the time: private enterprise and governments; the dominance of the Western nations over the non-Western world."[15] Laying copper meant shrinking space, a clear advantage for those developing empires, whether political or commercial in nature.

Yet if cables are rooted in a colonial past, their construction remains highly significant in the present. The production of more data has meant continuous demand for more capacity. As a result, the construction of submarine cables has accelerated significantly in recent years. Between 2013 and 2017 alone, the cable industry added an average of 32 percent capacity annually on major submarine cable routes.[16]

One of the recent entrants into this space has been Huawei Marine, a joint venture of Huawei Technologies and Global Marine Systems. While Huawei Marine is a relatively new player, only founded in 2008, already by 2012 its contracts included the ASSC-1 submarine cable linking Perth to Singapore, the BDM cable system linking Indonesia with Malaysia, and the Suriname-Guyana submarine cable system.[17] The timeline below (fig. 1), constructed from press releases and industry documents, charts Huawei Marine projects throughout the years. Beginning at a steady pace with cables like Hannibal and TECS, more projects were rapidly added to the company's portfolio, culminating in a flurry of submarine cables completed in the last few years, from Guinea to Greenland, Somalia to Singapore. Currently, the global map on the company's website lists 90 projects with a combined length of 50,000 kilometers.[18]

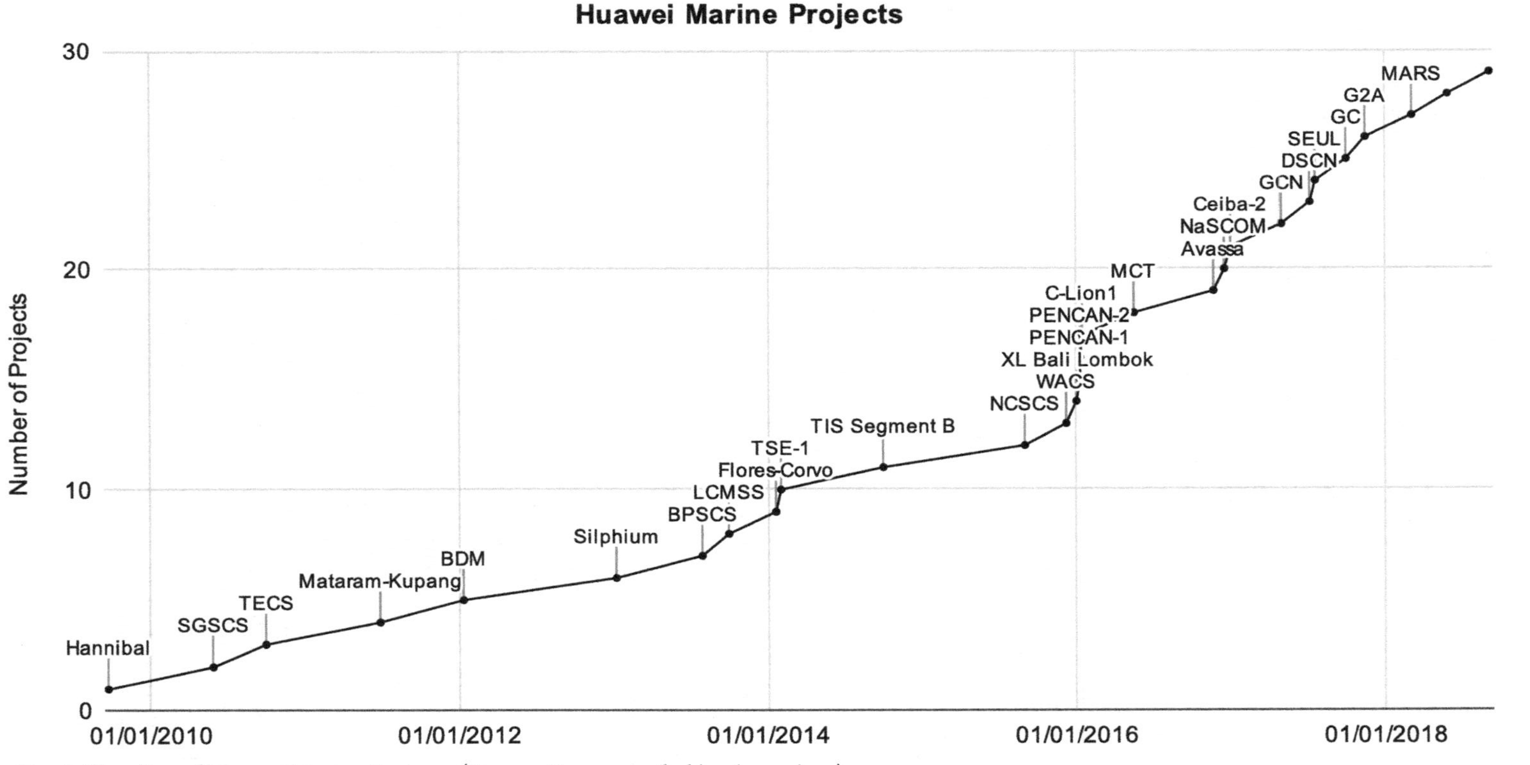

Fig. 1. Timeline of Huawei Marine Projects. (*Source:* Data compiled by the author.)

Alongside involvement in cable construction, other cable projects are tied to Chinese companies through financing. To raise the significant sums of investment required by a cable project, stakeholders typically form a funding consortium. For example, China Unicom, China Telecom, and China Mobile are three state-owned telecommunications providers listed as owners of the new SeaMeWe-5 cable connecting Europe, the Middle East, and Southeast Asia.[19] While these companies participate less directly, each company's capital investment still means they retain an ownership stake in the completed cable. Due to these substantial investments, noted cybersecurity analyst Stacia Lee, "between 2016 and 2019, Chinese companies will participate in 20% of all cable construction projects, over half of which take place outside the South China Sea."[20]

Taken together, the construction and financing of cable projects by Chinese companies presents a counter-movement to the colonial history of cable development dominated by Western empires such as the United States and Britain. Indeed, even by 2007, observed Edward Malecki and Hu Wei, the geography of submarine cables had evolved, signaling a shift to Asia.[21] Such investments seek to streamline the circulation of information, maintaining pace with the dual demands for larger data volumes and lower latency. Owning and constructing this infrastructure means retaining substantial degrees of control over such circulation. These projects, as mentioned earlier, dovetail into broader schemes such as the vast Belt and Road Initiative, which "seeks to facilitate flows of labor, goods, and raw materials across continents and oceans under conditions that advance Chinese economic interests."[22]

However, these moves to own or operate cables do not go uncontested, but are countered by cable systems constructed by US companies. In 2012 Facebook and Google banded together to finance the Pacific Light Cable Network, a 12,800 km cable running between Manhattan Beach in Los Angeles and Tseung Kwan O in Hong Kong.[23] The cable was explicitly designed to support Google Cloud customers situated across the two regions. Operational since 2018, the cable is currently the largest capacity trans-Pacific line, with a bandwidth of 120 terabytes per second. Indeed, the cloud giant claims the cable can carry up to 80 million simultaneous high-definition video calls.[24] Similarly, the HK-G cable, running directly from Tseung Kwan O to Guam, will be financed by Google through its subsidiary RTI Connectivity. The financial capital poured into these projects signals a growing awareness of hard infrastructures by cloud providers, a new push to build large network backbones that are dedicated exclusively to their own cloud services.

These investments foreground how submarine cables have become critical infrastructures. Drawing upon a leaked diplomatic cable, Sue Roberts, Anna Secor, and Matthew Zook discuss a map of sites around the world deemed critical to the US: "Global communication infrastructure dominates the map, with more communications locations than the number of shipping, port, minerals, and industrial sites combined," the researchers note. "Over 70 communication-related locations (landfall for undersea cables, satellite ground stations) are identified."[25] For those in the security and intelligence sectors, if infrastructures are critical, their relationship to territory is nevertheless straightforward. According to one former head of security, the failure of American corporations to match the rapid rise of Huawei Marine has meant that the United States "cedes space to China."[26] In this military framing, critical infrastructures are territorial choke points, strategic beachheads that hold or cede space. Losing control over critical infrastructures means losing territory.

Given this understanding, cable construction has been framed as a new kind of informational arms race. A recent article proclaimed that the ocean presents a new front "in the battle between the U.S. and China over control of global networks that deliver the internet."[27] For these commentators, control over cable infrastructure translates to control over the vital information that traverses it. The transatlantic cable, Project Express, provides one brief example of these growing geopolitical stakes. In 2012, Hibernia Networks awarded Huawei Marine with the contract to construct a new, four-fiber pair cable from New York to London, specifically designed to provide a low-latency link between these major financial centers.[28] However in September of the same year, the Permanent Select Committee on Intelligence of the US House of Representatives released a report suggesting that the "increased access to the telecommunications market" by Chinese firms posed a potential security risk.[29] Driven by these nationalist anxieties, major clients who had once backed the project began pulling their support, and in early 2013, Hibernia announced that Huawei would no longer contract for the project; instead, TE Subcom, a US-based company, had been selected as an alternate vendor.[30] This vignette demonstrates how, for cybersecurity analysts and policy makers, cable systems have become critical infrastructures with significant implications for national security, offering a foothold into the flows of data that increasingly underpin economic and political stability.

Yet if Project Express was "obviously" a Trojan horse for its critics, it was also an anomaly. The national affiliations and territorial claims of cable infrastructures are rarely so cleanly defined. Cable consortiums often comprise up to a dozen companies or state-owned enterprises. For instance, the consortium for the Southeast Asia Japan Cable, which connects to Tseung Kwan O, is made up of 13 different players, placing Google next to state-owned enterprises like China Telecom, Japanese firms like KDDI, and Indonesian interests such as Telkom Indonesia. Such alliances complicate the typical image of head-to-head rivalries and crushing the competition. Clearly each stakeholder retains its own identity, its own national affiliations. These visions and values may in fact be deeply incompatible with each other. And yet the benefits of infrastructure can only be achieved (and paid for) collectively. As Keller Easterling notes, these public and private players alternate "between competitive and cooperative stances in order to leverage goals" that benefit all parties.[31] The result is a strategic truce, a temporary alliance. The model here is collaboration rather than all-out domination.

The Asia Pacific Gateway (APG) cable is another major undersea cable that connects to Tseung Kwan O. The APG consortium includes Facebook, CAT Telecom, China Telecom, China Mobile International, China Unicom, Chunghwa Telecom, KT Corporation, LG Uplus, NTT Communications, StarHub, Global Transit, Viettel, and VNPT.[32] Here, US companies such as Facebook are partnered alongside state-owned Chinese enterprises like China Telecom and China Unicom. Alongside these investors, NTT Communications, or the Nippon Telegraph and Telephone Corporation, is a major Japanese corporation, while Viettel is Vietnam's largest mobile network operator. From social media platforms to legacy telcos, the APG forces an encounter between diverse stakeholders, each with their own visions and values.

To complicate ownership and influence further, the landing station for the APG cable has been constructed by China Mobile. Typically a small room located close to the shoreline, cable landing stations are nevertheless critical facilities where undersea cables literally surface and are connected into mainland telecommunications infrastructures. Landing stations are crucial "choke points"[33] through which all cable traffic passes before being routed to a diverse set of agencies, companies, and institutions. For precisely this reason, as the Edward Snowden revelations in 2013 disclosed, cable landing stations are key sites of mass surveillance and data harvesting. To tap cables, intelligence agencies place "intercept probes" on them, capturing the light as it flows through the cable but bouncing it immediately back without disrupting the original traffic flow.[34] Snowden's revelations suggested that after accessing this fire hose of raw data, data analytics software goes to work, forming profiles, finding relationships, and suggesting links. If the dozen stakeholders in the APG consortium arguably render it nation-state neutral, China Mobile's command of the cable landing station introduces a potentially more significant degree of sovereign control.

Control over cables and their associated landing station thus present an increasingly important geopolitical arena. "Everything you see in geopolitics . . . spheres of influence, national interests . . . has a counterpart in the structure of the internet," asserted the chief technology officer of one security firm.[35] The colonial geographies of cables have traditionally meant that a majority of internet traffic flows through either the United States or Britain. Indeed, the US National Security Agency has explicitly referred to this fact as their "home-field advantage."[36] However, the slew of new cables connecting Tseung Kwan O with other locations suggests a change in this dynamic. If the US hegemony of internet infrastructure was once commonly accepted, it is now a persistent myth.[37] Instead, in terms of both governance and geography, we see a tilting toward the East. "Keen to wrest control of core elements of the internet infrastructure that they perceive to have been excessively dominated by United States interests in the past, Asian governments and private investors have joined forces to change things in their favor," asserts Dwayne Winseck. "In terms of the geopolitical economy of the internet, there is both a shift toward the Asia-Pacific region *and* an increased role for national governments."[38] While these projects certainly present a complex mix of stakeholders, this shift suggests a growing awareness of technical infrastructures as a territory that can be constructed, contested, and operated, providing a degree of strategic influence over the information that passes through it.

Cloud

The cloud provides a second access point into understanding formations of technical power. Contrary to "cloud" rhetoric that suggests information is located in some ethereal realm, cloud services are underpinned by the hard physical infrastructure of data centers.[39] In these facilities, racks of servers store data on their hard drives, parse it with high-end processing chips, and distribute it to users or institutions who request it. While cloud giants may build and operate an entire data center themselves, most data centers are colocation facilities where multiple companies rent space, from a single server up to an entire hall.

The Tseung Kwan O Industrial Estate was set aside specifically for data centers and has become a major global hub, drawing on Hong Kong's unique political and geographical relation to China. American tech giants established an early presence in the Tseung Kwan O Industrial Estate. Both Microsoft Azure and IBM are located in the 50,000 square foot HKColo data center. The HK5 facility of Equinix, another major data center provider with headquarters in Redmond, Washington, is also located at Wan Po Road in the north of the estate. Close by is Sunevision's iAdvantage data center, an Amazon Direct Connect partner providing access to Amazon Web Services workloads and features—though Amazon does not disclose whether those services are based in the same facility or one nearby.[40]

Global Switch, a UK based company, launched their flagship data center in the estate in 2017. The 765,000 square foot space—officially Hong Kong's largest—was built at a cost of HK$5 billion.[41] Global Switch explicitly positioned the facility as a bridging opportunity for "Western" companies into China: "a hub for growth and a gateway into one of Asia's most dynamic regions."[42] Yet if the facility provides a gateway into China, it equally presents an opportunity for Mainland firms wishing to extend into international territory. Moreover, once again the lines of national affiliation at the facility remain ambiguous—the first announced customer was China Telecom and the data center itself is run by Daily-Tech, a Chinese data center operator. These kinds of collaborations mirror the highly heterogeneous affiliations of cable consortiums, demonstrating how the imperial directive of global expansion can in fact take the form of shared ownership and local partnerships.

Affiliations become more obvious when dealing with state-owned enterprises of China. For example, China Unicom, one of the largest telecommunication providers in the world by subscriber base, established a HK$3 billion data center in Tseung Kwan O in 2016. However, probably the best example in the industrial estate is the Alibaba Cloud data center. In 2014, Alibaba Cloud, the leader in the Chinese cloud market, partnered with TGT (Towngas Telecommunication) China to build a data center. Moreover, to supply the critical servers that would power the data center, these two companies partnered further with Huawei. As one case-study document notes: "TGT has deployed hundreds of Huawei . . . servers in the data center in Tseung Kwan O to offer Internet cloud data center services."[43] This close-knit partnership between a telecommunication provider, a cloud services platform, and a hardware technology supplier shows one way in which domestic companies branch out into the international sphere. As the document states: "The collaboration is a good example of the enterprises in Mainland China to expand their services through Hong Kong." This intersection of hardware and software, networks and services forms a "China-centric" infrastructural node even as it leaves the bounds of China proper.

Thus, if American companies such as IBM and Microsoft established an early foothold in Tseung Kwan O, Chinese enterprises have subsequently formed major infrastructural nodes of their own. Key to this territorial shift was an early event. In 2011, Google broke ground on a 2.7 hectare plot in the industrial estate, promising to invest US $300 million in a facility that would open later that year. However, throughout 2012 and 2013, a data center failed to materialize. "When news broke in December 2013 that Google had pulled the plug on its Hong Kong data centre project, there was plenty of hand-wringing and finger-pointing that followed as people tried to make sense of what had happened."[44] The Mountain View giant claimed that it needed to develop for economies of scale that Hong Kong couldn't provide, and instead opted to construct additional data centers in Singapore and Taiwan.

This decision would be formative in shaping the future configuration of the industrial estate. As infrastructure analyst Jabez Tan notes, "Four years later, the Hong Kong data centre market has moved on and now sees its growth inextricably linked to the ambitious development plans of large, nimble and deep-pocketed mainland Chinese companies."[45] If its data-hub designation, low-latency connectivity, and purpose-built grids make Tseung Kwan O a key infrastructural site, it is nevertheless a site with limited capacity. The estate can only support a certain number of plots, facilities, and companies. TKOIE thus demonstrates how a company's decision *not* to invest in a data center creates a void, a vacuum of technical power that is quickly filled by competitors. This dynamic is illustrated by the timeline below (fig. 2) showing Google's announcement, delay, cancellation, and the subsequent incursion into the space by others, which established their own major data center facilities in the industrial estate. Exit for one means entry for others.

These competing companies are not simply different brands, but rather comprise fundamentally different operational approaches. As the TGT-Alibaba-Huawei case study above suggests, each player within the technology industry brings with them a distinct infrastructural configuration of products, protocols, and processes. These technical assemblages, in turn, are linked in complex ways to government subsidies, intelligence agencies, and national interests.[46] In other words, technical configurations can be traced back to sovereign actors, who support them through national initiatives, financial incentives, and legal directives.[47] Of course, this relation is not unidirectional, nor frictionless. Ned Rossiter speaks of "a tussle between sovereign media and the ways in which modern sovereign entities such as the state have become dependent on nonpublic infrastructures in order to maintain and exert control."[48]

Yet along with the tussle of conflict, we might also attend to the synergies and alliances within these relations, the mutual advantages that state entities and corporate enterprises are able to grant each other. Indeed, if the coupling

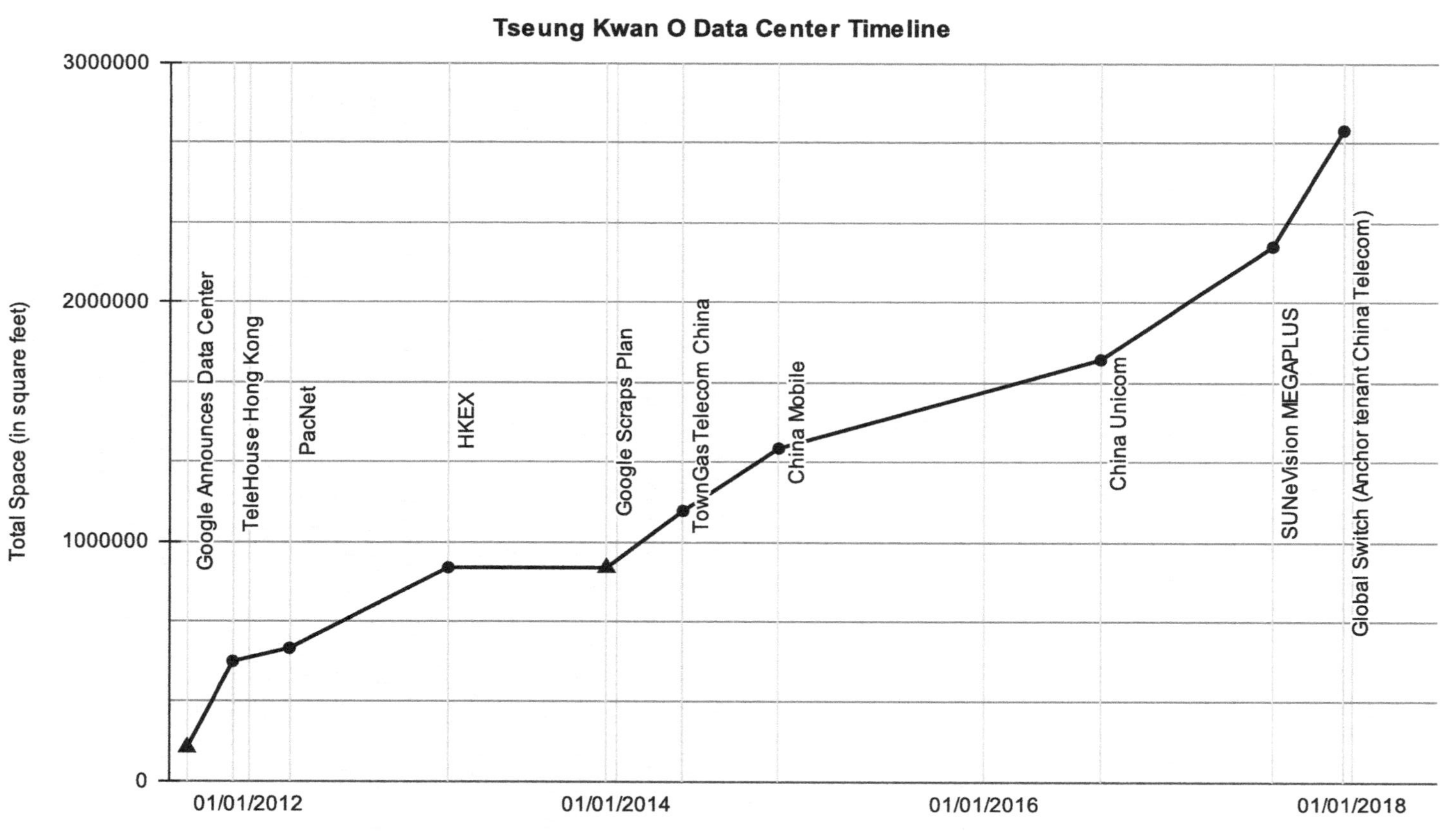

Fig. 2. Timeline of Selected Data Center Entries into Tseung Kwan O

of public and private interests occurs in both the West and the East, it is China above all where they dovetail together into a powerful parallel vector. "In China, two decades of state-led ICT development and a conception of cybersovereignty elevated to foreign policy spearhead have carved out a geopolitical enclave in which computational architectures and informational actors are coming together," notes Gabriele de Seta.[49] For some, the geopolitical stakes here are obvious. In a report titled "Red Cloud Rising," the authors warn that the "rise of China-based cloud computing services and solutions raises important concerns for US consumers, who may find themselves knowingly or inadvertently processing and storing sensitive data using cloud infrastructure located within Mainland China."[50]

But if data centers, like cables, can be understood as an infrastructure that extends or underpins territory, they do so in a complex way. This is not a matter of moving a fence or planting a flag. If these data centers are situated in Hong Kong, this infrastructural "Asia" encompasses a more nebulous territory of data storage, circulation, and processing. Such facilities, notes Rossiter, "while geopolitically belonging to the Asian region, are spatially tied through political economy and protocological interoperability to similar facilities distributed across the world."[51] Certainly, then, the location of a data center remains a critical question with strategic implications. But the territory of a data center should be understood not just as its physical footprint, but in tandem with the networks that it is connected to and the particular flows of data that it enables. As Rossiter reminds us, "The provenance of data may be territorially distinct at sovereign, geopolitical levels from the location of its storage."[52]

Indeed, evaluated purely by location, Hong Kong should never have become a critical data nexus. When location is mentioned within industry literature, it is typically in relation to criteria for site selection: ample land at low prices, protection from natural disasters, a cheap and consistent electricity supply, and ideally environments that supply free cooling through climate or water. Driven by this logic, data centers have been built in the vast plains of Idaho and the frigid north of Sweden. However Tseung Kwan O scores low in many of these areas. Land is scarce.[53] Electricity is expensive. The climate is hot. Locationally, Hong Kong makes little sense.

Instead, the specificities of Tseung Kwan O data centers point toward a logic of territory over location. While data centers certainly centralize data and concentrate power, they also functions as hubs or nodes, redistributing this data in particular ways. The data center is also an intermediary, a link in a chain, a hop point. A company hosted in a Tseung Kwan O data center can tap into the substantial infrastructure of submarine cables discussed in the previous section, an infrastructure that quickly overflows the tight borders of Hong Kong proper. Indeed much of the draw for data center clients in Hong Kong is that this special administrative region functions as a two-way territory: a bridge into China for Western interests, and a bridge out of China for Mainland players. "Springboard" and "gateway" are the two words that "encapsulate the China effect," asserted one industry analyst,[54] an effect that has led to the rapid growth of Hong Kong's data center industry.

In "Cloud Geographies: Computing, Data, Sovereignty," Louise Amoore suggests that the traditional understanding of the cloud has been geographical. In the "Cloud I" model, as she terms it, the questions are where are the data centers, where does data flow, and crucially, are these flows located inside or outside the boundaries of the nation-state? Among other limitations in this model, Amoore is particularly pushing against the naïve understanding of many governments, which seem unable to conceive of data as being in any way distinct from people or things. Instead, she suggests moving to a "Cloud II" model, which concerns a way of analyzing the world. In Cloud II, "it is not so much the 'where' of the data that matters as the capacity to extract patterns in information, indifferent to the location or data."[55] Here, it is the technical affordances that matter, the ability for a state to enhance its sovereign vision over the citizenry. More important than the flows of data are the functionalities that data offers.

However if such a model by no means reverts to the vague rhetoric of "the cloud," it also seems to lose something productive. It is no doubt true, as Amoore suggests, that the control enabled by data exceeds "the territorial geographies of the location of data centres."[56] But that control is also linked to and enabled by its territorial geography. The data center park of Tseung Kwan O provides a unique set of affordances that emerge from its unique location in a special administrative zone, a liminal space neither inside the Mainland nor entirely outside it. Put simply, situating a data center in Hong Kong allows a company to do things that could not be done from other spaces.

That Amoore must choose between a territorial model and a governmental model—between a bounded "somewhere" and an abstracted "everywhere"—suggests that the concept of territory itself needs to be rethought. Data centers, like the other informational infrastructure discussed here, challenge us to reconsider how technical infrastructures might carry out territorialization. Such territorialization draws on the distinct political capabilities established within a jurisdiction—but then uses technical means to immediately extend beyond it. Such territorialization may legitimate its activity through local laws—but then use that law as a loophole for cross-border data transfer.[57] Such territorialization may be embedded with the values or vision of the capital—but be instantiating them in nations halfway around the world. Indeed, both public and private actors have proven adept at navigating these ambiguities, forming operational spaces that work to their benefit. As Saskia Sassen observes, these technical territories openly exploit the vagaries of cross-border geographies, "with large sections of their operational chains functioning within existing law, but also partly beyond—though rarely in direct confrontation with—existing law."[58]

Sassen's "partly within, partly beyond" phrasing testifies to the complexities of contemporary territories. Territories are both situated *and* siteless, embedded *and* extended, within *and* beyond. These fluid formations, notes Sassen, "tend to unsettle what are often fairly deeply entrenched notions of interstate borders and sovereign national territory."[59] Such contradictory dynamics call for new theorizations that adequately capture these heterogeneous formations of space, capital, and power. However, territorialization is not just accomplished through the construction of cables and circuits, hardware and software. Influence can also be achieved through the formation and adoption of standards. The next section investigates the pursuit of 5G standards dominance as a recent vector for territorialization.

Fog

The fog, or edge computing, is the industry term for processing data closer to the source. As data volumes grow too large to send back to the cloud and low-latency applications emerge, the fog is seen as a critical supplement to the cloud (for more, see chapter 6). Key for the success of this vision is 5G technology, a broad term for the range of protocols, hardware, and software necessary to offer fifth generation cellular network service. 5G's ability to stream massive data volumes, support millions of devices, and reduce operational expenditure means it is viewed as desperately needed in the industry, a twin solution for revenue growth and data-driven crisis.[60] Huawei has won the contract for 5G deployment in Hong Kong, along with 40 other cities worldwide.[61] In the next few years, as 5G rolls out in various phases, Huawei telecommunications equipment will be installed in Tseung Kwan O and dozens of other locations globally.

5G is only just emerging and therefore its infrastructural presence in Tseung Kwan O cannot yet be documented. Indeed, 5G's focus on the edge of the network rather than the center means that future infrastructure will take the form of small signal boxes, radio waves, and distributed devices rather than hyperscale data centers and underseas cabling. Base stations, bearer stations, and terminals will be placed inside buildings and attached to civic infrastructure such as telephone and electric poles in order to support the millimeter wave (mmWave), C-band, and Sub-3 GHz frequency bands that form the basis of 5G.[62] This largely imperceptible infrastructure will form the critical backbone needed for the 10x speeds and low latency that fifth generation cellular service claims to deliver.

However, much of what renders 5G operational is its complex technical standards of processes and protocols. From radio access network technologies to new system architecture, 5G will require an array of new technical specifications and structures. For this reason, infrastructural theory needs to shift here, moving from its typical focus on facilities and networks to instead investigate the protocol standards at the heart of 5G networks. As Easterling reminds us, "the shared standards and ideas that control everything from technical objects to management styles also constitute an infrastructure."[63]

If the infrastructure of standards, like an undersea cable or a data center, also remains largely unseen, it nevertheless exerts a significant influence. Indeed, some of the earliest work on infrastructures from social theorists and science and technology studies scholars pointed to the importance of standards. Already in 2000, Geoffrey Bowker and Susan Leigh Star were arguing that standards were "invisible mediators of action" that often direct practices in structural and silent ways.[64] Nearly a decade later, Martha Lampland and Star stressed that these "quantifying, classifying, and formalizing practices shape everyday life."[65] This mediation and influence can be used to advance particular interests, including those of the state. For Paul Dourish and Scott Mainwaring, the formalization of knowledge into standards has long been a "technology of empire" and a line can be drawn between older colonial projects and contemporary computational technologies.[66]

In the context of 5G and fog computing, standards are set at a series of worldwide sessions coordinated by the 3GPP partnership project. Each meeting seeks to progressively hammer out the core aspects of 5G and how they should function. For example, RAN #74, conducted in Vienna in December 2016, described "scenarios, key performance requirements as well as requirements for architecture, migration, supplemental services, operation and testing."[67] In each meeting, proposals are submitted to working groups, which then discuss and develop them before submitting them to a vote. To ensure interoperability, the aim is for paper-based specifications and future technical processes to perfectly coincide. "Network-and-standard-based legal-institutional arrangements connect protocol and policy directly to one another and eliminate separation between them," observes Julie Cohen.

"Within such arrangements, the point of mandated standardization is exactly to specify the kinds of flows that must, may, and may not travel via the network."[68]

If standards are ostensibly universal, they are not equitable. Stakeholders can influence standards through various strategies, and the process allows firms to effectively carry out "competition through cooperation."[69] To draw on deep R&D investment in an area, to command executive positions in standards organizations, and to make sure these methods are written into global standards—these are the strategies necessary for what has been termed "telcogeopolitics."[70] In terms of telecommunication, China has shifted from importing foreign standards to developing and submitting their own, moving from "follower to leader."[71] Huawei in particular has been dominant. Even by 2014, it was clear that Huawei were sending more delegates to conferences, submitting more proposals, and claiming more patents.[72] The result, as of February 2019, is that the Chinese tech giant "owned 1,529 'standard-essential' 5G patents, the most of any company."[73] While 5G specifications are still being finalized and the trade war is still playing out, Huawei's current influence on this global standard is undeniable.

Such dominance takes on an amplified national character when combined with other firms from the Mainland. "Together with patents owned by ZTE, the state-owned China Academy of Telecommunications Technology, and Guangdong Oppo Mobile Telecommunications Corp., companies from China own 36% of all 5G standard-essential patents," noted one journalist.[74] In contrast, US corporations, such as Qualcomm and Intel, hold just 14% of critical 5G patents combined. In this sense, 5G standards have undergone a shift away from "Europeanization by standardization"[75] and toward Sinicization. As Julie Cohen notes, "Chinese trade policy and information technology policy have emerged as powerful and mutually reinforcing components of a larger strategy for pursuing dominance of standards for global economic and technical exchange."[76]

This rise of red power triggers fear. The anxiety around Sino standards dominance is that even cities that have chosen other companies as their contractor will nevertheless have Chinese-led technologies at the heart of their critical communications infrastructures.[77] Precisely how this presence might be translated into tangible geopolitical advantage remains to be seen. And how coupled these "strictly" technical and security-centered fears are with historical forms of Sinophobia and xenophobia can also be debated. Yet, at a minimum, the Huawei blacklisting demonstrates that, even if claims of government collusion remain unsubstantiated, these worries are enough to block products, cancel contracts, and sever long-established relations.

Like the material infrastructure of cables, the knowledge infrastructure of standards has been identified as another route for enacting and extending a China-centered technical territory. Peter Cai observes that the government sees telecommunications as a key component of the broader Belt and Road Initiative, one more potential vector for gaining acceptance of Chinese standards; as a Chinese official declared, "controlling standards means having an upper hand in negotiation, more bargaining chips and better profitability. To control standards is more important than anything else."[78] Standards are a knowledge infrastructure that can be invested in through finance, research, dedicated human resources, and so on. Establishing these standards, developing expertise in them, exporting them to other markets—these all become means of influence.

Adding standards into an understanding of technical territories stresses influence rather than ownership. From a power perspective, the imperative is to obtain a certain amount of force, control, or governance over practices within a territory, without formally annexing that territory (public states) or establishing a presence (private companies). In fact, to own a territory or lay claim to it would become a burden, entailing taking on responsibility for that territory and its inhabitants. A more economic mode of power desires authority rather than ownership. Here, information technologies allow remote forms of governance and extractive forms of capitalization.[79] Operations extend far beyond their points of origin in order to shape the environments and things that are mediated by them.

How might we picture this form of technical territoriality? Clearly it does not conform to the dotted border of the nation-state, with its clear inside and outside. But neither does it take the form of the concentric circle, with power radiating outward, or even the network diagram, with its ostensibly flattened structure. Instead, we might think of tendrils of territory, thickening at locations of concentrated power (which may in fact lay far from the center). Sassen echoes such language, describing "thick territorial moments" composed of the expected "networked digital structures and interactive domains" but also crucially underpinned by "some very material infrastructures and, often, massive concentrations of buildings."[80] These digital-material infrastructures are able to draw together disparate points across the globe, yet they do not extend everywhere to the same degree. If this is the case, then thin moments where territorial power becomes attenuated or interrupted are less the result of remote geography and more a product of weak technical influence—inadequate connectivity or incompatible data, for instance. In this sense, territorial density can be understood as a function of both infrastructural and informational density.

The previous section sketched a territoriality that attempted to move beyond both the "everywhere" of the cloud and the "somewhere" of the national border. Technical infrastructures draw upon the political, social, and financial specificities of their jurisdictions, often precisely in order to extend beyond them, establishing enclaves and shaping subjects far beyond their immediate facilities. The fog epitomizes the tension of territory, the both/and approach we need to adopt in order to understand technically driven geopolitical influence. On the one hand, the 5G technologies core to the fog are determined by global standards. Developed internationally through standards bodies like the International Telecommunication Union, standards must be implemented by all vendors that wish to offer 5G services. As suggested, this means that the Huawei influence over standards is a global influence. By dominating standards, the state-owned enterprise asserts a territorial influence that extends far beyond its headquarters. Yet, on the other hand, 5G technologies are enacted on a highly localized level. Standards must certainly be adhered to by device vendors, but these vendors will also implement their own routines, offer their own functionality, and privilege their own values. If global standards remain highly influential, they can also be amplified or undermined, inflected in particular ways as they touch down at the local level of urban space.

Tide

Tseung Kwan O has provided a productive lens to investigate the ways in which contemporary territorialization is enacted, a specific site to anchor the sometimes overly broad claims of geopolitics. The cables and data center facilities of the industrial estate demonstrate how territorial operations draw upon capital investments, infrastructural systems, and legal frameworks particular to a certain location.

However, these territorial operations also extend beyond borders and complicate boundaries. In this final section, then, I want to start putting the technical capacities discussed in sea, cloud, and fog together. What kinds of new relations might these combined infrastructures allow? How might they distort and stretch the conventional shape of the sovereign? And how wide might this technical territory extend? The term "tide" gestures to a distanced relation that nevertheless exerts significant force. If informational infrastructures provide new affordances for connecting spaces and extending influence, we should expect to see strange new territorial formations appearing far beyond their obvious physical footprints. One example of such a formation can be found in Africa.

Huawei has an extensive history of infrastructural projects in Africa. "Of the several dozen available commercial 4G networks in Africa, more than 70 percent were built by Huawei," admitted one representative at an industry conference.[81] Along with mobile telecommunications networks, the Chinese firm has also positioned itself as a leader in urban security systems. In a remarkably unabashed case study titled "video surveillance as the foundation of 'smart city' in Kenya," Huawei proclaimed that it had "deployed 1,800 HD cameras and 200 HD traffic surveillance systems across the country's capital city, Nairobi."[82] In 2015, Pope Francis visited the city, the post noted, resulting in eight million visitors and providing a useful test case for the surveillance system. The system, Huawei assured potential clients, worked "remarkably well"; through the use of "video surveillance and a visualized integrated command solution, the efficiency of policing efforts as well as detention rates rose significantly."[83]

China continues to make major investments in African infrastructure, often with the condition that Huawei is the key supplier. In April 2019 Chinese authorities and the Kenyan government signed a deal for the Konza Data Center Smart Cities Project at a cost of 17.5 billion Kenyan shillings. The technology vendor, unsurprisingly, was Huawei. As one journalist noted: "Chinese authorities immediately placed the tech firm at the centre of implementing key economic agreements with Kenya, in what could make the company's role more prominent in extending Beijing's influence."[84] The tech city will be built about an hour's drive from Nairobi in Konza. "In the deal," the journalist explained, "Huawei will build a national cloud data centre, smart ICT network, public safe city and smart traffic solution as well as a cloud centre for the government enterprise service."[85] If this future smart city will be based on African soil, its operations will emerge from infrastructures designed and developed in China.

One example of the unexpected possibilities of technical territories can be found in the data hack of the African Union building in Addis Ababa, Ethiopia. Built in 2012 with funding by the Chinese government, the buildings consist of a tower, conference center, and debating chambers. The primary IT provider for the entire complex was Huawei. As Danielle Cave outlines in detail, the Chinese company was deeply involved in the building's information architectures, from training technical experts to provisioning services and supplying hardware.[86] Cloud connectivity was one key service, and for this the African Union adopted Huawei's FusionCloud Desktop

Solution, which offers "computing, storage sharing, and resource allocation through cloud data centers."[87] Yet several years later, it was learned that these technologies had enabled a less legitimate form of territorializing. A 2018 *Le Monde* investigation, citing multiple sources, alleged that for five years, between midnight and 2 a.m., data from the African Union's servers had been transferred to servers in Shanghai, 8,000 kilometers away.[88] Upon discovery, the building itself was swept, revealing microphones hidden within desks and walls. Of course, such allegations were vehemently denied by the Chinese government, with the Chinese ambassador to the African Union dismissing the claims as "ridiculous and preposterous."[89] Huawei, for its part, has maintained that while it configured the systems for the building, it played no role in the theft of data.

While exactly who was behind this data theft remains disputed, the transmission of data, supported by highly specific dates and times, seems very probable. One could imagine that the hack drew upon not only the data center information (cloud), but also an array of connected devices (fog), bundling it up into nightly packages, and transmitting it via submarine cables (sea). The hack, then, combines all the layers of infrastructure already discussed in order to transmit data along networks to a location on the other side of the world, a territorial node far from its operating base. It demonstrates the prediction of Adrian Shahbaz that "as more of the world's critical telecommunications infrastructure is built by China, global data may become more accessible to Chinese intelligence agencies."[90] Like the imperial networks before them, the transfer of information in the form of digital documents and recorded conversations grants a geopolitical advantage to those who obtain it.

However, territory cannot be understood as a simple compression of space. Technical infrastructures must transform incompatible space into compatible territory. By providing the African Union building with their cloud platform solution, Huawei introduced a known set of protocols and platforms, rendering them interoperable with other Huawei infrastructures in other locations. As Rossiter reminds us, "The scalar dimension of software is dependent on the interoperability of protocols and the hegemony of standards."[91] In this sense, territory is less about domination than assimilation—about facilitating a mode of operations that can be parsed and processed by another set of operations. Here again we see the need to marry political geographies and network topographies when speaking of territory. Territorial expansion certainly might be accomplished through establishing a contract in a foreign market or infrastructure in an offshore location, but that geographical incursion must also be accompanied by technical translation, in which informational architectures are reworked in order to make them functionally congruent.

Addis Ababa joins a host of other cities adopting Chinese-centered technical infrastructures. The design, construction, and operation of critical infrastructures around the world by Chinese firms has not gone unnoticed.[92] Huawei in particular has been highly successful in bringing together cable networks, cloud computing, and cellular technologies to form a complete "safe city solution," a total securitization package based on mass surveillance. Along with locations like Nairobi and Konza, the system has been deployed in the Bonifacio Global City in the Philippines, Gelsenkirchen in Germany, Belgrade in Serbia, and other locations in Zimbabwe, Uzbekistan, Pakistan, and the United Arab Emirates. Huawei proclaims that these urban security solutions are now serving 120 cities in more than 40 countries. Despite Western pundits decrying these as totalitarian,[93] these systems are adopted by nations because they are utilitarian—functional service offerings that deliver security. In this sense, territorialization proceeds less through subjugation than integration, where an infrastructural solution can be refined, packaged, and installed, scaling out to dozens of cities across the globe. These informational technologies "derive their power to govern as a result of standardization across industry sectors coupled with algorithmic architectures designed to orchestrate protocological equivalence and thus connection between software applications and workplace routines."[94] By transforming the incompatible into the compatible, technical infrastructures shift spaces from exterior unknown to internal territory.

Today, territorialization proceeds through infrastructural operations. By tracing the construction of cables, the operations of data facilities, and the formalization of standards in Tseung Kwan O and the infrastructural "Asia" beyond, this chapter has explored one such technical territory. For a number of commentators, the coupling of this extensive technical influence with the political values of China represents a dangerous trend of exporting "digital authoritarianism."[95] Yet while the oppressive possibilities of this particular "end-to-end digital ecosystem"[96] are certainly concerning, these anxieties should stress how data infrastructures—regardless of national affiliation—have become key sites of contestation.

Such technical territories are not constituted through soil, but through the construction and operation of technical infrastructures. The submarine cables of the sea, the data centers of the cloud, and the 5G technologies of the fog are key information infrastructures. By controlling the ways in which data is stored, circulated, and processed, these systems become strategic. As the everyday lives of citizens become increasingly mediated by data, these capacities become political. And as the promises and pitfalls of data begin to touch everything from economic transactions to security concerns and the broader national imaginary, these capacities also become geopolitical. Such influence is powerful precisely because it is not a grand and spectacular strategy but a functional and often invisible reality, anchored in cables and copper, standards and protocols, switchgear and server racks.

This shift in power requires an accompanying shift in focus. For political theory, technical territories productively complicate purely legal or theoretical framings of territory, suggesting that researchers must attend to the ways in which state power becomes mediated and extended through contemporary technologies. For governments and policy makers, technical territories anticipate a future in which retaining meaningful political sovereignty will mean actively investing in—and grappling with—layers of technicity, from low-level telecommunications networks up to secure storage facilities and the management of their wireless spectrum. And for citizens and civic groups, technical territories indicate how asymmetries of power might be maintained through infrastructures and the pervasive influence of their low-level technical conditions.

In all these cases, technical territories stress that geopolitics is not limited to the capitol, nor is politics constrained to parliaments and parties. Instead, technical infrastructures become a key new site of political and geopolitical power, exerting influence at scale through their processes and protocols. Such forms of spatial power draw upon the legal and jurisdictional but extend it through the operational. What can be done with this territorial power? The next three chapters explore this question, showcasing the kind of force that can be exerted on subjects and spaces through these technical territories.

Part II • How to Do Things with Territory

3 • Countering the Protestor in Hong Kong

The sea of bodies sways forward, gaining in inertia, before breaking like a wave on the wall of plexiglass shields held by police. A protestor stumbles back, jostling against the sweat-soaked T-shirts of her comrades. Her plastic goggles and mask are knocked to the side. She retreats from the front to adjust them, lowering her face covering. It is only the briefest of moments, but it is a moment not overlooked by the always-on cameras dotted throughout the city. With only a frame or two to work with, software isolates the signature pattern of eyes, nose, and mouth that constitutes a human face. Sitting on a camera or on a local server, this data is relatively benign. It is only when it is transmitted—joining up with other pools of data and systems that seek to identify and incriminate—that its dangerous potential is unlocked.

In Hong Kong, a proposed extradition bill has triggered a series of sweeping protests across the city. This bill would open up the possibility of fugitives being sent to Mainland China for detainment, prosecution, and sentencing.[1] Both the immense popularity and intense ferocity of the protests that have since erupted demonstrate the extent to which Hong Kong citizens fear this possibility. They anticipate that by being shifted into this jurisdiction, their former freedoms would be stripped and they would be exposed to a fundamentally different legal system. As critics point out, this is a system that has failed to uphold basic human rights,[2] that has established so-called black jails,[3] and that conducts internal "trials" where every verdict is guilty.[4] Transfer into a new territory is therefore not merely a geographical movement, but a fundamental shift in the types of forces that can be wielded against a subject.

But while this traditional form of extradition remains a justifiable concern, a different form of extradition is already at work in these protests. Personal data has emerged as a secondary battleground of contestation, with authorities trying to capture data while activists attempt to stop its capture and control its spread. A key concern for protestors is that such data will be sent to the Mainland, where it could be stored and processed in particular ways, triggering a set of insights or flags that could be wielded against them in the future. The result, as one protest organizer observed, is that "Hong Kong people's private information is already being extradited to China."[5]

This chapter explores this concept of *data extradition*. How does the transfer of information from one territory to another confer a novel set of technical and political capacities? To examine this question, this chapter traces a notional data journey from the moment of capture in a Hong Kong street to its transmission along network cables and its eventual arrival in Beijing. The first section focuses on capture, suggesting that the struggle over protestors' data is a struggle to halt data extradition by never allowing it to be collected in the first place. The second section investigates transmission, showing how information infrastructures come together with strategically absent cross-border regulation to support the flow of data out of one territory and into another. And the third section concentrates on processing, identifying some of the strategic advantages gained by moving data into the computational and legal environment of Mainland China.

If this specific scenario is notional, it is by no means unfeasible. Indeed, as the lines between the city and the Mainland become increasingly blurred, both researchers and protestors see it as a real possibility, one underpinned by the "smart city" systems and informational infrastructures already operating in both Hong Kong and China. "What about the Chinese companies that are assisting or involved with the collection of data in Hong Kong?," asked Human Rights Watch researcher Maya Wang, "Would they be passing that data back?"[6] A data extradition approach pays particular attention to how the territorial movement of data modulates the insights and advantages that may be extracted from it. This chapter will argue that resituating data in a different jurisdiction also resituates it differently vis-à-vis legal conventions and computational infrastructures, granting it new capacities. Put simply: shifting data also shifts its affordances.

The approach taken here differs somewhat from other geographical studies. When the phrase "data geographies" is used in earlier work, it typically refers to census data containing geographic information about neighborhoods[7] or counties.[8] Data geographies in these contexts concerns the statistics associated with a particular suburb or spatial area. This understanding is not dissimilar from the extensive work on geographic information system or GIS technologies.[9] Here "space" is something that gets encoded into data in the form of coordinate systems, topographical maps, and physical geometry.

In this view, data becomes geographic when it contains geographic information: longitude, latitude, elevation. In a similar way, media only becomes "spatial media" when it contains overtly spatial data like location.[10]

In contrast, the approach here understands media as inherently spatial. Regardless of whether or not it is geotagged, data has a spatial life. Data is constructed or captured at a certain location. It may lie dormant on a drive or be immediately distributed across the globe. And its intersection with the social, technical, and political environments it inhabits alters its abilities. This resonates with approaches such as the data journey that strive to "situate data across interconnected sites of practice distributed through time and space, drawing attention to the movement of data between these sites."[11] Data is material; data moves. Artist and theorist Hito Steyerl, drawing on her familiarity with networked media, has long pointed out this spatial dynamic. Whether as images, transactions, or biometric information, packages of data "are dragged around the globe as commodities or their effigies, as gifts or as bounty. They spread pleasure or death threats, conspiracy theories or bootlegs, resistance or stultification."[12] Steyerl not only stresses the circulation of data, but the way that this movement changes its context and transforms its capacities. Data does different things in different places.

To sharpen this distinction, we could push against a widely cited article in human geography. In "Digital Turn, Digital Geographies?," James Ash and his colleagues argue that geography is in the midst of a digital turn, exemplified by locative media, mapping tools, and spatial databases.[13] Yet as the borderless fantasy of cyberspace fades out and we witness increasing moves to regulate cross-border data transfer,[14] to "balkanize" the internet,[15] and to see data "operating differently in different places" according to sovereign wishes,[16] we could reverse this proposition, arguing that the digital is in the midst of a geographical turn. Ash and his coauthors asked how the "digital mediates the production of geographic knowledge." This chapter turns that question around, investigating how the geographical mediates the production and instrumentalization (or indeed weaponization) of digital knowledge. The possibilities of data change as data moves from place to place, entering into different jurisdictions, linking up with centralized repositories of information, and encountering distinct regimes of computation. "The analytical techniques available in the cloud do not strictly act upon the earth from some novel spatial dimension 'above' or 'below' the ground," argues Amoore, "but rather enroll the very space of calculation itself."[17] How might the territorial movement of data intensify its political force?

When writing this chapter, academic scholarship on the protests was scant. The handful of existing articles focused on the economic power of this pro-democracy movement and the solidarity between its moderate and radical elements.[18] Because of this gap, I drew frequently from both mainstream and investigative journalism, splicing these accounts together with the technical capacities of data infrastructures in the region. Of course, there is a wealth of scholarship on the earlier Umbrella Movement of 2014. These accounts are often very positive, arguing that technologies like social media encouraged individuals to more significantly support or partake in the protests, and that this deeper participation ultimately empowered the wider movement.[19] Network technologies were framed as new, alternative media that provided both a community and a counternarrative to the pro-government account disseminated via traditional media like newspapers and television.[20] Digital media, underpinned by digital infrastructures, enabled new ways to organize and fostered new forms of democracy. Tech was emancipatory. Yet in the current wave of protests, the stance toward such technology appears more critical and cautious. Led by this disenchanted attitude, the chapter paints a far darker portrait of the ways in which technology can be used to impinge on democratic freedoms.

The aim is to explore how a technical territory operates and show why it matters deeply. Hong Kong crystallizes these dynamics in an intense way and clarifies what is at stake here. Exploring these sociotechnical conditions advances our understanding of how contemporary technologies intersect with their spatial environment in order to shape democratic protest and individual freedoms. Today, the politics of protest cannot be adequately grasped by attending only to the relations witnessed on the street. Instead, both the agency and the insecurity of protestors are formed by a complex and far more expansive set of operations, where techniques like facial detection and location tracking draw upon information infrastructures and remotely exerted state power.

Yet if the violence and oppressive state actors in Hong Kong certainly make it an intense example, the ability to capture, recirculate, and computationally instrumentalize data can be found elsewhere, whether in Silicon Valley start-ups or presidential political campaigns. Indeed, even as data sovereignty and cross-border laws strive to limit this movement, the ability to extradite data will take on an increasingly urgent nature and offer distinct advantages. Hong Kong thus provides insights for activists and communities in other contexts, for those striving to maintain civic liberties, to retain democratic freedoms, or simply to assert their right to exist as equal subjects within society. Understanding the rights of subjects means going beyond abstractions to understand the technical regimes that directly facilitate or undermine these rights.

Capture

The Hong Kong protests have been visceral, marked by tear gas and tense standoffs between opposing forces in the sweltering city. Like other protests, activists have sought to draw attention to their cause by literally embodying it. In some of the largest protests, millions have come together to march and chant, to oppose the government, and to stake their claims. These protests have been met with responses ranging from dispersing participants to police cordons and outright physical violence in the form of beatings and bloodshed. Undoubtedly, then, bodies and the control of bodies remain key to protest.[21] But it is also apparent that the digitization of those bodies has emerged as a form of meta-struggle in recent years. The identification of individuals through information technologies has now become a critical theater of operations, a secondary front interposed on the conflicts taking place in the street. For protestors, the capture and control of their data matters, driving a new set of tactics.

One tactic designed to defeat data capture has been refusing to use Octopus cards. The Octopus card is a stored value smart card for making electronic payments. While it can also be used at supermarkets and vending machines, the card is most closely associated with Hong Kong's train network, the MTR. Metro riders use the now familiar tap-on, tap-off mechanism to pay for their fare, making the card a normally ubiquitous object seen throughout the city. However, since the protests began, the card has been seen as a potential capture point, a means to log the movements of protestors and identify them as individuals. As one female protestor simply explained: "We're afraid of having our data tracked."[22]

This fear is not unfounded. In 2010, Octopus Holdings flatly denied that it sold the personal data of cardholders to third parties—only to confess two weeks later that it had made HK $44 million over the last four years by doing exactly that. Over two million individuals had joined their Octopus Rewards scheme and had their data unknowingly sold, including "names; partial identity card numbers; partial date of birth, including year and month; mailing address without block and floor details; occupation; gender; range of salary; and spending on the reward scheme."[23] The Office of the Privacy Commissioner ruled that this unauthorized sale of data was clearly a violation of data protection principles, yet, despite this decision, the company was not punished or fined, only asked to delete identity card numbers and birthdates from its database.[24]

Instead of using the Octopus card, protestors have elected to purchase single-trip paper tickets with cash, an option typically only used by tourists. The result has been unusually long queues snaking back from machines in metro stations. These paper tickets are not only less convenient, they are also more expensive compared to using the stored value card. Yet this expense in both time and money is seen as a necessary trade-off for anonymity.[25] In some metro stations, these one-way tickets have been left on top of machines along with bottles of water and clothing.[26] Here, the paper ticket becomes a basic essential, providing the ability to move without being digitally tracked.

Along with paper tickets, protestors have also adopted an internet-less app in order to communicate. Bridgefy is a mobile application that allows users to send messages with Bluetooth across a "mesh network." Rather than being connected via servers, users in a mesh network connect directly to each other, provided they are physically close enough. As more users join the network, it can become larger and more stable. Bridgefy has typically been positioned as a tool for disaster relief scenarios, where the internet has been disconnected, or in music festivals, which can often be remote. But with thousands or even millions of individuals in close proximity with one another, the protests also provide optimal conditions for a mesh network. In its new life as a protest tool, the application has enjoyed a surge in popularity. Over a two month period, the app saw a 4,000 percent spike in downloads as users switched away from applications like WeChat, which is monitored by the Chinese state.[27] While the security of the Bluetooth protocol and mesh networks can certainly be debated, the point here is that protestors are aiming to avoid the capture of data. The rationale is that the app "does not use the internet and is therefore harder for the Chinese authorities to trace."[28] Once data enters the more open spaces of the internet, it can be copied, circulated, and instrumentalized in potentially damaging ways.

Taken together, paper tickets and offline apps signal a new unease around networked technologies, a deepening of distrust. In the earlier Umbrella Movement of 2014, technology such as social media platforms were seen as positive vehicles that contributed in numerous ways to the success of the protest. One Hong Konger asserted that "digital media have empowered the participants in the Umbrella Movement to effectively communicate, organize, construct identity and gain public attention to their social movement."[29] Others also argued that "digital media and the emergence of connective actions have empowered the movement."[30] Yet in these antiextradition protests, there is a more cautious and perhaps more nuanced engagement with digital technologies. This is not to suggest a neo-Luddite refusal of such technologies. Certainly some media have been strategically employed to great effect. From highly successful crowd-funding campaigns to social media groups, these have contributed by raising money and raising the public profile of the Hong Kongers demands.[31] But there is also fear and skepticism—particularly among protestors on the front lines—that location-based services and social media have the potential to be highly damaging. "Many said they turned off their location tracking on their phones and beefed up their digital privacy settings before joining protests, or deleted conversations and photos on social media and messaging apps after they left the demonstrations."[32] While encrypted messaging apps like Telegram are used, protestors have established a set of best practice guidelines to avoid leaking incriminating or identifying data. One protestor recalled that he was told to change his username to sound nothing like his actual name, to change the phone number associated with the app, and to only buy SIM cards without a contract.[33]

Such tactics of going "digitally dark" represent a kind of counterlogic. Transparency is not only the business model but the broader imperative of much networked media. Individuals are encouraged to photograph their life, moment by moment, as the selfie phenomenon attests. Platforms ask users to tell them "what's on your mind?," translating their inner thoughts into a public update. As Byung-Chul Han observes, these technologies embody a friendly and more positive form of power, one that "is constantly calling on us to confide, share and participate: to communicate our opinions, needs, wishes and preferences—to tell all about our lives."[34] These documents and desires are wrapped up into digital packages designed for distribution. They are shared with friends and peers, but also the wider world. Content is produced and shared by exposing the self, leaving nothing hidden.

Yet as is increasingly pointed out, there are personal, political, and societal drawbacks to this pressurized transparency. In this respect, the tactics of protestors dovetail into a broader disenchantment with information technologies and their ability to capture personal data and impinge upon individual privacies. "In our digital frenzy to share snapshots and updates, to text and video-chat with friends and lovers, to 'quantify' ourselves, we are exposing ourselves," argues Bernard Harcourt, "rendering ourselves virtually transparent to anyone with rudimentary technological capabilities."[35] The tactics of protestors strive to limit this exposure, recognizing the stakes should their data reach the wrong hands. Rather than transparency, the protestor strives for anonymity and obscurity.

These tactics of preventing data capture reach their apex in the facial mask. It is the face above all that is seen as the gateway to unlocking identity, the particular configuration of eyes, nose, mouth, and other morphological features unique to an individual. "What we've seen as the protests have gone on," observes one journalist, is that "the face has become weaponized and identity itself in a way is weaponized."[36] Faces may be captured either as still images or in video feeds by one of the many surveillance cameras dotted throughout the city. To defeat these digital eyes, protestors don neoprene masks, safety goggles, ventilators, reflective sunglasses, hardhats, or even full gas masks.[37] In covering over their identifying features, protestors hope to shut down the face as a potential capture point.

The mask recognizes that the territory of the Hong Kong street, with its confluence of militarized police power and digitized network power, is by no means a level playing field. Indeed, the advantages such public space offers to the government regime make it highly asymmetric. This is a territory deeply embedded with surveillance cameras, tracking devices, and other information infrastructure that can be taken up by state actors. In this sense, the protestors see "the public sphere not as a utopia of reason and transparency but as a Foucauldian nightmare of surveillance and coercion."[38] To protect herself, the protestor must not only avoid the physical threats of gas canisters and police batons but must also don a mask, concealing her particular identity when moving through this digitally antagonistic space. The mask obfuscates, refusing the imperative to communicate. Along with this obfuscating apparel, handheld laser pointers are the latest tactic to be employed by protestors, a swarm of multicolored lines that strives to confuse facial recognition, preventing photographs or even burning out sensors entirely.[39] The aim is to remain a leaderless mass, where individuals cannot be singled out and harmed because of their participation.

The police, for their part, wear riot gear with black helmets and a highly reflective mono visor that covers the entire upper portion of their face. In addition, protests have often seen the Special Tactical Squad deployed. Known locally as the "raptors," this unit's military style garb features dark goggles, a cloth mask over the mouth and nose, and respirators, a highly concealing uniform that only leaves the eyes uncovered. This renders them unidentifiable in a lineup, removing any form of individual accountability. Unique ID numbers on each police uniform are designed to address this issue, but since the protests began, these have sometimes been strategically absent. Activists have filed formal complaints because police failed to display identification numbers; the secretary for security responded weakly by claiming there was "no room" for identifying numbers on the uniforms.[40] Together, masks, uniforms, and ID numbers demonstrate the tussle over the ability to capture facial features and single out a single person. The aim is to establish an informational asymmetry, where authorities can identify protestors while themselves remaining anonymous.

How is the identification of protestors through facial data carried out? In Hong Kong, one method of facial recognition is enacted through Hikvision technology. Specializing in surveillance cameras, the company is situated under the umbrella of the state-owned China Electronics Technology Group Corp. Its mandate, according to a promotional video, is to "unleash the power of machine vision, to add an intelligent eye to everything."[41] A perusal of the company's offerings reveals cameras like their DarkFighter model that can operate in low light, that can capture an environment at 30 frames per second, and that can stitch together multiple feeds to form high-resolution panoramic views of urban environments. Moreover, Hikvision cameras "can recognize people's faces, analyze biometrics and check against a database of wanted persons or dissidents simultaneously."[42]

"Across the border in China, the police often catch people with digital fingerprints gleaned using one of the world's most invasive surveillance systems." writes one journalist. "The advent of facial-recognition technology and the rapid expansion of a vast network of cameras and other tracking tools has begun to increase those capabilities substantially."[43] Given these kinds of capabilities, protestors were quick to notice when an array of the company's cameras was installed in Admiralty, a district that houses many key legislature and government buildings. The cameras were subsequently blocked with umbrellas, spray painted black to obscure their lenses, or even destroyed entirely, with protestors using buzz saws and ropes to rip down a "smart lamppost."[44]

For both sides in Hong Kong, then, capturing or preventing the capturing of identifying data is seen as important. Biometrics, as the statistical analysis of biological data, is a core technology in the spheres of securitization and surveillance.[45] Biometrics are technologies of both identification ("Who are you?") and verification ("Is this you?"). In carrying out these processes, biometrics often claims a certain pragmatic functionalism, delivering up an identity as a solution, swiftly and accurately, to whoever the client happens to be. Yet the identity of an individual, far from being a static and self-contained field, constantly shifts based on its immediate geographical and political context. As Joseph Pugliese emphasizes, "'Who are you?' pivots on the specificity of a subject's embodiment and her or his geopolitical status."[46] In Hong Kong, identification at a protest site is immediately more fraught than at a shopping mall.

Of course, the fact that protestors are targeted by facial identification is hardly a novel point. From the Occupy movement to Anonymous and Antifa, masks and tactics of obfuscation have emerged as a common theme in recent protests around the world. As Zach Blas observes: "At the intersection of biometrics, governmentalities of the face, and contemporary protest, a global political struggle has ensued over visibility, recognition, and representation."[47] However, here I want to situate capture in a longer chain. Capture is the fundamental first step in the process of data extradition. The body of the protestor is certainly present at the protest site. But it is at the moment their face becomes digitized—when the bios of the body starts toward the biometric of data—that this presence becomes identifiable and doubly dangerous. The digital photograph initiates an extended data creation process where a face can be detected within the frame, isolated for analysis, and evaluated by using the eyes, nose, and mouth as distinguishing features.* This data can then be circulated, cross-indexed against other profile data, or integrated into broader informational repositories. As Btihaj Ajana stresses, the ascendancy of biometrics as a means of verification and securitization is not just due to its ability to "automate the process of linking bodies to identities" but also because it provides a way to "*distribute* biological and behavioural data across computer networks and databases" (emphasis mine).[48] Biometric data can be packaged and shifted, linking up with more extensive datasets in ways that facilitate governance and control.

This explains why capture is often the flashpoint of contestation. Once data is captured, it becomes difficult to control. Restricting the location and authorization of data remains difficult both technically and juridically. After ripping open the "smart lamppost" mentioned above, protestors discovered a number of electronic components alongside the cameras. These included a Bluetooth locator, a wireless router, and most tellingly, an industrial Ethernet switch model that has been granted a "Network Access License" by the Ministry of Industry and Information Technology, meaning that it can be connected to China's domestic public telecommunications network.[49] Such components provide an ability to immediately pass on collected information into the wider network.

So if scholars have certainly demonstrated that the digital is by no means immaterial,[50] it is also true that encoding information into bits allows it to be rapidly replicated and recirculated to a unique degree. The digital package can be copied and shifted in ways that a stone or a tree cannot. Indeed, it is interesting that one of the first modern uses of the word "data" leads off with this property, defining it as "transmittable and storable information."[51] Given this ability, capture is the crucial a priori of circulation. For protestors, better

*There are a number of different techniques for facial detection and recognition. While the technical details of these mechanisms are not the focus here, an accessible summary of the Viola Jones algorithm and Haar cascades, which remain fundamental to many facial detection technologies, can be found in Gupta, "Breaking Down Facial Recognition."

than a reliance on data rights is never having data captured at all. For authorities, data capture catalyzes the rest of the chain—once it is captured, it can be transferred, stored, and processed, yielding productive insights. The struggle to prevent capture is an effort to prevent the devastating transmission and processing that swiftly follows it.

Transmission

Once data is captured, it can be transmitted. In our notional scenario, an image of a protestor's face is momentarily captured by a Hikvision camera in the Admiralty district as she adjusts her mask. In order for this data to be leveraged, it cannot merely remain at the site of capture. If an image remains stuck in a camera or sitting in memory, it is useless. Instead, it must be distributed and circulated, sometimes far from its initial location. To extradite data is to eject it from one territory and into another.

Extradition can be initiated through a data request, where a government requests information in another jurisdiction, either through specific single requests or via an ongoing arrangement. To comply with the request, the original data holder hands over this information, resulting in a forced transfer of data across territories. China's newly drafted Cybersecurity Law, for example, requires operators to provide the government with full access to data along with technical support as necessary.[52] Similarly, the new US CLOUD Act paves the way for bilateral agreements where data must be transferred across territories: foreign governments can request data on an individual from US operators and vice versa.[53] These acts essentially allow states to pursue this circulating data in order to extradite it back to a "national" jurisdiction.

Alongside state institutions and law enforcement agencies, data requests may also be directed at corporations. Researchers have already noted at least one instance of a Hong Kong–based company admitting it would hand over user data to the Chinese government if asked.[54] Of course, in a post-Snowden world, we also know that states have circumvented such formal requests and official channels, choosing instead to adopt extralegal measures.[55] By tapping information infrastructures, state agencies accessed the data flowing through them without alerting foreign governments.[56] This information was transferred back to their territory, forming a vast repository of information that could be processed by data analysts with custom tools. These abilities suggest that both the infrastructural and the legal are key for understanding the transmission of data. This section examines both in turn, demonstrating how the increasingly "blurred lines" between China and Hong Kong that concern protestors are not just ideological but operational.

First, transmission requires infrastructure, and, in this respect, the Hong Kong government has been highly supportive. Undersea cables are one aspect of this infrastructure. Hong Kong, long a nexus for telecommunications in the region, is connected to no less than 11 cables, from the Asia Pacific Gateway to FLAG Europe Asia, the REACH North Asia Loop, and the South-East Asia Japan Cable System.[57] While the exact route of our notional protestor's data cannot be known, of particular interest here is the EAC-C2C cable, which runs directly from Tseung Kwan O in Hong Kong to Qingdao in northern China, only a short hop away from the government capital of Beijing.[58] Close collaborations at the network level with Chinese companies, together with a surge in network construction and upgrades, have meant that the transmission of high volumes of data between the island and the Mainland can be done almost instantaneously. One Hong Kong-based network provider boasted that its "30Gbps direct peering with China Telecom CN2, China Unicom and China Mobile" provided the lowest latency connectivity to Mainland China, enabling the transmission of data to Shanghai and Beijing in under 40 milliseconds.[59]

Data centers are another key transmission infrastructure. Alongside cables, their construction has fostered the vision of Hong Kong as a critical nexus for informational flows. "Data is the lifeblood of the digital economy," stressed one tech pundit. "Southeast Asia must allow data to flow freely across borders for the digital economy to thrive."[60] Beginning in 2013, the Hong Kong government earmarked land specifically for data center development in Tseung Kwan O, and since then dozens of data centers have sprung up.[61] Notable from a data extradition perspective is that a number of these are operated by Chinese state-owned enterprises. Both China Unicom and China Telecom have major data centers in this industrial estate, and China Mobile is not only situated here but also operates one of the key cable landing stations, where undersea cables exit the water and connect into the local telecommunications infrastructure.[62] These informational infrastructures, with strong technical and corporate links to Mainland Chinese institutions, suggest some feasible possibilities for the routes that data extradition might take.

If the details of these undersea cables and data centers are somewhat arcane, they stress the materiality of data and the investments in time, labor, and capital required to shift it. Against terms like "the cloud" and its discourse of the global and ethereal, data is situated and material. Its movement depends on a vast infrastructure that encompasses copper and cables, servers and switchgear. This is particularly the case for big data, due to its volume (file sizes and number of entries) and its velocity (rate at which it is produced and must be captured).[63] The transmission of data is not effortless, but encounters friction in diverse forms. Data friction "refers to the costs in time, energy, and attention required simply to collect, check, store, move, receive, and access data," explains Paul Edwards; whether packets are traveling from place to place or machine to machine, "data friction impedes their movement."[64] Major investments in high-speed cables and hyperscale data centers by the Chinese state and state-owned enterprises aim to reduce this friction, to smooth data's journey. These infrastructures overcome the resistance that physical distance and financial cost entail, rendering the movement of data not just feasible but economical.

While infrastructure is one means of facilitating transmission, legislation is the other. Hong Kong was actually one of the first countries in Asia to pass laws governing the collection of personal information, with its Personal Data Privacy Ordinance enacted as early as 1995.[65] The ordinance lays out a number of key principles concerning the use of such information, ensuring that personal data is not captured excessively, specifying that it must be accurate, that it must be stored securely, and so on. Alongside these general principles, such privacy legislation generally includes clear stipulations regarding cross-border restrictions.[66] These specify what types of data may be legally moved out of the country under what conditions. Within frameworks like Europe's General Data Protection Regulation or the EU-US Privacy Shield arrangement, for example, a key point is that data may only be transferred when the destination country is a "substantially similar" environment in terms of data protection, upholding the same personal data rights.[67]

Yet here Hong Kong law departs from more well-known frameworks. As one law firm noted, while a cross border data transfer restriction was included as a section in the broader ordinance that was passed, that particular section "has not been brought into operation."[68] This means that cross-border restrictions, while technically included in the ordinance, never legally came into effect. Here law is never triggered or made operational, but rather lies dormant as nonfunctional lines within a functional piece of legislation. If cables and data centers are a positive move by the government to support the transmission of data, this is its negative mirror, a form of legislative infrastructure that remains strategically deactivated.

The result, from a data extradition perspective, is that Hong Kong may transfer personal data to any country without explicitly notifying the data subject. This ability fuels protestor fears of their data being transmitted to Beijing. As a data protection lawyer cautioned: "There is no restriction on cross-border data transfer. All this can be sent to China. It's like throwing a stone into the sea. You don't know how they are going to use it."[69] Yet for some, this lack of regulation simply reflects the realities of attempting to corral data in a globalized and connected world. "In the era of smartphones and cloud computing, it is very difficult to see how 'hard' cross-border transfer restrictions (i.e., localization or consent-based systems) can realistically be complied with in practice," asserted one lawyer.[70] Such data fatalism neatly coincides with Hong Kong's broader laissez faire approach to markets and corporate actors. Throughout its history, the entrepôt has consistently sought to encourage the circulation of commodities and capital, not hinder it. "Hong Kong imposes few controls on capital and currency flows across its borders," observed the same lawyer. "To restrict international transfers of personal data would be perceived by some to be counter-productive to wider economic and trade agendas."[71] Based on this strategy, barriers to entry and exit should be minimized or removed entirely. Data, like other commodities, must be allowed to flow smoothly in and out.

Transferred via undersea cables and unchecked by cross-border laws, the protestor's data in our notional scenario crosses over the Hong Kong–China border. For two journalists who have long worked across these spaces, the border is a critical "digital cutoff" point, a "virtual divide" that separates two highly divergent internets.[72] Each internet has its own set of norms, rights, and responsibilities, its own understandings of censorship, privacy, and security. In crossing the border, data enters a new political and technical environment, a distinctly different realm in terms of both juridical and operational possibilities. Hong Kong is famously ruled under the "one country, two systems" approach. However, this shift in data jurisdictions might better be summed up as "two environments, two systems." If transmission is momentary and invisible, it is nevertheless highly consequential. As discussed more specifically in the next section, things can be done with data in China that cannot be done in Hong Kong.

Such leveraging of borders is hardly limited to this particular case, nor even to state-based actors. As Sassen has observed, companies or institutions increasingly use emergent technologies to exploit conventional nation-state borders and achieve a kind of legal gray zone, "with large sections of their operational chains functioning within existing law, but also partly beyond—though rarely in direct confrontation with—existing law."[73] From a data extradition perspective, then, a territory might be understood less as a bounded space of restrictions, and more as a collection of capacities. Shifting the territory presents an opportunity to unlock new abilities, either by drawing on local legislative norms, (partially) exceeding them, or gaming the in-between zones enabled by technical circulation.

Transmission thus seeks to use the law, not to break it. The transmission of data from Hong Kong is an operation that instrumentalizes (inoperative) cross-border legislation to its benefit. Indeed, Sassen's observation resonates with the comments of legal scholar Julie Cohen in a recent review of Shoshanna Zuboff's work. Throughout the book, Zuboff had argued that surveillance capitalism asserts a right to a "lawless space."[74] Yet Cohen counters that the relationship between them is "both far more complex and far more productive" than this understanding allows.[75] The proponents of surveillance capitalism do not seek to entirely toss aside existing regulations, but to pinpoint potential legislative supports and then alter them so that they work for them. As Cohen asserts, they "create zones of immunity (and corresponding legal disability), and they do so by mobilizing changed understandings of legality."[76] If these codes can be reconfigured, they can be leveraged toward the same imperatives, legitimating technical operations with legal authority. In this particular scenario, shifting data across the Hong Kong–China border uses local law while simultaneously seeking to escape its clutches. For data extradition, the law too is a machine that can be used.

Processing

Finally, we arrive at processing. In our notional scenario, a Hong Kong protestor's data arrives in the national capital of Beijing, a transfer that, based purely on network latency, might take as little as 47 milliseconds. What are the operations available as a result of this data extradition? Put simply, what can be done to data in Beijing that cannot be done in Hong Kong?

First, data can be centralized. Without centralization, data remains scattered throughout a number of law enforcement agencies and state departments. Often, each one of these institutions has their own method of inputting data and storing data, their own database structures, their own tool sets for querying results and drawing out potential insights.[77] Dispersed across information systems, data remains locked within the proprietary systems employed by each agency, each constituting their own isolated Tower of Babel.[78] These institutional silos enact a double barrier, not only firewalling data from the outside world but also rendering it incompatible with other datasets. Even if this information could be physically linked up with other datasets, divergent standards and custom structures would prevent integration, hamstringing the insights to be gained. From the perspective of the state, this results in a highly fractured image, a collection of shards that fails to adequately apprehend the protests.

Centralization, then, is not just a translation in location, but in information. By assembling this data at one point or even under one roof, it can be transformed by a single institution and integrated into a unified system. Bringing this data together is a way to smooth out its irregularities and differences, to carry out the translations necessary for "protocological equivalence."[79] The goal is to render these heterogeneous pieces into a homogenous whole, a common architecture that is compatible and interoperable. China already maintains national lists of criminals with over 300,000 entries, and is slowly building up a similar list of ethnic Uighurs through its surveillance infrastructures.[80] It is not a stretch to imagine that a similar index of dissidents in Hong Kong could be assembled. Once data is assembled and integrated, fields can be clustered, compared and cross-indexed, approaching the kind of gaze desired by the state. These kind of agglomerated lists are "not dead information," media theorist Geert Lovink reminds us, but "a potent, dense form of rule that shows us the power of organization, and the organization of power."[81] Centralization draws together data spatially but also computationally.

Second, shifting data allows it to be more intensively and intelligently computed. Data does not possess some innate value of its own. Rather, its value can be amplified or diminished by the environment that it is situated in. This environment comprises both the software-based analysis able to be deployed and the hardware infrastructures available to power them. It's worth noting, for example, that the computer systems of Hong Kong police are so outdated that manufacturers have stopped supporting them, forcing the department to employ contractors to maintain obsolete hardware and software.[82] In contrast, China would seem to be the ideal environment for processing. Though the particular processing abilities of the government in Beijing remain unknown, the country possesses a number of concrete advantages when it comes to parsing information in order to extract intelligence. CloudWalk, for instance, now valued at over a billion dollars thanks to recent government contracts, is a facial detection company that offers to detect "sensitive groups" of people with its technologies.[83] Similarly, Megvii is a Beijing-based company employing 1,400 computer scientists and offering a facial recognition product that touts its "robust technique" and "high accuracy."[84] Another company, SenseNets, touted the use of its technologies in helping local police identify individuals from an "illegal gathering" in 2016, a code word for protests in China.[85] These indicate, albeit broadly, both the software analysis and the hardware infrastructures that might be drawn upon in the Mainland capital.

The value that can be extracted from information is related to the environment it is situated within. As Rob Kitchin reminds us, this "data infrastructure" does not just consist of software and hardware, but also aspects such as "access, licensing, use, reuse, privacy and ethics policies," "ownership, copyright and intellectual property rights policy," and "administrative arrangements, management organization and governance mechanisms."[86] This more expansive understanding of a technical environment goes beyond circuits, frameworks, and protocols to bring in the role of policy and governance. Despite the claims of "everywhere" that pervade cloud rhetoric, data is located in the "somewhere" of a jurisdiction—a territory with particular laws and legislation. Locating data in an ideal computational environment is not just a matter of deploying faster processors or smarter scripts, but a more fundamental challenge of *aligning* the computational and the legal.

This leads into the third advantage for relocating data: transferring protestor data to the Mainland provides a better alignment with broader national imperatives. China's stance against collective assembly and the Hong Kong protests in particular has been very clear, a position enacted through political rhetoric, internet censorship, shows of military force, and media propaganda.[87] One specific example of this stance has been the pro-government site HK Leaks. The sole purpose of the site is to "dox" democracy activists, revealing their personal details online so they can be targeted and harassed. Since launching in August 2019, the site has doxxed about 200 protestors, with individuals reporting that they have received hate mail and hundreds of threatening calls. While officially hosted in Russia, the site has been actively promoted by Chinese state media like China Central Television (CCTV) as well as the nationalist *Global Times* newspaper. Echoing the battle of masks and data capture described earlier, the Chinese Communist Youth League linked to the site and called its audience to participate: "Netizens have produced a website called HK Leaks. . . . These hideous people have been categorized according to surname. Let's remove their masks, take action!"[88] This nationalist rhetoric demonstrates how data extradition to the Mainland could provide a more supportive environment for those wishing to explicitly use data against protestors. Shifting data means obtaining a better fit between the possibilities available from the data (identifying protestors, suppressing collective organization) and the values of the data processor (pro-surveillance, anti-collective action).

This is not to suggest a lawless space where anything goes. In fact, China has passed its own version of the General Data Protection Regulation called the Personal Information Security Specification. Although not yet legally binding, it does provide strong guidelines for the collection and use of personal data by private companies. However, it does nothing to restrict the state. This double standard creates a "split identity" where "Chinese citizens will soon have broad protections from commercial data collection" while continuing to experience "growing, perhaps total government surveillance."[89] This one-sided application of privacy would seem to intensify existing asymmetries of power, allowing the state to retain its control while hamstringing corporations. This provides an environment where the state can continue to pursue goals "without the constraints present in other jurisdictions," as one scholar rather diplomatically put it.[90] These kind of considerations demonstrate the extent to which political, legal, ethical, and even cultural norms may shape the ways data is handled. Processing is not perfunctory, a technical performance made slightly faster or slower depending on hardware. Instead, the insights derived from data and the way these are wielded against subjects emerge from the complex interplay of factors within a broader sociopolitical environment.

For pro-democracy advocates, the convergence of data-driven surveillance and state values can already be witnessed in Xinjiang. Indeed, when protestors fear what could be done with their data, it is often Xinjiang that they refer to.[91] This autonomous region in northwestern China is home to the Turkic Uighur people. Pervaded by ethnic tensions, religious suppression, and moments of violence, the Chinese state has intervened in increasingly brutal ways in recent years to crush what it sees as separatist tendencies. The region has become notorious for its so-called re-education camps, which are thought to be holding over a million Uigher and other ethnic Muslim minorities.[92]

While such claims of incarceration and indoctrination are certainly disturbing, of particular relevance here is the mass surveillance deployed in the region.[93] Inhabitants are subjected to a highly invasive regime of data capture and control on a daily basis. Cameras are everywhere in the city, smart gates are set up in public spaces, and facial recognition is widely used, including in mosques. Journalists investigating surveillance in Xinjiang were shown a database "contained facial recognition records and ID scans for about 2.5 million people, mostly in Urumqi, a city with a population of about 3.5 million."[94] Granted, Hong Kong is not yet Xinjiang. Yet for protestors, the region exemplifies a state imaginary that has (partially) become reality, a vision of the dystopian future that awaits them if technological capabilities and antidemocratic values are allowed to align.

The Politics of Circulation

Data does not exist in a vacuum, but is situated within a particular environment. While this environment is certainly technical, composed of specific hardware and software configurations, it is also organizational, legal, and political, shaped by the capabilities that can be drawn on in an institution, the policies and frameworks governing data use, and the broader visions and values of significant data processors like the state. All these factors come together to shape the potentiality of data—the ways in which it may be handled and the insights and advantages that may be gained from it.

Given this broader understanding of an informational environment, transferring data from one location to another is more than a locational shift. Instead, data extradition assumes from the beginning that the political and the computational are linked—that resituating information in another jurisdiction is not just a matter of convenience or access, but provides a fundamentally different set of capabilities. Certainly there is a pragmatic danger in that a government now has the data pertaining to an individual, whereas formerly they did not. But attending to the data environment goes beyond this, highlighting the affordances that particular spaces grant. Circulation is a way to centralize information, to render it interoperable with broader systems and processes, and to situate it within an ideal political context where local norms, rights, and values allow it to be leveraged towards particular ends.

"Where our data 'lives' and how it circulates is rarely a question we are confronted with," Mél Hogan has observed.[95] The notional journey of data traced here has attempted to inquire into this overlooked issue, to confront the question of circulation and its deeply political consequences. As Jo Bates stresses, the "circulation of online communications data brings ordinary citizens into new forms of relationships with state agencies and commercial organizations that mine such data."[96] Indeed, a key benefit of focusing on the Hong Kong protests is that it foregrounds the very real stakes of this ability—the potential weaponization of circulation. If data can be locked down by cross-border laws or prevented from being constructed altogether by protestor tactics, then it becomes disarmed, losing much of its potency. Conversely, once data is able to be requested and circulated, it can be repositioned into an environment with the optimum mix of technical and geopolitical properties. In doing so, a powerful new set of affordances can be unlocked.

The Chinese state arguably provides one of the clearest examples of how such abilities might be devastatingly deployed against individual citizens and collective freedoms. These conditions provide a potent example of what Rossiter has called the "logistical state."[97] This sovereign entity leverages the power of communication technologies to exert forces through and across borders, blurring traditional boundaries and engendering new forms of territoriality. Rossiter observes that infrastructural forms like cables and data centers and their "circuits of movement governed by protocols of storage, transmission and processing" enable the extraction of new forms of value from populations.[98]

Yet if this logistical power exerts a generative financial force, we might also note its normative political force. The anxieties of Hong Kong activists suggest that these same circuits of movement might also be wielded to exert control, manage dissent, and punish individuals. Such techniques are not just an intensification of state power, but a more fundamental transformation of it, allowing more articulated and extended forms of governmentality. As such techniques become refined and widely deployed, attending to such power will mean attending to the capture, transmission, and processing of the massive volumes of information generated and associated with subjects. Understanding political geographies will require registering the data geographies that underpin them.

While this chapter has focused on China, it is one overt case among many. The conditions found in Hong Kong can increasingly be witnessed in other nations, from technologies that monitor opposition activists in Ethiopia to citywide surveillance networks in Ecuador and Dubai's "Policeman without Police" program.[99] These moves exemplify a broader and more pervasive paradigm shaping the politics of protest, where technologies are actively deployed to amplify the insecurity of those wishing to exercise their rights and freedoms. The capture, transmission, and processing of information contributes toward an asymmetry of power, securing hegemony while intensifying the vulnerability of those who oppose it.

Data extradition can be witnessed in a diverse array of contexts. On the one hand, there is *state-based extradition.* A governmental institution or agency has the ability to request information in another jurisdiction, either through specific single requests or via an ongoing arrangement. By complying with the request, the original data holder hands over this information, resulting in a forced transfer of data across territories. China's newly drafted Cybersecurity Law, for example, requires operators to provide the government with full access to data along with technical support as necessary.[100] Similarly, the recent US CLOUD Act paves the way for bilateral agreements where data must be transferred across territories: foreign governments can request data on an individual from US operators and vice versa.[101]

Certainly there is a pragmatic advantage to these transfers in that a government now has the data pertaining to an individual, whereas formerly they did not. But the stress on the data environment outlined above would also suggest that this transfer is a way to centralize information, to render it interoperable with broader systems and processes, and to bring it into the realm of an organizational structure with a particular expertise and value set.

The introduction of these legal acts demonstrate one way in which states are grappling with new technological capabilities, where data may flow in and out of the bounded space of the nation-state. These acts essentially allow a formal request to pursue this circulating data in order to extradite it back into national space. They preserve sovereignty while also supplementing it in response to contemporary conditions, carving out a space of exception that forces data to be transferred into a desired jurisdiction.

On the other hand, with perhaps a similar outcome but a different mode of operating, is *nonstate extradition*. A private corporation has the ability to technically transfer information on individuals or entire populations from one territory to another. Amazon's Alexa device, installed in the homes of millions throughout the world, is one clear example of this. Every day, the audio recorded by these devices is transferred to Amazon data centers. Here the data can be cleaned by thousands of workers and integrated into broader training sets for use in machine learning.[102] While this data is used to improve Alexa's understanding of language, it also provides a gold mine of consumer information that advertising agencies and consultancy firms are clamoring for.[103]

Another example of this nonstate extradition has been Facebook's transfer of European data to the United States. The social media giant regularly sends vast amounts of personal data from its users in the European Union to its servers across the Atlantic. However, this practice has been repeatedly challenged, spearheaded by the efforts of Austrian privacy advocate Max Schrems. After getting the Safe Harbor Law declared invalid in 2015, his campaign is now taking on the so-called standard contractual clauses that enable such transfers; if successful, "many organizations will be left without any practical solution to legitimize the international transfer of personal data."[104] For privacy advocates like Schrems, these transfers are violations of fundamental rights. For technology giants like Facebook and Amazon, these transfers are fundamental to both business and technical operations.

Whether seen as impinging on privacy or fueling growth, both groups recognize the fundamental importance of data transfer and circulation. While tech critic Evgeny Morozov has long pointed out the pathologies of this model,[105] others have also begun to note how "the collection and circulation of data is now a central element of increasingly more sectors of contemporary capitalism."[106] These critiques highlight how extradition is often rationalized in economic terms, justified as a vitally needed mechanism for fueling growth, enhancing products, and driving innovation. However, the activism of individuals like Schrems reminds us that this circulation is also political. In extracting, transferring, and accumulating data, corporations increase their revenue, consolidate their position, and amplify their control in comparison to individual users, intensifying existing asymmetries of power.

Such power dynamics do not just touch the protestor or the activist, but spin out to exert their forces on a far broader set of publics—"normal" people and their everyday lives. In that sense, the technical and infrastructural forces investigated here are never "merely digital" but instead ontological in shaping our wider political environment. Such forces shape both our ability and our desire to voice dissent: to attack hegemonies, to draw together counterpublics, and to construct alternative infrastructures and services. Unpacking these conditions provides a first step in critically engaging with them or even intervening against them. Data extradition draws renewed attention to the movement of information, to the intersection of data with its broader environment, and to the ways in which its political force varies across territories.

In the next chapter, we turn to another instance of technical territories on Christmas Island. This tiny island, far off the northwest coast of Australia, differs fundamentally from Hong Kong in its histories and cultures. And yet here too we witness a significant political force, one that aims to expel migrants, police the border, and simultaneously reinforce "Australia" as a cohesive nation.

4 • Filtering the Migrant on Christmas Island

Head northwest of Australia for over 1,500 kilometers and you would eventually see a dot of green in the distance, a lone cluster of rock and rainforest emerging improbably from the sea. Christmas Island comprises just 135 square kilometers and is designated as an external territory of Australia. Surrounded by the vast Indian Ocean for hundreds of kilometers, the island is marked above all by its isolation. For the state, such isolation is both a blessing and a curse. The island is home to the Christmas Island Immigration Detention Centre, where migrants and asylum-seekers are held while their applications are processed. At the same time, the island has recently become a hop point for two undersea cable projects, key infrastructures striving to connect citizens into broader communication networks.

On the one hand, then, the territory forms a key location for arresting the physical and legal progress of subjects—holding them back or expelling them. On the other hand, it demonstrates the state imperative to facilitate the free flow of information and connect citizens with circuits of social and financial capital—including and integrating them. This chapter explores this tension, examining the disparate political conditions that particular individuals and communities inhabit. It argues that territory enacts a logic gate or filter, impacting populations in different ways. In demonstrating this difference-making potential, the chapter contributes insights into the broader complexities of contemporary territory.

For a key concept, territory has often been taken for granted. Across a number of fields, the term is deployed without any explanation, a concept that is supposedly presupposed. As Stuart Elden has noted, territory is "assumed as unproblematic. Theorists have largely neglected to define the term, taking it as obvious and not worthy of further investigation."[1] After conducting an extensive survey of territory, Joe Painter concluded that it remains generally undertheorized: "While the implications of territory are hotly debated, the concept itself, its genealogy, conceptual preconditions and even its precise meaning have been given less attention."[2] The result is a nebulous concept with various meanings used across political science, international relations, ethology, and even psychology.

If an ill-defined territory is one result of this gap, a conventionally defined territory is the other. Definitions of territory such as "a portion of geographic space that is claimed or occupied"[3] or "land that has been identified and claimed by a person or people"[4] convey a very traditional framing. Granted, these definitions are introductory statements, which are then unpacked and expanded. And of course these experienced scholars are highly aware of the numerous articulations and nuances of the term. Nonetheless, these excerpts gesture to an understanding of territory in which state and land continue to play decisive roles. While territory certainly has a deeply embedded political history, it seems strangely untouched by the new conditions ushered in by contemporary technologies and information infrastructures.

So if the dangers of the "territorial trap" have by now been made clear,[5] the response here is not to jettison the concept of territory altogether, but to both trouble and thicken it. This means moving beyond the simplistic, mutually exclusive world of states to acknowledge something more complex—the overlapping and often conflicting forms of spatialized power exerted by both state and nonstate actors. Sovereignty has become diffused or "unbundled," suggests Agnew, ushering in a dynamic where "a wide range of private, supranational, and international actors are licensed or enrolled in the exercise of various types of authority beyond the confines of individual territorial states."[6] And this also means moving beyond theoretical sovereignty and generic subjects in order to explore the highly disparate experiences of individuals as they encounter and inhabit these spaces.

To follow this last point, territorial framings have often linked the state with the ideal and generic subject of the citizen. For James Caporaso, states "relate to the population within their borders as citizens (*Staatsangehörige*, those belonging to the state)."[7] He argues that the Westphalian model of territoriality, while challenged by the forces of globalization, nevertheless persists as a powerful norm, a model in which "state, border, citizen, national, territory, and authority have come together with such regularity" that they form a recognizable unity.[8] This link is echoed in Deborah Cowen and Emily Gilbert, who open their volume by thinking "territory through social and political subjects—or, in other words, through the lens of citizenship."[9]

Even when space is foregrounded, the entwining of state and citizen remains paramount. "The territoriality of the state" rests on its role as place-maker, asserts Avery Kolers, "making places by harnessing or determining citizens' agency, shaping its citizens by setting ground rules for the kinds of places they can make, and creating a spatial background against which the citizens act."[10] In this view, states do things for and on behalf of citizens. Perhaps there is some historic residue here, an echo of a past in which the singular identity of a nation and the simplified identity of an ideal citizenry were strongly connected. As Guntram Herb observes, in some of the earliest examples of self-determination such as France and the United States, there was no difficulty "conceiving of the entire population within their territories as a unified group with a common identity."[11] If the citizen is the only subject, then the territory tends to become a monolithic realm that establishes a comparable set of conditions for all.

This framing presumes that these inhabitants share the same status, that they all enjoy the privileged and protected role of the legitimate citizen. Such a view is not only myopic, but possesses a hegemonic bias that is powerful precisely because it is invisible. In seeing territory like a state, we reinforce the privileging of the citizen and overlook those more marginal populations who may experience this spatialized form of governance in very different ways. Indeed, Kunal Parker explicitly characterizes the "emerging relationship between citizenship and territory as a state strategy" for refusing the rights of immigrants.[12] For these and other groups, rights and responsibilities may vary greatly; agencies and freedoms may look very different. Indeed, for the subaltern, their presence within a territory may be characterized not by inclusion and protection, but by debilitation and expulsion.

Taken together, these conventional assumptions about territory work to stress the legal and theoretical, while occluding the individual and the material. These viewpoints continue a rich lineage of historical work around territory: Jean Bodin on how sovereignty might be legitimately imposed upon it or Carl Schmitt on what juridical law it rests upon.[13] Yet without discounting such significant (if problematic) contributions, such work tends to take the state's perspective and treat its realm in the abstract. These texts aim to legally justify sovereign power. Once done, territorial power washes across the kingdom, affecting all of its inhabitants in the same way. The result is a strangely generic realm: if a territory is teeming with subjects, it has no place for subjectivity.

The chapter here begins from a different premise: territory impinges upon lives in specific ways, intersecting with thoughts and feelings, hopes and dreams. It bears down on some while supporting others, it alters abilities and relations, and it facilitates or frustrates desires. Territory discriminates, in more ways than one. With Sven Opitz and Ute Tellmann then,[14] I want to ask about the phenomenology of Christmas Island—what this territory does to people and things. What does a territory feel like? How does this lived experience differ between "legitimate" and "illegitimate" subjects? And how are these different conditions established and enacted?

Immobilizing the Asylum-Seeker

Christmas Island, like other isolated islands, originally drew interest for its rich phosphate deposits. In 1887 Captain Pelham Aldrich visited the island with a naturalist, hacking his way through the thick undergrowth and collecting rock specimens, which were found to contain almost pure phosphate of lime. After this discovery, no time was wasted: "In the year 1897 a Company acquired the lease of the island, and arrangements were immediately made for its thorough exploitation."[15] Annexed in 1888 by the British, phosphate mining began a decade later, a typical colonial project that leveraged indentured labor from Malay and Chinese workers. For the next 50 years the island would remain under the Crown, with administration carried out via Singapore. In 1958, the United Kingdom transferred sovereignty to the Commonwealth of Australia, which paid $20 million for the Crown's loss of phosphate revenue. Yet until the turn of the century, the island largely remained a sleepy backwater, far removed from the public eye.

A key turning point came in 2002, when the Australian government announced it would build a detention center on the island. By 2007 the Department of Immigration had constructed an 800-bed complex at a cost of $400 million, a facility officially known as the Immigration Reception and Processing Centre on Christmas Island. The buildings, situated on a former phosphate mining site of 40 hectares, comprise eight accommodation units, a medical center, administrative offices, and utilities, among others. While regular operating capacity for the Centre is set at 1,000 people, in 2013 the Centre held up to 2,960 individuals.[16]

To be sure, the population of the Centre and its use has shifted over the years. The Centre closed down completely at one point in 2018 before reopening again the following year. Rather than its earlier population of thousands, the Centre's main inhabitants throughout 2019 and 2020 were a single Tamil family of four. And the relationship between Christmas Island and other immigration detention facilities in Nauru and Manus is complex and has also evolved significantly. Yet if these details certainly matter, this chapter synthesizes some of these distinctions in order to focus on the overarching logic of this territory, a logic that persists even as the particulars of asylum shift over time. What is this territory designed to achieve? What operations does it aim to enact against the asylum-seeker?

Detainment is designed to retard the progress of the subject, to halt her geographical and legal advancement. For migrants, arriving at the mainland unlocks a distinct set of resources. Once the individual has set foot on this soil, then a set of rights may be claimed. Detainment seeks to arrest this movement, to hold her back from this border and its claim-making potential. At the same time, detainment impedes the asylum-seeker's momentum on a legal level. Rather than being integrated into a national body, detainment strives to drastically slow down or even halt any assimilation into the nation entirely.

Detainment thus introduces a deceleration, a friction, a delay. As Sean Anderson and Jennifer Ferng observe: "Only a slight temporal lag marks the difference between an asylum-seeker and a refugee, the one with unrealized intentions, and the other with sanctioned recognition."[17] For the government, the prime directive is to extend this temporal lag, to defer the moment between asylum-seeker (unrecognized) and refugee (recognized) as long as possible. Indeed, this time lag has steadily been extended, moving far beyond what could be described as a temporary delay. Taking into account both on- and offshore detention facilities, the average detention period is now 500 days.[18] Immobilized in a facility for months or even years at a time, the subject never "arrives" at her destination, but instead is placed into a kind of legal-juridico gray zone, where rights can be almost indefinitely deferred.

Detain, in fact, is too gentle, failing to capture the full force exerted on migrants within this territory. Detain implies a temporary inconvenience, a momentary impediment, a brief hurdle. In a legal context, detainment enables a subject to be held for an interim period while claims are assessed and processed. Here the legal status of an asylum-seeker should be stressed. These are individuals who claim they will be oppressed, harmed, or even killed if sent back to their home country. Under international and much national law, states have an obligation to nonrefoulement, to not return refugees to a place of persecution.[19] Until this claim can be properly assessed, they are neither "illegal migrants" nor "queue-jumpers," neither hijackers nor criminals. In short, asylum-seekers have done nothing unlawful and should be treated accordingly.

Yet if the bureaucratic rhetoric of "reception" and "processing" suggests a mere formality, a gentle if bureaucratic touch, the conditions experienced by migrants shatter this image. This is an architecture specifically designed to exert an intensive degree of control over the bodies of asylum-seekers and their potential movements. After visiting the new facility, Senator Chris

Evans penned a letter to the minister for immigration, noting the "high security, prison-like character" of the buildings and stressing that it was an "extremely harsh and stark environment to detain people."[20] Similarly, a Human Rights Commission report from 2010 criticized "the use of a maximum security environment to detain virtually all single adult males"[21] and the broader architecture of "caged walkways, perspex barriers, and electrified fencing" comprising the facility.[22] These reports suggest a disjunction between the official rhetoric of immigration and a set of far harsher realities experienced by detainees. "In detention you are routinely reminded that immigration detention is not a prison and you are not prisoners," wrote Leo Jai in reference to his stay at Christmas Island, "but the regular room searches and pat-down body searches say otherwise. So do the restraints."[23] Despite the careful language used, the Christmas Island detainment complex is carceral, an enclosed space for locking down bodies.

Indeed, in a perverse sense, the detention center represents the apex of a long anti-immigration history, a distillation of past architectures that were designed to encircle and imprison, to capture and confine. As Heather Johnson notes, the Christmas Island facility rolls all the "learnings" from previous centers into its design specifications:

> The Christmas Island centre was built from advice from American military consultants from Guantanamo Bay . . . and represents all the lessons that Australia learned during the period of unrest in the onshore detention centers at the turn of the century. The hooks in the walls and on the doors were designed to collapse if too much weight is placed on them, in order to prevent attempted hangings by detainees. Similarly, shower heads were embedded into the ceilings. The roofs of the complex were set at such an angle that it was impossible to climb onto them. The centre is subject to twenty-four-hour video surveillance in all areas, and to twenty-four-hour lighting. There is motion-detector technology under the ground, which tracks the movement of the detainees.[24]

While restricting the freedom to move, this architecture also restricts the freedom to end one's life. The "innovations" of collapsing hooks and showerheads suggest a morbid regime of care that encloses and oppresses a life, suppressing its potential but never allowing it to die. Such a situation, of course, could expose the government to claims of barbaric treatment, increased scrutiny, and legal battles.

Along with the physical enclosures of walls, barriers, and cages within the detainment center, the video surveillance listed by Johnson suggests a suite of newer technologies deployed by the state. In his study of both Christmas Island and the island of Lampedusa in the Mediterranean, Joseph Pugliese notes the increasing use of techniques like satellite surveillance and fingerprint identification that attempt to identify and repel asylum-seekers long before they arrive at their destination. "In biopolitical terms," suggests Pugliese, "biometric technologies inscribe borders on bodies that are effectively located well beyond the physical borders of the nations of the global North in order to preemptively foreclose the movement of irregular migrants and asylum-seekers by attempting to 'fix' them at the very locus of the pre-frontier."[25] These technologies attempt to identify each individual, augmenting physical barriers and checkpoints with a digital identity coded with an illegitimate status. Even if the cages and walls of the detainment center were removed, this digital identity continues to flag the individual, policing the border and foreclosing any onward movement.

The selection of Christmas Island itself as the location for the detainment center doubles this degree of enclosure. Much of the island's edges are dominated by steep cliffs, which prevent easy access between the coast and its central plateau. The landmass of the island only spans around 19 kilometers by 14 kilometers, with a national park dominating over half of this space and the main township of Flying Fish Cove pressed hard up against the shoreline. Beyond these tight confines lies the vast expanse of the Indian Ocean. For this reason, Pugliese describes geography like Christmas Island, Nauru, and Lampedusa as examples of a "carceral archipelago,"[26] strings of offshore islands strategically selected in order to isolate and entrap. As one Iraqi detainee on Nauru stated: "The detention camp is a small jail and the island is a big jail."[27] The island provides a natural boundary that doubles the architecture of the detention center, hemming in asylum-seekers and preventing wider movement.

Excising Australia, Excluding the Asylum-Seeker

The reference to the "island as a jail" suggests that the territorial conditions surrounding the asylum-seeker are not only formed by the detainment center, but by the island itself—in particular its legal designation. The territorial status of the island has been carefully designed, constructing a juridical zone that enables a particular set of activities and disables others. This territory transforms the asylum-seeker, producing a figure with a far more restricted set of rights. To understand this ability, it is necessary to briefly sketch how the status of Christmas Island has evolved in response to the pressures of immigration.

Throughout the 1980s and 1990s, asylum-seekers began landing on Christmas Island, many coming from nearby Indonesia. In August 2001, the captain of a Norwegian ship, the *MV Tampa*, rescued 433 Afghani refugees from a distressed fishing ship in international waters. However, when the captain tried to enter Australian waters to disembark, the government refused permission and instead sent in Special Forces to board the boat. The now infamous event not only created a diplomatic dispute between Australia and Norway, but became an issue in the next election, triggered a flurry of responses in the news media, and produced analyses across international law, immigration studies, and social and cultural theory.[28]

In response the Howard government announced the Pacific Solution, a package of legislation enacted over the next several years that collectively worked to formalize borders, close down perceived loopholes, and harden Australia's official stance to refugees. Almost immediately, in September 2001, the Migration Amendment Act was passed. The act cut Christmas Island and several others out of Australia's migration zone, meaning that migrants who landed on the island could not apply for refugee status. Legally, the island was no longer part of the territory where Australia's visa policy applied. According to the amendment, when migrants now landed on the shore of Christmas Island, they set foot on an "excised offshore place."[29]

Pushed through less than a month after the *Tampa* affair, and closely coinciding with the September 11 attacks, the act rode a wave of anxiety around security, terror, and the "erosion" of national identity. Indeed, the demonization of "boat people" proved enormously successful as a key issue in the following election campaign. The act demonstrates how territorial conditions are not permanent nor simply given, but rather subject to public sentiment and partisan leanings. "Rather than neutral lines," asserts Anssi Paasi, "borders are often pools of emotions, fears and memories that can be mobilized apace for both progressive and regressive purposes."[30] Territories can be reconfigured and borders redrawn, updated to reflect a current climate of xenophobia.

For the cartographer or the jurist, Christmas Island is formally part of Australia. Yet for the asylum-seeker, it is part of a new geography of "not-Australia."[31] It joins other excised sites like the Ashmore, Cartier, and Cocos Islands in strategically working the slippages in traditional concepts of territory. Such concepts are not merely abstract but concrete in that they allow the government to treat people in distinct ways. Indeed, what should be stressed here is how this legally decoupled territory allows for the construction of a unique new subject. As Opitz and Tellman explain: "The excision of offshore places coincided with the creation of a distinct legal persona: the 'offshore entry person' who possessed limited rights in comparison to the regular onshore claimant."[32] Migrants who reach the "migration zone" of the mainland have the right to apply for a protection visa, whereas migrants who are detained outside this zone rely on the discretion of immigration authorities, who may "allow" them to apply but are never required to by law. In excising the island, the government also excises a bundle of rights.

Since the passing of the Migration Amendment Act in 2013, the "offshore entry person" has been substituted with the newer phrasing of the "irregular maritime arrival."[33] Regardless of the terminology used, these terms are not merely bureaucratic descriptions, but the forging of a new figure entirely. The associations of the refugee—a person escaping persecution and able to draw on a rich bundle of long-established rights under international law—are largely stripped away. Instead, the "irregular maritime arrival" strives to conjure up a less politically charged and pettier figure, someone who has attempted to bend the rules and bypass the normal way of entering the country taken by everyone else. Excision thus manipulates territory in order to alter identity: by not arriving in "Australia" the individual also never arrives at the recognized legal status of "asylum-seeker."

The Migration Amendment Act decoupled the island from the migration zone of the mainland—and, crucially, from the humanitarian obligations attached to it. For this reason, Suvendrini Perera refers to the act as a "technology of excision,"[34] a juridical-geographical operation that enabled special forms of governance to be applied within this space. This is Australian sovereignty but without Australian juridical responsibility.[35] For Victoria Palmer and Julie Matthews, this territorial excision is also a moral excision, "a mechanism that distances, dehumanizes and alienates so that extraordinary measures can be presented as normal and justifiable."[36] Excision isolates asylum-seekers from democratic communities and ethical responsibility by presenting them as the enemy. In situating them outside the national boundaries, they become outsiders. The disconnection of territory, then, also results in disconnection from spheres of accountability and care.

Excision joins other technologies to create a fluid and ultimately unreachable border. For the asylum-seeker, the boundary of "the nation" is constantly adjusting its contours, snaking back and forth, hemming in and darting away. In a remarkable article on Christmas Island and the broader "archipelagos of enforcement" established by the government, Alison Mountz observes how the "mobile border was perpetually reconstituted around the body of the asylum-seeker in a proliferation of sites between states, national and international legal and security regimes, state and nonstate actors."[37] These measures construct an asymptotic boundary, a horizon lying perpetually out of reach.

This reconstitution around the body stresses that, for the migrant, the territory of Christmas Island is designed above all for exclusion. Here geography and legality come together. By containing migrants on an isolated island, immigration regimes not only establish a thousand mile buffer between her body and the mainland, but a buffer between excluded "boat person" and recognized refugee. The right to have rights is an embodied possibility, one altered by the "creation of new political spaces on the grounds of and across sovereign spaces and nation-state territories."[38] Expulsion blocks the asylum-seeker from "entering the system" colloquially understood, the broad array of governmental services and bureaucratic mechanisms that provide an individual with a legitimate identity, a recognized status understood by the sovereign. If this juridical stability were ever attained, it might become a technique of counterpower, instrumentalized in order to validate her presence in the country and sanction claims to remain. Indeed, the broad array of measures implemented under the Pacific Solution—the excision of islands, the turning back of boats, the construction of securitized detainment facilities—are about vigilantly policing this exclusion. Of course, this vision cannot always be realized; many migrants have eventually been resettled in Australia. Yet these cases run counter to an overall exclusionary logic. The prime directive for this spatialized form of power is to excise the migrant herself from the territory of "Australia," to ensure that she never enters a space where rights can be asserted and a wider community can be drawn upon. The asylum-seeker is detained by a nation-state precisely so that she may never enter the "nation."

Integrating the Villager

To provide contrast to the asylum-seeker, we can briefly examine the villager—shorthand here for the other inhabitants of Christmas Island who are already recognized as legitimate citizens. While these two groups occupy the same island, they are subject to vastly different territorial conditions. Rather than being detained, immobilized, and expelled from the national body, this villager encounters a number of initiatives designed specifically to connect her with the world and integrate her into its circuits of social and financial value.

As a small population located thousands of kilometers from the mainland, the inhabitants of Christmas Island have long felt isolated. Commuter planes, while increasing from one to four per week, are still infrequent and highly expensive; a freight plane once a week carries in supplies such as groceries; visitors flying to the mainland are required to fill out an "outgoing passenger" card, as if they are visiting another country altogether.[39] In terms of communication, inhabitants have long relied on satellite dishes for connectivity, a precarious solution that only offered limited bandwidth and was often interrupted during cloudy weather. For users, this meant that internet access was slow and expensive in terms of monthly fees. For Christmas Island business owners, network interruptions could mean a failed payment, resulting in lost business and frustration.

In 2010 a major report was released that directly responded to these conditions. Authored by the Joint Standing Committee on the National Capital and External Territories, the report paints a picture of an island community unsure of its future. It begins by noting that the Indian Ocean territories of Christmas Islands and the Cocos (Keeling) Islands both shared the "economic and social challenges posed by isolation and remoteness."[40] Phosphate mining has been the bedrock of the economy since the island's inception. But easily accessible deposits have been exhausted, and production is expected to plateau before ceasing completely. While lucrative, mining operations are degrading the island's other obvious asset, the environment. Some believe that a fledgling eco-tourism industry of diving and fishing might be expanded, but worry that ceasing mining altogether would kill the economy before it could diversify. In essence, the report investigates how the state might best support citizens through this transition period.

If the fear of the migrant is based around her illegitimate movement—her contagion of sovereign stability and erosion of national borders—the anxiety here is that the villager will become a stagnant subject stuck in the past, "left behind" while the rest of the world races ahead. Isolated in the middle of the Indian Ocean, she is disconnected from the mainland and from the regional and international links found in global cities, unable to leverage the economic opportunity they purport to provide. In doing so she becomes too secluded, too static, failing to conform to the "always on the move" entrepreneurial subject envisioned by neoliberal governance.[41] As one intervention to counter these concerns, the government sponsored an "Entrepreneurial and Leadership Program," a five-day course that sought to help villagers "build skills in leadership, communication, presentation, networking, business development, marketing and accounting, and increase cultural awareness within these communities."[42]

Echoing broader rhetoric, the island here sees digital technologies and information infrastructures in particular as a path forward, allowing inhabitants to learn new skills and create novel forms of businesses. "The future of Christmas Island will increasingly be determined by our ability to produce services and products that must utilize the most up to date communications systems," stated the Shire, the island's local governing body. "We will not be able to compete at home or abroad if we are not at the same level of speed and efficiency attainable in Perth, Jakarta or Broome. Our future will depend increasingly upon communications based businesses including research and education."[43] Another submission to the report stressed the shift to digital services and the need for villagers to have high-speed connections to the mainland. "With the trend to e-government and e-business, Christmas Island will be increasingly disenfranchised through substandard connectivity to the internet. Without improved links to the mainland, development of better telecommunications on the island is a waste of money as effective use of any enhanced infrastructure is effectively nullified."[44] In this vision, information infrastructure not only provides citizens with access to state services online but also allows their businesses to branch out into global markets.

These desires for communication and connectivity have eventually been granted. In 2018 and 2019, two major undersea cable projects were completed, transforming the telecommunications abilities available to villagers. The Australia-Singapore Cable is the first project that contributes to integrating this community with the modern world. Stretching 4,600 kilometers underneath the ocean, the newly completed cable runs from Perth in Western Australia through to Flying Fish Cove in Christmas Island, then on to Jakarta before terminating in Singapore. The cable is seen as a vital piece of infrastructure in bridging markets, a crucial backbone providing high speed connections between trading partners. On its website, Vocus claimed the cable would offer "an approximate 30% reduction in latency from Sydney to Singapore compared to alternative routes."[45] In making this connection, the project seeks to not only build links to the attractive economic powerhouse of Singapore but also to use it as a springboard into the broader Southeast Asia region.

The cable represents a broader surge in infrastructure construction attempting to handle the region's voracious needs. One report, noting in particular the surge in demand as China comes online, stressed that "digital connectivity subsequently results in a sharp growth in the amount of data generated, consumed, stored and transferred."[46] Data, like capital, must continually circulate. "Data is the lifeblood of the digital economy," asserted one tech pundit, "Southeast Asia must allow data to flow freely across borders for the digital economy to thrive."[47] In this view, the bottleneck or the blockage of information circuits must be avoided at all costs. By decreasing latency and increasing bandwidth, these infrastructural projects aim to smoothly deliver immense flows of information. Almost immediately after being switched on, capacity in the cable began to be bought up. "Since launch, we have nearly sold 10-times the entire capacity of the [previous] Sea-Me-We3 cable system on ASC," stated Vocus. One year later, in 2019, Vertiv increased the speed of the cable, ramping its end-to-end capacity up to 60 terabits per second.[48]

Yet while such rhetoric focuses largely on global hubs like Sydney and Singapore, these cables also usher in significant changes to the inhabitants of Christmas Island. In an interview, one Vocus spokesperson stated that the $170 million cable would offer Christmas Island an "unlimited pipe to the rest of the planet."[49] The cable is seen as a solution that will resolve the limited bandwidth and interrupted connections that have plagued former satellite links. For internet users on the island, latency is no longer an issue, allowing the use of a broader range of online services. For business owners, problems like dropouts in cloudy weather are gone, facilitating faster and more reliable transactions, and potentially setting the stage for new business ventures.[50]

Closely following the arrival of the Australia-Singapore cable has been a second cable project termed Indigo-West. In late 2018, the first section of the cable was laid from Christmas Island to Fremantle in Western Australia, a distance spanning around 3,000 kilometers in mostly deep waters. In 2019 the second component was installed, a 1,600-kilometer section running in the shallower waters between Singapore and Christmas Island. From Singapore, the cable will branch off into neighboring Indonesia, providing low latency connectivity to this burgeoning economy. The cable has been backed and financed by a consortium of six partners, including Singtel of Singapore, Telstra of Australia, and Google.

A Singtel vice president echoed the rhetoric of Vocus and the Australia-Singapore cable, asserting that "this new submarine cable will usher in a new era of high speed communications between the growing economies of Southeast Asia and Australia."[51] Along with purely economic incentives, the infrastructure project also aims to boost "future growth in collaborative data-intensive research and transnational education."[52] These goals link strongly to the state's historical role in establishing institutions, educating subjects, and offering vocational training.

The rhetoric surrounding both cables thus conforms closely to the typical infrastructural imaginary of collapsing space and enabling novel forms of value. In a post on its website, Vocus goes further, claiming that we have now entered the fourth industrial revolution, "an era where a proliferation of new data experiences and ubiquitous connectivity will deliver tremendous value to all."[53] The fourth industrial revolution is a concept coined by World Economic Forum founder Klaus Schweb. In a report prepared for the Forum, the contributors caution about "the potential impact of conflicting regulation and data-localization requirements on digital trade and commerce, which is reliant upon cross-border data flows and which helps distribute economic benefits across the globe."[54] For its proponents, what is required is a two pronged approach, where data must be accelerated through infrastructures and simultaneously unhindered by legislation. In this vision, the unrestricted circulation of information will bring prosperity to all.

Discriminating Territories

The territory of Christmas Island, then, is a space of contradiction and juxtaposition. On the one hand, the detention center attempts to isolate and enclose the individual. For the asylum-seeker, both the center itself and the broader territory of the island are means of expulsion, disconnecting her from the legal rights and social communities she might draw upon on the mainland. On the other hand, new cable projects facilitate flows of data between the Australian mainland, Christmas Island, and the broader regions of Southeast Asia. More than simply bandwidth, these "pipes to the planet" slot into broader initiatives striving to connect villagers into social and economic circuits, to enhance their lives and livelihoods.

Connection for some; disconnection for others. For Opitz and Tellman, this duality is characteristic of offshore spaces, a disjunction registered in their phrase of "dis/connectivity."[55] To immobilize and exclude, to mobilize and integrate—these are the antagonistic imperatives at work in this single space. With Brett Neilson then, we might ask "how the practices of exclusion and differential inclusion that characterize border and migration regimes intersect modes of capitalist valorization and extraction."[56] These contradictory dynamics jostle and push, each an attempt to balance and correct the other. Indeed, for Perera, immigration policy in Australia exemplifies the attempt of states to retain some semblance of stability amid global flows, to somehow "take control of a world where the borderless flow of information, goods, and finances also inevitably involves the movement of people across borders."[57] Yet if identifying these opposed imperatives is important, the key is understanding how these disparate conditions operate on their respective subjects.

One way to understand the asylum-seeker and the villager is as inhabitants of separate territories. Geographically, of course, these two groups occupy the same space, sharing the small parcel of soil and sand that constitutes the island. In fact, before the construction of the detention center, migrants waiting on their claims roamed relatively freely across the island, mingling with villagers. As one longtime resident recalled, "Pieces of yellow flagging marked a no-go-zone perimeter outside the old basketball courts, the hot tin shed near the jetty where the new arrivals were taken, and the supermarket and petrol station from which they were to stay away."[58] Detention was a far more casual affair. Yet even today, with a purpose-built detainment facility and heavily enforced separation, the villager and the asylum-seeker inhabit the same island, the same mound of land surrounded by ocean.

Yet while separated by a few kilometers, these two groups inhabit vastly different worlds. When arriving on the beach in Christmas Island, asylum-seeker Behrouz Boochani recalls seeing a little blonde girl playing on the beach, completely unaware of the boatload of refugees filing past her. "In the world view of that child there is no place for affliction," writes Boochani, "in her world, there is no space for the hardship that comes from injustice."[59] While spatially proximate, these territories produce disparate conditions. They establish not just a different set of expectations and norms, but an entirely different understanding of who a subject is, what kinds of agencies and abilities they possess, and what the governing of that subject entails. Indeed, the excision previously discussed means that the asylum-seeker, in a strange way, has never set foot in "Australia" proper, has not entered the bounded space that might afford her a distinct set of legal rights. The villager lives within the Commonwealth; the asylum-seeker held nearby lives outside it.

Seen as twin territories, Christmas Island recalls the premise of *The City & The City* by science fiction author China Mieville.[60] In the novel, the two "crosshatched countries" of Beszel and Ul Qoma lie interposed on top of each other, each with their own states and subjects, their own histories and exigencies. Inhabitants of each city have learned to "unsee" the other territory, to consciously ignore the individuals and architectures that do not belong. While occupying the same terrain, those sights and sounds belong to another world. Walking through the streets, the narrator is "hemmed in by people not in my city,"[61] people who are not recognized by his territory and who possess an entirely different set of rights and responsibilities.

If Mieville's novel is fictional, it gestures to the complex interweavings of contemporary territories, their mingling and splicing, interlacing and interfacing. In an article on asylum-seekers, scholar Alison Mountz asserted that "*who* one is relates to where one is located."[62] Yet what Christmas Island demonstrates is the multiplicity of territories that can pervade a single location. In this sense, the island exemplifies a broader condition, albeit in a more explicit way. "What might seem as an anomaly both within a Westphalian and a post-Westphalian frame," suggest Optiz and Tellman, "could in fact be a paradigmatic phenomenon of the 'present logics of territory' that find their visible expression in the proliferation of different types of zones."[63] These zones mean that inhabitants of the same island, located just a few kilometers apart, can possess a very different status. While the "valid" citizen and the "invalid" migrant may share the same soil, they are subjectivated by two fundamentally distinct territories. These intermeshed spaces are constructed not only through physical borders, but through legal distinctions, sociocultural divisions, and technically constructed differences.

But, perhaps more speculatively, we might also ask to what extent these twin territories might be two sides of the same coin, two modes of the same spatialized power. Is this ability to enact difference, to support the subject and exclude the subaltern, not a core ability for regimes of governance? Territory is "essentially classificatory, it may have the function (or at least the effect) of reifying forms of identity and difference," observes David Delaney. "It is very often a means of controlling what is 'inside' the lines by limiting access or excluding others."[64] Following the disparate conditions experienced by the migrant and the resident on Christmas Island leads us toward this classificatory role of territory, this ability to formalize and intensify difference.

What all migrants share, asserts Thomas Nail, is that their attempted movement has resulted in a "certain degree of expulsion from their territorial, political, juridical, or economic status."[65] Yet this expulsion is not inherent or automatic, but must be enacted. In *Expulsions*, Saskia Sassen argues that the acute conditions endured by marginal populations like migrants mean they are effectively expelled from circuits of social and financial capital. For Sassen, there is a "savage sorting" enacted on these subjects, an intense differentiation that exacerbates classical divides of citizen and noncitizen, resident and migrant, rich and poor.[66] Yet rather than cast the blame on the forces of globalization and the breakdown of state-based safeguards, this dynamic remains closely tied to the nation-state and questions of territory. Far from a borderless world of global flows, Sassen asserts that we're witnessing "a multiplication of these systemic edges within our national sovereign territories."[67] These systemic edges not only construct difference, but formalize it, delineating the inside from the outside, the included elite from the expelled remainder. "In play in all these processes," asserts Sassen, "is the question of membership and constitutive participation."[68] Sorting determines who is in and who is out.

Immigration procedures help surface the racializing element at work in the sorting carried out by the state. For Michel Foucault, difference was what created a "caesura within a biological continuum,"[69] a break or rupture in a formerly smooth spectrum of population. Where once there was an undifferentiated mass, there are now classifications and divisions. Where formerly there was a singular totality, there is now a friend and an enemy, an us and them. Indeed, enacting difference—the isolation and exclusion of those deemed illegitimate in order to protect those deemed legitimate—is integral to biopolitics. For Foucault, this form of state-based racism explained how governance predicated on protecting life could rationalize its destruction. Such destruction is not framed as militant or adversarial, but as the necessary response to "threats, either external or internal, to the population and for the population."[70] The repulsion and subjugation of a marginal group is necessary for the health and strength of the hegemony. Some lives are privileged while others are denigrated. Jodi Melamed's work on racial capitalism extends this approach, updating it to account for contemporary neoliberalism where the state and private companies often work hand in hand. For Melamed, the logic of differentiation is at the very core of such state-capital orders because "accumulation requires loss, disposability, and the unequal differentiation of human value."[71] Appropriation for some necessitates dispossession for others.

Taken together, these theorists suggest difference-making as a kind of core routine. As Melamed asserts, sorting creates "discrete identities, distinct territorializations and sovereignties, and discontinuities between the political and the economic, the internal and the external, and the valued and the devalued."[72] On Christmas Island, the differentiation between valued and devalued is accomplished through a multivalent logic that accounts for where an individual was born, how they arrived at the island, and what kind of documentation they possess. The villager benefits from extensive state support, ranging from educational opportunities to improved telecommunication infrastructures. These initiatives aim to reduce her isolation, to integrate her with wider social and economic circuits, and to bolster her future potential. The valid citizen is a valued life. The asylum-seeker, by contrast, bears the brunt of state antagonism aiming to hinder her movement, to detain her for months or years on end, to disconnect her from the legal and social resources of the mainland, and ultimately in many cases to expel her from its sovereign territory. The noncitizen is a nonvalued life.

Offshore sites are territories that crystallize this difference, rendering this calculus disturbingly visible. Here we must confront the extent to which the alien and the citizen are linked; the government justifies the brutal treatment of the former as necessary to secure the lives and livelihoods of the latter. Despite its tiny footprint, argues Peter Chambers, Christmas Island is "an integral site for the reproduction of Australian society."[73] In the imaginary of immigration, the island allows the danger posed by the asylum-seeker to be carefully corralled. For Nadine El-Enany and Sarah Keenan, the small islands surrounding Australia such as Christmas Island and Nauru are "sites for the isolation and punishment of racialized people whose very existence on the continent threatens the fragile skeleton of white Australian sovereignty."[74] This offshore site offers invisibility and isolation, a space where the "illegitimate" individual can be detained and processed without threatening the stability of the national populace on the mainland. Chambers explicitly draws out the difference-making potential of these offshore spaces, the way in which they "separate the mobile, 'high-value' lives of some from the immobilized 'no value' suffering inflicted on others."[75] For the state, the formation of a special territory and its pathologic treatment of particular lives will always be rationalized by pointing to the majority of lives, an uncomfortable but necessary intervention made in the national interest. The alien is expelled to sustain the health of the citizen.

Of course, one of the primary mechanisms for establishing difference is the border. In encountering the border, the subject is exposed to the scrutiny of the state, revealing details such as her sociocultural origins, her past migrations, and her desired goals. These details come together to form a highly selective portrait that is graded against immigration criteria. This evaluation, in turn, allows for classification or filtering, a decision that results in acceptance, detainment, relocation, or outright deportation. "Australia's border security apparatus uses Christmas Island to scrupulously and anxiously screen the region for threats," notes Chambers, "which, having interdicted, it transfers and detains until such time as they can be recognized by the state as either recipient-objects deserving of protection or unacceptable, unworthy risk entities who should be rejected and returned, depending on the decision."[76] The border is thus a decision-making mechanism, a logic gate or filter that allows individuals to be assessed and responded to in powerful ways.

Indeed, if the border is one of the great differentiators, then the extension of borders into offshore processing zones and island detainment sites suggest an attempt to move this mechanism outwards. This shift toward externalization, occurring not just in Australia but across the European Union, for instance, has been noted by many scholars.[77] Today the border has become "less the contour of a sovereign administrative unit and rather a reactive process,"[78] an instrument to manage, channel, and control the flows of migration. But rather than a "reactive process," this instrument is better understood as proactive or preemptive. For immigration regimes, the entry point at the airport or seaport comes far too late; the subject has already reached the territory of the mainland, where rights can be asserted and support drawn upon. Offshore sites like Christmas Island remedy this tardy intervention, establishing a geography that essentially provides a form of prescreening. This allows the state to establish difference earlier, to introduce the sovereign decision further forward in the asylum-seeking journey. In this sense, the vast geographical expansion of borders seeks to carry out a temporal anticipation, where movements can be predicted, deflected, and discouraged. As Chambers stresses, border security forms "a general horizon of future-oriented, future-orienting anxiety."[79] The island territory contributes toward an imaginary of preemptive power, where immigration threats can be anticipated and defused with early interventions, kept from developing into more potent dangers.

Christmas Island crystallizes some of the key dynamics of contemporary territories, registering their complexities and contradictions. In diving into this particular site, this chapter has aimed to inject a degree of subjectivity into the often abstract notion of territory, moving past the theoretical and juridical to explore the way it intersects with individual lives, physical bodies, and fervent aspirations. These conditions are not universal but particular; they are discrepant rather than generic. For the asylum-seeker, this territory is one striving to impede their geographical and legal progress, to incarcerate them for an indefinite amount of time, and potentially to expel them altogether, forcing a return to a dangerous situation in their homelands. For the legitimate citizen inhabiting the same patch of sand and soil, conditions are very different. For these villagers, this territory provides informational infrastructures that aim to integrate them as modern subjects, to facilitate their education and livelihoods, and to connect them into wider economic and social circuits.

Territory, then, bears down on some while supporting others; it impinges on the lives of the marginal while enhancing the agencies of those deemed central. Rather than paradoxical, this difference-making can be understood as fundamental. From Sassen's "savage sorting" to Foucault's "caesura" and Melamed's "discrete identities," this differentiation is integral to regimes of governance. Territory assists in constructing and enacting this difference. In doing so, it becomes a kind of filter or logic gate, formalizing a populational division. Those deemed to be dangerous or worthless are detained and expelled, while those deemed valid are supported and integrated. Indeed, the state rationalizes its hard stance on immigration by linking the two groups. "*We* remain standing here to ensure that *they* don't come," proclaimed Prime

Minister Scott Morrison in a recent press conference.[80] Some lives are kept precarious so that others may be secured.

The next chapter continues two of the key themes here: the nation and disparity. It examines how Singapore constructs multiple types of territory through landmass expansion, informational networks, and computational processing. This empire-building carries out a heavy physical toll on the ecologies and laborers it extracts from. Yet it also enacts a more subtle inequality through digital technologies, privileging some groups while rendering others invisible.

5 • Constructing the Nation in Singapore

Just off the coast of Singapore, a barge appears and levers a hose off its bow. A switch is pressed and the hose begins shooting tons of sand into the surrounding water. The sand will settle along the bottom, eventually forming a new, extended coastline to the island. This "land reclamation" is one way in which Singapore constructs its territory. The footprint of the nation-state is literally expanded, grain by grain, truckload by truckload.

Under the waterline of Singapore, a submarine cable snakes along the ocean floor. To avoid getting snagged by anchors or damaged by sharks, it is buried meters below the ocean floor. Underneath its layers of protective steel sheathing, the fiber optic cable is composed of silica strands. This cable provides the ability to transfer vast amounts of data at lightning fast speed. Together, these cables form an undersea network, a territory that allows the tiny nation of Singapore to distribute capital globally, to connect with far off continents, and to rapidly circulate data in various forms.

Deep within a data center in Singapore, a server spins up. Its processor has been specifically designed to accelerate complex queries on huge datasets. Together with the other machines in the server rack, it checks millions of entries for certain variables, dynamically assembling a population and visualizing them in real time. The silicon of the chip here stands for the range of capabilities that Singapore, with its "Smart Nation" imaginary, might wield. Such technologies enable new modes of governance and control, unlocking new ways of conceiving and constructing territory. In each of these cases, a distinct formation of territory emerges, one drawing upon divergent technical, political, and governmental understandings.

This chapter investigates territory through the lens of sand. It seeks to productively complicate established understandings of territory by presenting several distinct yet intersecting versions of territory. Territory has traditionally been understood as a bounded space that is claimed by a government. Storey, for instance, begins his exploration of territory by defining it as "a portion of geographic space that is claimed or occupied."[1] Cowen and Gilbert frame it as "land that has been identified and claimed by a person or people."[2] Stuart Elden is perhaps the foremost thinker around territory with his comprehensive genealogy of the concept in *The Birth of Territory*. Elden initially appears to offer a fascinating alternative, arguing that territory is a "political technology," a bundle of diverse political techniques deployed by the state in order to enact, maintain, and contest their spaces of governance. Yet while this framing seems promising, Elden seems to conclude toward the end of the study that these techniques are "techniques for measuring land and controlling terrain."[3] Territory reverts once more to a bounded space, only this time with high-resolution edges and computational tools. In these conventional framings, territory retains strong links to the soil and the state.

Such framings fail to adequately grasp both the modes and means of contemporary territoriality. In terms of modes, rather than solely the bordered space of jurisdictional control, we witness a proliferation of different forms of territory. Over the last decade, work has explored networks and territory,[4] "territories that deborder territoriality,"[5] logistical territories,[6] and "territories beyond terra."[7] These spaces reconfigure or extend beyond conventional borders, but are still spaces where influence is asserted, labor is organized, and capital is extracted. In terms of means, they signal a shift from the strictly political to the politico-technical, where information infrastructure and technological operations enable new forms of governance. This governance may be taken up by the government, but also intersects with private enterprise and contains its own embedded logics.

The danger here is that we would continue seeing territory as state-based and one-dimensional, rather than multiple and technical. The state capitol and the ruling party are not the only sources for spatial power. In essence, conditions have changed, but we keep looking in the same place. This is not merely a theoretical point, but a practical and political one in that we fail to direct our critical energies into more targeted or strategic interventions. To understand how and why migrants are excluded or environments damaged, we need to also attend to these contemporary territories and the ways in which they come together.

So this chapter aims to weave together updated understandings with older insights, putting often siloed disciplines in conversation with one another. On the one hand, we have political studies that stress how traditional forms of empire building are forged by taking or claiming land, by appropriating natural resources, and by employing violence on individuals and environments. Emerging from Marx's work on primitive accumulation, political geographer David Harvey has developed this concept into "accumulation by dispossession."[8] Here, wealth in its many forms is produced for some by taking from others. This mode is characterized by direct or physical force exerted on both human beings and nature.[9] On the other hand, we have media studies that focus on the newer forms of informational technologies that are leveraged by both state and nonstate actors. As our lives become increasingly mediated through data, the control over the production and circulation of this information becomes a key political hinge.[10] While such technologies are often surrounded by forms of technopositive rhetoric, they are also forms of governance that enact systemic power relations. Embedded with norms, values, and bias, they privilege some while excluding others.

The triple territories of sand, silica, and silicon, then, while unorthodox, begin to combine these twin strands. Interposing these territories on top of each other starts building a richer, messier, and more multilayered view. Within these portraits, contradictions certainly abound, but intersections also become apparent. Ours is a moment in which the sand-based territory of land reclamation, with its brutal excavation of beaches and riverbeds, exists alongside the silicon-based territory of computation, with its privileging of the smart citizen and filtering out of the migrant. Overt ecological and anthropological violence sits side by side with the more subtle racial inequalities and class-based invisibilities of information communication technologies.

To examine these intersections, this chapter focuses on Singapore. This city-state, built atop reclaimed land, linked with fiber optic cable, and incessantly processing data, brings together sand, silica, and silicon. Singapore certainly epitomizes these dynamics, illustrating these territories more clearly than other nation-states could. Singapore's technical connectivity and extensive influence, despite its tiny physical size, highlights the ways in which territories go beyond a geophysical footprint. However, Singapore is far from being an isolated case. Dubai, the Netherlands, Korea, and Hong Kong are also undertaking vast land reclamation projects.[11] The United States and China also increasingly see undersea cables as a new geopolitical territory.[12] And the United Kingdom, Finland, and Estonia also have their own smart or digital nation initiatives.[13]

The encroachment of the state far beyond its immediate territory has not gone unnoticed in urban studies. Two decades ago, Kris Olds and Henry Yeung were already citing Singapore as a global city-state that was able to develop a "terrain of extraterritorial influence" through "both attracting in material and non-material flows, and in functioning as a command and control centre for the flows and networks that reach out at regional (for the most part) and sometimes global scales."[14] This vein of work looks beyond the all-too-easy label of "the global city," asking what globality means, how we might distinguish between different forms of it, and how it is established. Yet if there are certainly insights here, I want to move from the abstract to the concrete. What are these flows? How is this terrain of extraterritorial influence established? And how are forms of command and control operationalized? In particular, I'm interested in the role of contemporary data infrastructures, and their ability to structure practices, transmit information, and facilitate labor and trade, exerting influence in material ways. In this sense, sand, silica, and silicon ground this inquiry, giving us flows to focus on and mechanisms to home in on.

Singapore, then, is a useful case study for a broader set of dynamics that apply to a variety of nations around the world. It demonstrates the diverse forms of territory at work, the ways these are leveraged to advance national interests, and the force they exert over subjects and spaces. It provides a specific site of focus, even if the global links of smuggling, supply chains, and transcontinental connections mean that scalar operations are also constantly spiraling outward. Benjamin Bratton has called for new "ways to account for the intersecting complexities of computational globalization, its thickened geographies, its mysterious weaving of geometries of governance and territory, seen on their own terms, not as transgressions of some other system."[15] This chapter takes up that challenge. Contemporary territories emerge from the contested interplay of people and things, from the friction between governmental institutions and computational operations—from the messy meshing of sand, silica, and silicon.

Sand

After water, sand is the most consumed natural resource on earth. Much of this consumption takes place in the construction industry, where sand is used in mortar, tile, bricks, and, most of all, concrete. In these contexts, only sand of a certain particle size can be used. While the desert contains vast expanses of sand, such ultra-fine particles, worn into perfect spheres by the wind, are unsuitable for most applications. Indeed, countries like Qatar continue to import large quantities of sand, and the value of sand-like material brought into Saudi Arabia each year equates to hundreds of millions of dollars.[16]

For Singapore, sand is not only a material for constructing buildings, but for fabricating the very ground of the country itself—for expanding outward as well as upward. In land reclamation, land is formed by claiming back space from an ocean, river, or waterway. Sand, whether dredged from the bottom of the sea, mined from lakes, or imported from other countries, is the crucial material in this process. Through a process called "in-filling," thousands of tons of sand are dumped, piped, or pumped from barges, enlarging the coastline and the usable footprint of the country. Grain by grain, a territory is slowly extended outward into the water. In this sense, land "reclamation" should properly be termed "land fabrication," a technique allowing the design and production of landmass at the scales required by the sovereign.

Land reclamation can be considered a technology that dovetails into broader narratives of technically driven progress. "Less than a century ago, Singapore was a small swamp-filled island," begins one description of the island-nation, but "in a span of less than 50 years, the city-state has transformed into a major global commerce, financial, and transportation hub."[17] The swamp here symbolizes the country as a cultural backwater, a nation-state still sloughing through the bogs when compared to the productivity and progress of its global competitors. In draining the swamp and reclaiming the land, the state starts to assert control over the territory, to shape its environment by technical means. As Elden reminds us, "measuring land and controlling terrain" are key for this more conventional form of territoriality.[18] Jurong Town was constructed by filling mangrove estuaries, covering ponds, resettling farms, and leveling hills. Jurong Island was fabricated by amalgamating seven offshore islands to form a single island with squared-off edges, a tidy and highly artificial landmass now used as an industrial park. Here, nature is domesticated, the shoreline tamed and extended. Singapore lifts itself out of the mud, becoming an informational and economic nexus and ascending into the echelons of the global elite. This is the tale of the "Singapore Miracle."[19]

As Singapore grew, pushing up against the hard boundary of the sea, its territory has been incessantly remade. Over the decades, various state agencies have transformed "useless" oceanic space into useful terrestrial space. For the Maritime Development Authority, land has been used for port facilities and airport terminals. For the Jurong Town Corporation, land has become industrial parks aimed at the lucrative petrochemical industry. For the Housing and Development Board, land provided urgently needed apartments for a booming population. Following the spirit of technical progress, these major projects have aimed to maximize the island-state's territory, optimizing it as a kind of variable. Indeed, over the last 40 years, Singapore has used this technique repeatedly, increasing its land area by 20 percent and extending its territory by 130 square kilometers in total.[20] The result, as one cartographer described it, has been a "permanent territorial revolution."[21]

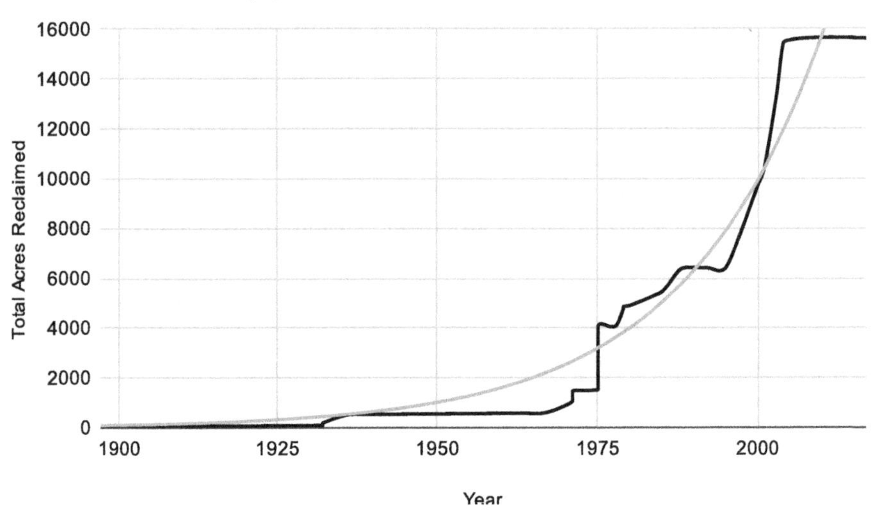

Fig. 3. Total Acres Reclaimed by Singapore. (*Source:* Compiled from figures taken from Lim Tin Seng 2017.)

A time-lapse film of these changes has been assembled, stitched together from satellite photos over the years. As the decades flick past, landmarks come and go, making the video a disorienting experience. The landscape buckles and folds; the shoreline undulates and then extends; the edge suddenly becomes the interior. These alterations not only adjust the coastline but also shift the identity and memory of its inhabitants, rewriting what Singapore is and what it means to be Singaporean.[22] Familiar landmarks and the ways of life that accompanied them are deleted; kampongs are erased and more "desirable" neighborhoods of high-rise apartments shimmer into existence. Territory has been made fluid.

Singapore is one of the largest importers of sand worldwide. One project in Singapore involved the reclamation of 1,500 hectares of land, requiring 500 million cubic meters of sand to be dredged at sea and brought ashore.[23] Table 1 draws on Singaporean scholar Lim Tin Seng to construct a timeline of Singapore's major land reclamation projects in the 20th century, from the smaller forays carried out by British administration to the vast transformations in the 1980s and 1990s. One of the most recent projects aims to extend the usable land around the Pasir Panjang seaport, fabricating space for two new container terminals.

Early on, sand was heavily imported from Indonesia, where a resource-strapped government was unable to curb illegal sand mining. Based on the

Table 1. Singapore Land Reclamation Projects by Year

Description	Year	Acres	Total Acres	Agency
Telok Ayer 1	1897	42	42	British
Beach Road Reclamation	1932	47	89	British
Telok Ayer 2	1932	88	177	British
Kallang Basin	1936	339	516	British
Connaught Drive	1939	6	522	British
Jurong Industrial Site	1963	46	568	JTC
Keppel Harbour	1967	23	591	MPA
East Reclamation Phases 1 and 2	1971	458	1,049	HDB
Kallang Basin	1971	400	1,449	HDB
East Reclamation Phase 3	1975	67	1,516	HDB
East Reclamation Phase 4	1975	486	2,002	HDB
Jurong and Tuas ("string of projects" over the 1970s)	1975	2,000	4,002	JTC
East Reclamation Phase 5	1977	34	4,036	HDB
Clementi New Town	1978	89	4,125	HDB
East Reclamation Phases 6 and 7	1979	660	4,785	HDB
Pasir Panjang	1979	61	4,846	MPA
Pasir Ris	1980	44	4,890	HDB
Pulau Tekong	1985	540	5,430	MPA
Punggol	1986	277	5,707	HDB
Tuas	1988	650	6,357	JTC
Urban Waterfront Promenade	1992	38	6,395	HDB
Woodlands Checkpoint and Tuas Checkpoint	1995	30	6,425	HDB
Pulau Tekong enlargement	2000	3,310	9,735	MPA
Pasir Ris to Seletar	2001	685	10,420	HDB
Jurong Island	2003	3,000	13,420	JTC
Changi Airport	2004	2,000	15,420	MPA
Pasir Panjang Terminal Phases 3 and 4	2017	200	15,620	MPA

MPA = Maritime Port Authority, HDB = Housing and Development Board, JTC = Jurong Town Corporation lucrative trade, islands became "buried treasure" for these sand pirates, who dug up entire beaches, sold the sand and gravel to suppliers, and left the rest to erode in the waves.[24] Nipah Island was an early casualty. The island, lying between Singapore and Indonesia, was mined so heavily that in 2003 it disappeared from sight altogether, "with only 3 to 4 palms trees visible to mark the island's location."[25] This matters because Nipah Island serves as a point of reference for Indonesia's sea borders; "if the island sinks completely the international boundary between Indonesia and Singapore will change—to Singapore's advantage."[26] Here we see a territorial shift on two fronts. Sand mining extracts resources from one country in order to fabricate land, grain by grain, in another. At the same time, sand mining works to erode and eliminate, deleting an entire landmass as a point of reference and reconfiguring the territorial boundaries between the two nations.

Since then, rapacious mining activities have resulted in at least 24 more sand islands in Indonesia being erased entirely.[27] In 2007, Indonesia officially banned exporting sand, although black-market operations undoubtedly continue. Yet this move has simply resulted in Singapore turning to other neighbors: Vietnam, Cambodia, China, and Malaysia. "What these people are doing is selling a little bit of Malaysia," decried one local about operations that "dig, keep digging Malaysia and give her to other people."[28] Similarly, Cambodia has suffered extensive sand mining, where 300 ton barges are filled, transferred to 5,000 ton barges upriver, and then transported directly to Singapore for construction and reclamation projects.[29]

As the island extends further into the sea, depths get larger and larger, requiring more material to fill. And as supplies close to home become exhausted, the island-state turns to sources further away or more ethically dubious. The result is that sand mining continues unabated, particularly in underdeveloped countries, where cheaper labor and lack of regulation produces conditions ripe for exploitation.[30] Singapore successfully extends its sovereign footprint, but this becomes progressively more difficult, requiring more material, from more suppliers, under more precarious conditions.

Territories of sand are territories built by violence. There is an ecological violence already alluded to. Beaches are stripped back to bare rock; rivers are dredged, clouding the water and killing marine life; lakes are carved into, lowering water tables.[31] In the Koh Kong estuary, a pristine site of dense mangrove islands, sand mining has led to concerns about shore collapse, the smothering of benthic organisms, and large-scale shifts in fragile marine ecosystems.[32] These ecological shifts have human impact, affecting the lives and livelihoods of those who occupy these environments. In Malaysia, two rivers have dried up, with water receding and the land barren, halving one fisherman's income from RM30 to RM15, the equivalent of around $3.50 US dollars per day.[33] In destroying environments, sand mining also erodes the life that depends on them, stripping away the traditional means of subsistence long relied on by its human inhabitants.

Alongside this damage to waterways and species is also a direct bodily violence. Sand has now become a black market activity, with sand mafias controlling territory, bribing officials, warring with competitors, and forcibly subjugating those who would stand in their way. In Indonesia in 2015, two farmers, Salim and Tosan, protested against an illegal beach sand-mining operation: "The mine operators threatened to kill them if they kept interfering; the farmers reported the threats to the police and asked for protection. Soon after, at least a dozen men attacked Tosan, ran him over with a motorcycle and left him for dead in the middle of the road. Salim was battered and stabbed to death. His body was left on the street with his hands tied behind his back."[34] These acts are stark reminders that violence persists even in modern day nation building. They slot into a longer historical arc of empires built upon an edifice of coercion, subjugation, and domination.[35] Sand mining demonstrates how territorial expansion—whether through the horizontal vector of sand for land reclamation or the vertical vector of concrete for housing and urbanization—still depends on regimes of labor largely indifferent to both ecological and anthropological forms of life.

Sand-based territories tap into a deep historical vein of sovereign space and imperial expansion. For Schmitt, it is land—whether constructed from sand, soil, or stone—that constitutes the legal basis of territorial authority. According to the jurist, the "great primeval acts of law remained terrestrial orientations," with the appropriation of land being key among them. The formation of legal power can be traced back to its designation and allocation, to "an initial measurement and distribution of usable soil."[36] Others have also observed this close coupling. As Schmitt notes, Immanuel Kant spoke of "*territorial sovereignty* or, more preferably, of *supreme proprietorship of the soil*."[37] Here, ownership and control over the earth is the substrate for legal sovereignty—the immensely complex scaffold of the law sits atop this primal foundation. Indeed, land reclamation closely resembles Schmitt's description of one kind of land appropriation, in which "a parcel of land is extracted from a space that until then had been considered to be free."[38] For the Singapore government, the space of the sea is a free space, unallocated and unclaimed. In this sense, their choice of land reclamation as the path of least resistance is one that Schmitt anticipated. "It is not difficult to comprehend," he observed, "that acquisition of formerly free territory, lacking any owner or master, presents a different and simpler legal problem than does acquisition of territory with recognized ownership."[39]

Yet these territories also diverge from Schmitt's understanding. Technologies enable territory to be fabricated, synthesized, and imported, a set of operations that introduce a difference in kind, not just in degree. In describing the taking (*nehmen*) of nomos, Schmitt asserts that a kingdom was first forged through the "seizure of land" followed by an "appropriation of the sea."[40] But what Schmitt could not have foreseen is how these ancient drives have been amplified and coupled together through technological development such as river dredging, material in-filling, and global logistics. Land reclamation accomplishes both the seizure of land and the appropriation of the sea in a single movement and at vast scales, grasping uncontestable territory by encroaching further and further into oceanic space. Indeed, Bratton has stressed that informational technologies and global platforms mean that the classical Schmittian understanding of territory must now be updated. For Bratton, this "space of planetary-scale computation is a new kind of 'free soil'" that challenges conventional Westphalian models.[41] The next section explores these new technical capacities, examining how subsea internet cables forge new forms of territoriality.

Silica

If sand constructs one form of territory, silica forges another. Fiber optic cable is composed of long filaments, each the thickness of a strand of human hair, drawn from molten silica glass. Signals are transmitted down these filaments at the speed of light, kept from escaping by the reflective properties of silica. It is this fiber optic cable that provides the basis for contemporary data transmission. Laid along the seabed and interspersed with repeater stations, these cables stretch thousands of kilometers, forming intercity or even transcontinental connections. There are currently about 500 undersea cables worldwide, with new cables constantly coming online. Thus, while these undersea cables have a long, colonial lineage, they remain key technical infrastructures in the present, continuing to carry the vast majority of internet traffic.

In Singapore, cables provide the backbone for information infrastructures, underpinning financial services, video streaming, mobile applications, and social media platforms. Here, cables are subjected to twinned pressures. On the one hand, data consumption is growing exponentially, with higher data volumes produced by rich media and a growing constellation of sensors and devices. On the other hand, activities like financial trading or real-time gaming demand lower latency, with millisecond delays considered inexcusable. "Our way of life is changing," stated one PricewaterhouseCoopers report on Asia Pacific infrastructures, with smartphone use, rich media, and digital solutions resulting in "sharp growth in the amount of data generated, consumed, stored and transferred."

New cable projects, with new designs, attempt to keep pace with these needs. They aim, as Rossiter observes, to "probe the territory of the technical in an attempt to graft increased processing speed and operational performance upon the transit of people and things."[42] The new Australia-Singapore cable, for example, has a capacity of 40 terabits per second, allowing it to stream eight million high-definition movies simultaneously; completed in 2018, it allows data to travel from Perth to Singapore in under 50 milliseconds.[43] The Indigo cable has also been recently lit up, following a similar route. Funded by a consortium that includes Google and Singtel, it connects Sydney, Perth, and Singapore, supporting data transmission of 36 terabits per second.[44] In fact—harkening back to the previous section—the cable connects into Singapore at the cable landing station in Tuas, a peninsula constructed entirely from reclaimed land that did not exist 20 years ago. Here we see one of the ways in which multiple forms of territory intersect with each other, feeding off the gains and new capacities that each offers.

Singapore has long realized that cables and connectivity would be key to its territory. Singapore is "by far the most important station in the East," proclaimed Stamford Raffles in 1819, "of much higher value than whole continents of territory."[45] In this vision of a territory, the tiny island leverages networks to extend far beyond itself. As far back as 1870, the Penang-Singapore cable was established, integrating the island-nation into the British Empire's All Red Line system of electric telegraphs. Looping from the Straits of Malacca outward into the Pacific, the city would hook into a high-profile network of world cities, expanding in both reach and significance. This long-standing dream was formalized and further catalyzed by a 1992 government report titled *A Vision of an Intelligent Island*. "Too small to rely on its own resources, Singapore has always plugged into the global networks," the commission observed; if informational infrastructures could be supported and successfully deployed, it would "turn Singapore into a highly efficient switching centre for goods, services, capital, information and people."[46]

The state has embraced this vision of Singapore as a switching center, an intelligent island connected to the world. To this end, the government has established the Infocomm Media Development Authority, which provides information to companies wishing to land new submarine cables in Singapore.

Their regularly updated documents walk applicants through the application process step by step, detailing what infrastructure is available, which agencies to inform, and which permits are required.[47] Initiatives like these have made Singapore one of the most highly connected territories in the world.[48] The city-state is hooked into the East Asia Crossing, the Bay of Bengal Gateway Cable System, the Tata Indicom India-Singapore Cable System, the Asia-Pacific Gateway, the Asia Submarine-Cable Express, and many others.

These existing systems will be joined by new cables currently under construction. The 10,500 km Southeast Asia Japan cable will soon come online, connecting nine markets.[49] Bundled into fiber, sheathed in protective layers, routed from point to point, and shot through with information at the speed of light, these strands of silicate become a vast communications system, one leveraged by the state for strategic advantage and national interests. Here "infrastructural power" becomes a "territorial program" in itself,[50] one that establishes a set of key imperatives and pursues them by adding more routes, more volume, and more connection points. In doing so, these networks support a vision begun with trade routes, intensified by telegraphy, and vastly expanded through submarine cables, a dream in which the city-state becomes a key informational nexus, a larger-than-life player on the global economic stage.

Table 2 below traces a timeline of undersea cable construction in Singapore. Starting slowly with projects such as ASEAN in the early 1980s, subsea cables connected to Singapore have quickly proliferated. The turn of the century saw a large cluster of cables being built such as the Thailand-Indonesia-Singapore cable and the i2i cable. Since then, construction has exploded, with new projects coming online almost every year. These include infrastructures that are touted to be highly strategic for both commercial and governmental reasons, such as the Asia Pacific Gateway network and the high-speed, high-volume Australia-Singapore Cable. These projects have resulted in a densely networked island-state. Today, Singapore is plugged into 22 undersea cables, which link it to close neighbors like Cambodia, Vietnam, and Indonesia, as well as nations further afield: Japan, China, the United States, and India.

Yet it would be overly simple to state that cables merely connect one territory to another, as if data exchange was the informatic equivalent of a package conveyed along a very long string. Certainly in a physical or material sense, fiber optic cable extends beyond the borders of one nation-state, running along the seafloor, and then emerging from the ocean to hook into the communications infrastructure of another state. But as Bratton reminds us: "Network edges and lines produce interiors and exteriors, and so networks are not just superimposed on a given territory, they also produce a real terri-

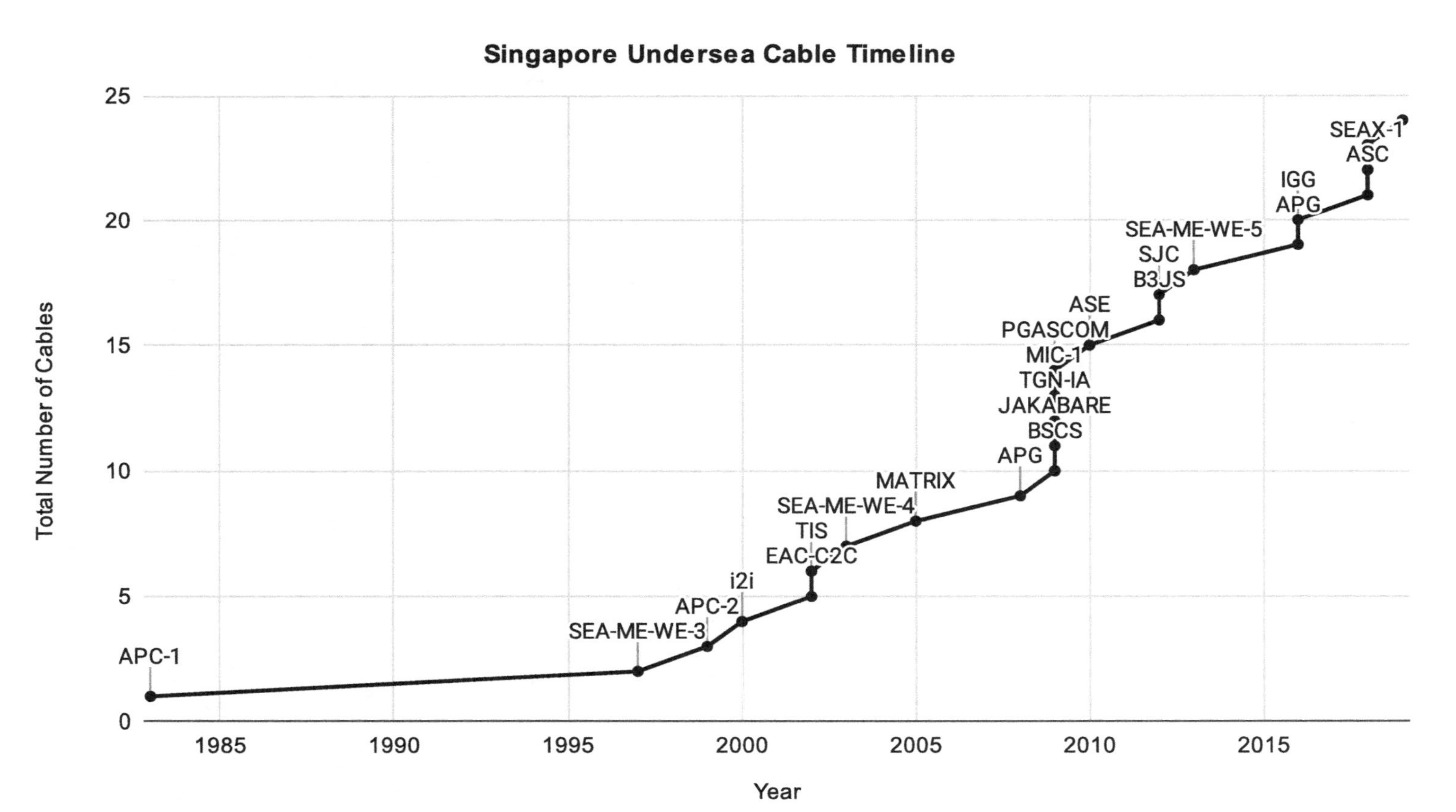

Fig. 4. Singapore Undersea Cable Timeline

Table 2. Singapore Undersea Cable Projects by Year

Cable Name	Year
ASEAN	1983
Asia-Pacific Cable Network	1997
SeaMeWe-3	1999
Asia-Pacific Cable Network 2	2000
i2i	2002
EAC-C2C	2002
Thailand-Indonesia-Singapore (TIS)	2003
SeaMeWe-4	2005
MATRIX	2008
Asia-America Gateway	2009
Batam Singapore Cable System (BSCS)	2009
JAKABARE	2009
Tata TGN-Intra Asia (TGN-IA)	2009
MIC-1 (Moratel International Cable)	2009
PGASCOM	2010
Asia Submarine Cable Express	2012
Jakarta-Bangka-Bintan-Batam-Singapore (B3JS)	2012
Southeast Asia Japan Cable (SJC)	2013
SeaMeWe-5	2016
Asia Pacific Gateway (APG)	2016
Indonesia Global Gateway (IGG) System	2018
Australia-Singapore Cable (ASC)	2018
SEAX-1	2018
INDIGO	2019

tory by striating it."[51] From a territorial perspective, we might say that cables draw zones together so that events that occur in one territory quickly propagate to another, so that capital accumulated in one territory might smoothly be transplanted into another, and so that media produced and packaged in one territory can be readily consumed in another.

While these territories are physically disparate, they are informatically aligned: it becomes faster and easier to exchange news, greetings, documents, and money between these two places than between others. If this territory is a diagram, then, it is not two cleanly divided spheres, connected by a line. As John Allen suggests, these spaces are "not linked together or merely brought into contact, but coextensive with the presence of others acting elsewhere."[52] There is a kind of interposition of one territory on another, in which the sights and sounds, events and activities, transactions and relations of one place are more likely to appear or be responded to in another place. Rather than geographically, this territory might be understood topologically, a reach that "is more about *presence* than distance; it is *intensive* rather than extensive, a *relational* arrangement where power *composes* the spaces of which it is a part by stretching, folding or distorting relationships to place certain outcomes within or beyond reach."[53] In this sense, if silica produces a distinct territory, it does through a redistribution of life.

Such a redistribution spills beyond borders, undermining control. Of course, Singapore is known for control, for being a smoothly managed technocratic state. Schmitt once stated that the fundamental problem of sovereignty is the "connection of actual power with the legally highest power."[54] If this is the case, then Singapore, more than many other nation-states, can be said to have "solved" the sovereignty problem. And yet there is also a sense in which these territories—even if planned and authorized by the state—set in motion a whole chain of encounters and interactions that were not anticipated and cannot be entirely corralled. The state actively supported the fiber optic connectivity of the intelligent island, but this has brought new influences and complicated censorship.[55] Singapore wants to become "a coherent city of information, its architecture planned from the ground up," stated William Gibson in his infamous critique, "they expect that whole highways of data will flow into and through their city. Yet they also seem to expect that this won't affect them."[56] Territories may be consciously desired and meticulously erected through top-down hierarchies, but the operations that emerge can create surprising knock-on effects that undermine assumed power.

Indeed, we might ask whether these territories are also deterritorializing. Do these new spatial conditions disorient subjects by putting formerly stable aspects of life in flux and introducing a global set of influences? Networks of cables are key accelerating infrastructures for an informational society, designed expressly to intensify the circulation of data, to increase the volumes and velocities of information that can be transmitted. To what extent must the government buffer its populace and counterbalance these dislocations? For Nur Amali Ibrahim, it is clear that the state must step into this rapidly fluctuating space, asserting order and control; Singapore's "everyday authoritarianism" is a direct response to the "insecurities caused by the rapid movement of people, capital, and ideas in the neoliberal economy."[57] The state, as discussed, has certainly encouraged cable projects and landing stations, facilitating the nation as an intelligent island, a sophisticated interface to the world. Yet what Ibrahim suggests is that these transnational flows are also destabilizing. There is a need to anchor the populace, to maintain a unified national identity in the face of a disaggregating globalization. Singapore's reputable "rule of law," its meticulous sense of order, and its overall pro-business environment provides this counterweight, a sense of stability that entices global corporations, cloud platforms, and financial firms to the island. Here the nation-state—in a very traditional sense, with its associated sovereignty and its grounding in juridical law—must intervene in order to anchor the global city. One "territory" is propped up by another.

Silicon

The third form of territory is one constructed in the silicon of the processor chip. If this material is highly refined—the 99.9999 percent purity or "seven 9s" of electronics-grade silicon—processor production can still be summed up in the phrase "sand to silicon."[58] Here the processor becomes a proxy for a set of data-driven processes, processes used to track individuals, to evaluate their behaviors and routines, to cross-index them against others, and to form an overarching vision of the "nation" as a whole. Rather than a mere technical translation of government processes, this technology offers distinct new forms of governance. As Aihwa Ong suggests, technology allows the nation to "be conceptualized as a kind of problem-space," where "administrative techniques construct social space that becomes a constitutive element in the problematization and creation of human subjects."[59] How might data-driven processes and informational architectures constitute a distinct territory, a computational space with a particular vision of governance and a particular set of subjects?

One access point into this silicon-driven territory is Singapore's Smart Nation program. Launched in 2014, this government-led vision seeks to integrate technology into the daily life of citizens and foster innovation. Smart Nation ushered in an overwhelming number of pilot programs, public-private partnerships, and innovation hubs, from the National Digital Identity framework, to an e-Payments framework, a Smart Nation Sensor Platform, a Smart Urban Mobility architecture, and many others.[60]

One specific example of this silicon-driven territory is DataSpark, a subsidiary of Singtel whose website boasts that they collect "one billion data points per day" from "4.1 million mobile subscribers." Once collected, their proprietary "mobile genome" API, or application programming interface, then segments this data into a distinct set of packages. The People package "reveals demographic signatures," showing home and work location, hangout location, and radius of gyration; the Content package indexes "users' online behavior at different locations," revealing their web visits, categories of apps used, and topics of content; and the Movement package tracks routes made throughout the city, as well as "footfall" outside retail locations and tourist hotspots.[61]

Already then, DataSpark begins to reveal a certain framing of territory, one conducted through the mass capture of mobile information and the classification of users into particular consumer profiles. As Rossiter suggests, such a realm is "not territorial in the geographic sense but is rather derived from amassing colossal amounts of data that enable the centralization of analytic and economic power."[62] These vast repositories of information function as a highly articulated lens for the state, allowing agencies to survey the movement of subjects, to track trends over time, and to zoom in to particular demographics. The borders of the nation-state melt away, replaced by a "queryable" territory, where populations can be combined, cross-indexed, and called up in seemingly limitless permutations.

Yet if this exhaustive data tracking composes a fine-grained territory, it is also an exclusionary one. Programs like DataSpark and the broader Smart Nation initiative promise a brighter future only for those who embrace it, the smart citizen who rushes eagerly toward a technocratic tomorrow. They prompt a fundamental question: Who is included in such imaginaries? Drawing upon ethnographic work, Singaporean scholars Lily Kong and Orlando Woods show how these visions exclude elderly individuals, who have protested that pilot smart home programs make them feel incompetent or surveilled and who have responded with everyday rebellions like draping towels over sensors.[63] They also note how this technically driven dream excludes the migrant workers who preferred using legacy 2.5G mobile networks, networks that have now been shut down by the government for "efficiency" reasons.

Indeed, for an island-nation of five million, Singapore's population of roughly 1.5 million migrants is vast, stretching from domestic carers to construction workers. Where is the place for these marginal demographics and subaltern populations in this silicon-driven territory? Ho Rui An asks: "What does the Smart Nation mean for the workers, sourced largely from the region, whose lives are made vulnerable by transnational capitalism and for whom data is often missing, falsified, or withheld?"[64] In being unwilling or unable to adopt the latest mobile technologies, the movements and behaviors of these "dumb citizens" are never integrated. As Lily Kong and Orlando Woods conclude: "Those that fall outside—whether by choice or circumstance—of the competencies and characteristics of a smart citizen" are incomprehensible.[65] They are left outside the boundaries, failing to be registered within the territory constituted by data collection and computational analysis. In not being counted, these publics do not count.

In this sense, the codification of the territory enacted by Smart Nation initiatives is a double-edged sword. On the one hand, it works to formalize the territory, integrating fragmented public services into all-encompassing platforms (e-Payment and the National Digital Identity initiatives, for instance), and bolstering the everyday capacities of subjects by offering them new technical features and enhanced informational architectures. Here, silicon-driven technologies offer an enticing clarity to governance, transforming the messy, heterogeneous city-state of Singapore into a Smart Nation with a new degree of cohesion and oversight. In this "whole-nation" approach,[66] seemingly every subject is known within the totalizing system; every subject has access to the same set of national services.

On the other hand, this formalization also establishes a hard filter, a territorial boundary that clarifies that the Smart Nation is for the smart citizen. Such computational filtering matters deeply because territory is meant to be a means of "providing security to those 'inside' from those ever-present dangers located 'outside.'"[67] For those formerly on the margins, digital governance enacts a strict delineation, placing them more firmly on the outside. "More than just a technocratic solution to manage the urban ebbs and flows of the city-state," stresses Kenneth Tay, "Singapore's Smart Nation is deeply implicated in the question of citizenship."[68]

This specificity of silicon-driven territory appears again in a DataSpark demo. As populations shift around the island, they tap into the closest cell tower. The platform taps into this "big telco data" in order to visualize the footfall of millions of individuals during a multiday Formula 1 race in the city. In the visualization that results, stacked blocks fluctuate up and down, indicating the number of people at each site. The blocks spring upward at midcity during the race final, and surge again at a nearby concert venue following the competition. In these visualizations, the national border drops away. Indeed, the geography of the state, with its divisions and boundaries, regions and place names, disappears entirely. Distributed across the island, the blocks allow the shape of Singapore to still be vaguely deduced, but it is a territory defined by the cellular activity of telco customers. Here, the nation-state becomes an "abstract and emptiable space"[69] and the population is defined by those individuals whose signal is registered by Singtel.

Homing in on a particular subset of this data, the visualization highlights the number of tourists present within this population, going so far as to isolate the percentage of Australian, British, and Japanese tourists. In this visualization, like the broader Smart Nation, a data-driven logic renders some legible while erasing others. Here, those who count are cellular consumers who move, shop, and spend, digitally registering their activity at the closest cell tower. Given this logic, those who must stay fixed, like the elderly, or who must leave their phones off, such as a care worker, would appear faintly or not at all. The digital territory of silicon does not register all equally. As Ern Ser Tan observes: "There is a digital divide between those in the service and intermediate class, on one side, and the working class, on the other side."[70] The result of this logic, as the visualization highlights, is that the tourist from a desirable country is counted more than those who may be citizens, residents, or migrants within Singapore, yet whose activity remains digitally unmediated.

Territorial Conjunctions

Examining the territories of sand, silica, and silicon in Singapore begins to draw together two disparate understandings. On the one hand, we have a strand focused on the appropriation of land, the exploitation of the environment, and the violence done to bodies. This strand highlights materiality, physical force, and the key role of the centralized state. We might label this the political geography perspective, referencing the rich body of work by scholars like Marx, Harvey, and Moore.[71] On the other hand, we have a strand focused on the unequal ways in which technologies mediate information and facilitate extraction. This strand highlights the flows of data, the values embedded in variables, and the decentralization of governance broadly understood. We might label this the media theoretical perspective and point to work by Gillespie, Kitchin, and Gray.[72]

Sand, silica, and silicon bring these two views together, suggesting the ways in which environmental degradation, for instance, can sit alongside computational inequalities. Contrary to some accounts, there is not a historical progression in which former modes are sloughed off and replaced with more modern equivalents, a "passage from one territoriality to the other."[73] Rather than abandonment of the supposedly outdated, we see the ways in which divergent modes of spatial power persist side by side.

First, we see the splicing together of the *technical and terrestrial.* In an earlier era, we were told that information was borderless and the cloud was somewhere "out there." And of course to a certain extent, information infrastructures do establish new technical conditions that reconfigure spatial dynamics. The silicate-driven territory of cables, for instance, links together high speed financial transactions in Singapore and Hong Kong, transmitting a sell order in a matter of milliseconds. It temporarily brings together a mother in Singapore with her son in Indonesia for a video call, rapidly shuttling images and audio between two points to establish a form of telepresence. If these subjects and spaces are terrestrially distant, these affordances render them technically proximate.

Such a territory, then, certainly stretches across other places and nations. But despite the rhetoric of cyberspace or the cloud, new technologies do not suddenly usher in an ethereal world where space is collapsed. Scholars like Jussi Parikka[74] and Sean Cubitt[75] have demonstrated how technologies are always terrestrial and material, drawing upon the earth's resources to construct their infrastructures and sustain their operations. There is a material underlayer to these territories, from truckloads of sand dredged out of a river bottom to the silicate of fiber optic cable running from one landmass to another. The sinking island of Nipah, for instance, demonstrated how national borders became contested through ecological violence that erased key landmarks. These territories are underpinned by material substrates and situated in the soil of specific places. Matter continues to matter.

The intersection of technicity and materiality is perhaps best demonstrated by the silicon-powered territories discussed earlier. In the DataSpark scenario, for instance, data is sourced from cell towers dotted around the island. This historical infrastructure, built up over time, required the acquisition of parcels of land for towers, the burying of fiber cable in the earth, the mobilization of a local labor force, and significant investments of capital by the state. This is hard infrastructure, embedded in the dirt, that takes up increasingly scarce space. And yet once cell towers are operational and cell data can be captured, this informational matrix begins to form a space all of its own. This "data space" has its own ways of mapping relationships, its own architectures, its own internal topology. The national population, rendered into data, can be cut, queried, and sliced in a multitude of ways, each time forming a new territorial portrait with a distinct set of borders and patterns.

Second, we see the conjoining of the *technical and the imperial.* The exploitation of nature and humans associated with former empires has not vanished. Land "reclamation" adopts a conventional understanding of territory, literally extending the geobody of the nation by pumping sand onto its shoreline. As this sand becomes scarcer, the environmental and anthropological destruction that accompanies it also becomes more violent. As Harvey stresses, "accumulation based upon predation, fraud, and violence" is not some "original stage" that is now past, but a dynamic that can still be witnessed in the present.[76] From police brutality in Hong Kong to the reeducation camps of Xinjiang in China, we see the ways in which physical violence exerted on bodies remains a key state strategy for obtaining and "securing" territory.

However, this direct force on skin and soil is now accompanied by data-driven mediations. The Smart Nation initiatives discussed earlier gestured to some of the ways in which inequality can be embedded into technical systems. These architectures are based on a particular imaginary, they are built with particular assumptions, and they enact particular norms. These work to privilege the "smart citizen" while further excluding marginal populations such as migrants. These inequities do not take the form of physical violence, but they are harmful nonetheless, rendering individuals algorithmically invisible and expelling them from the social, political, and "national" circuits that support their lives and livelihoods.

Indeed, we can start to see how technical mediation could be framed as a newer form of accumulation by dispossession, one which provides wealth, space, and security to some while taking from others. As our lives and activities become increasingly determined by such data, these mediations matter, removing job prospects, altering credit scores, or undermining visa applications for instance. This insight begins to suggest a form of computational violence, albeit one that is procedural rather than physical. This kind of violence is "inscribed into machine architectures," asserts Jonathan Beller, and these inequalities predicated on racial, social, and gender difference are key to what he terms "computational capital."[77]

Whether it takes new forms or old, these negative conditions and unequal experiences begin to erode the dominant "techno-solutionism"[78] of the smart city and the broader narrative of nation-state progress, imaginaries where progress ticks steadily upward. In Singapore's own fable, the Singapore Miracle, the state marries political and technological control to bring about economic prosperity for all. Yet the unevenness apparent here stresses how territories are powerful formations that redistribute the life capacities of both individuals and environments. Some national spaces are extended, others are erased. Some individuals are empowered, others are ignored. Some subjects are granted prosperity; others, like Thai migrant workers, clutch onto "bare life."[79] These disparities recall Gibson's assertion that "the future is here, it's just not evenly distributed."[80] Rather than the happier, healthier tomorrow of state rhetoric, they foreground the fallout of national dreams.

These layered territories are messy, multiple, overlapping. Each has its own logics, its own imperatives, its own forms of spatial production and subjectivation. Together, they challenge us to rethink traditional framings of territory. While a renewed investigation into this concept has certainly been undertaken in previous years, this work remains largely grounded in a state-led tradition. The focus on contemporary Singapore highlighted heterogeneous forms of territory: territories based on smuggled sand and illegal supply chains, territories underpinned by undersea cables that stretch across oceans and connect into continents, and territories where populations are altered every time a data query is run. Each exerts influence over a diverse array of actors and a broad spectrum of spaces. These diverse forms of spatialized power should prompt us to reconsider the concept of territory for our contemporary moment.

Territories come together, conflicting at points yet also complementing each other. Indeed, one of the contributions of sand, silicate, and silicon is that they highlight the *coextensive* nature of territory. Far from being supplanted or superseded, empire and its material violence continues alongside newer forms of data-driven technologies and their systemic inequalities. In these formations, the environmental destruction of sand mining occurs alongside the flows of an undersea cable and the smooth calculations of machine learning. Here the imperial and terrestrial coexists with the technical. While these forms are distinct, their underlying logics sometimes mirror one another. Expropriation can occur through extracting a natural resource or extracting social capital via data.[81] Territories, then, do not just exist in parallel, but intersect and augment each other. As Singaporean scholar Kenneth Tay concludes, "The more Singapore communicates, the more its territory expands, the more it extracts resources from its less-affluent neighbors."[82]

The three chapters in part II of this book have demonstrated "how to do things" with technical territory, from countering the protestor to filtering migrants and constructing the nation. In moving from Hong Kong to Christmas Island and Singapore, the aim has been to show why data infrastructures matter by grounding an analysis in real-world situations. These sociotechnical conditions stress the stakes of information infrastructures, the force they exert on subjects and spaces, and the novel reconfigurations of governance and labor that they unlock. The next chapter continues to think through these stakes while turning to the future and exploring the coming shift from the cloud to the so-called edge. This new computing paradigm hopes to alter the network in profound ways, solving the weaknesses of its predecessor by extending its territory spatially and functionally.

Part III • The Future of Territory

6 • From the Cloud to the Edge

In Asia and around the world, information infrastructures are becoming swamped with data. Over the next few years, 30 billion devices will be connected to networks, from self-driving cars to smart city sensors.[1] Yet existing cloud infrastructures are not designed for their needs. "Moving all computing tasks to the cloud has been an efficient way to process data because there's more computing power in the cloud than in the devices at the network edge," explain two computer scientists, however "the bandwidth of the networks that carry data to and from the cloud hasn't increased appreciably. Thus, with edge devices generating more data, the network is becoming cloud computing's bottleneck."[2]

The sheer weight of this data is certainly a problem. But it is not the only one. These connected devices will usher in new applications and capture new kinds of data. Autonomous vehicles, for instance, cannot afford the delay caused by transferring back to the cloud and waiting for a response. Data must be processed in real time; decisions must be made instantly. Connected cameras and connected medical devices will capture extremely intimate information. Transferring this personal data back to the cloud and storing it would trigger an array of privacy legislation and come with risks of data leaks and breaches.

All of this points to the limits of cloud architectures. If the previous chapters have explored the tremendous force of data infrastructures in constructing territory, this chapter begins by pointing to its weaknesses. Even by 2015, major industry players like Cisco were flatly admitting that "today's cloud models are not designed for the volume, variety, and velocity of data that the IoT generates."[3] The IoT here is the internet of things, that catchall term for smart-home appliances, self-driving cars, medical devices, networked cameras, and a thousand other devices. These diverse things—small, localized, and highly mobile—will all require connection, transmission, and coordination. But traditional cloud architectures cannot accommodate this new list of specialist demands. As one computer science paper simply stated: "The cloud is not enough."[4]

If this moment is a crisis point, the industry also sees it as a window of opportunity. Their solution is to move computation and storage closer to where it is needed. Over the next few years, this will mean shifting many applications from centralized data center facilities to highly distributed devices at the periphery of the network—from the center to the so-called edge. What does this look like on a practical level? The edge is the autonomous car that processes gigabytes of driving data in real time, while funneling a fraction of that back to cloud servers. The edge is the camera that runs its own facial detection model, only sending shots to the cloud when a condition is met. And the edge is the personal health device worn on your body that collects intimate information but anonymizes this data before transmitting it to the manufacturer.

The edge is a distinctive vision, a distributed layer of intelligence deployed at a local level.[5] The dream, in essence, is to evade the growing problem of "data gravity" by moving computation into the nooks and crannies of everyday life. Data is captured and processed on the spot without overwhelming cloud infrastructures. But the edge also refers to the new architectures, infrastructures, and protocols needed to realize that vision. Conceived in 2012, researchers described it as a "non-trivial extension of the cloud"[6] that would introduce a whole new array of challenging technical problems such as networks with thousands of heterogeneous devices. The edge, then, is both paradigm and protocol, both model and mechanism.

In one very pragmatic sense, the edge extends the territory of the cloud. In the rhetoric of industry professionals, transmission of data "all the way back to the cloud" is no longer feasible. Given this urgent problem, edge-based devices, mounted on cell towers or installed in workplaces, provide a way to expand the network. The cloud can no longer be siloed in the major metropolitan center, but will need to stretch all the way down to the level of the regional hub, the neighborhood, and the home. Data processing must take place at the site of data production. Certainly, then, this represents an extension of technical territory. Governance drawing on these infrastructures expands its operational space, moving across a greater array of sites and situations, becoming more distributed, more diffuse.

But to understand the edge as merely extension would be simplistic. The edge is not simply a matter of enlarging the territory of the cloud, of continuing the same kinds of techniques and logics over a larger area or more diverse set of spaces. Instead, this extension is also a fundamental recalibration. Leaving the data center means operating with less security, less power, and potentially less stable connectivity. Digging down into the hyperlocal level thus requires not only a different set of hardware, software, and protocols, but a different set of imperatives. Moreover, once instantiated, this territory provides a novel set of conditions—connected to, yet distinct from—the cloud. Driven by rapidly developing edge technologies, these conditions often outstrip existing safeguards associated with cloud-based architectures, presenting both state and nonstate actors with a new array of capabilities that may be wielded against subjects. The aim of this chapter, then, is to highlight how the territorial extension of the cloud to the edge is not just technically but politically effective, facilitating the apprehension of the individual and extraction of valuable data in new ways.

The edge is seen as a crucial augmentation to the cloud, a counterpart that will provide critical new functionalities. The first section of this chapter compares the cloud and the edge, revealing not only their distinctive technical architectures, but their fundamentally different models. Indeed, from the perspective of power, the edge provides both a distinctly different epistemology, in the sense of knowledge production through data, and topology, in the sense of how technicity is situated vis-à-vis the subject. The second section discusses the result of extending the cloud with the edge: what kind of territory emerges from coupling these opposing architectures? The third section draws on Foucauldian theory, examining how this formation conforms to the notion of "intensification" while complicating it in particular ways. Moving past the blinkered approaches of engineering and pro-business that currently dominate edge rhetoric, the chapter explores this conjoined cloud-edge territory as a form of spatialized power. This twinned architecture is at once technical and political, providing new methods for governance and subjectivation.

Cloud-Edge Comparison

The cloud and the edge comprise a number of important distinctions, from the size and power of devices to how data is handled. From all the small differences that might have been explored, the differences featured below were chosen because they are not just technical but territorial in enabling new forms of spatial power to be taken up. These differences demonstrate how the cloud and the edge are two fundamentally distinct models. But—to anticipate the argument of the next section—they can also be read as highly complementary. In this sense, differences in hardware specifications or network protocols go beyond the merely technical to form a distinctive architecture of control that complements the strengths and weaknesses of its counterpart.

Copper vs. Air. The cloud is connected by cables. Fiber optic cable, sheathed in protective layers, forms the connective tissue that supports data center connectivity. Subsea cables in particular have a long history, comprising an "instrument of power" that contributed to the "shrinking of the world" in the 19th century.[7] Cable placement followed preexisting routes and were understood to be strategically important for these empires, a dynamic that Starosielski terms "copper cable colonialism."[8] Thus, if cables span the globe, they do so unevenly, forming thick striations across the Atlantic, for instance, while leaving sections of Asia and Africa relatively uncovered. This geography is not only asymmetric, but fixed. Cables are ultimately hard infrastructure, requiring the installation of repeater stations, the laying of cable, the onshoring at particular cable landing stations, and so on. Whether set into the seabed or buried in the earth, cables are a pattern of hard lines that cannot be shifted.

Cables excel at ferrying massive electronic payloads, continuing to carry 95 percent or more of the internet's data.[9] Far from being a legacy technology, then, cable construction has accelerated in recent years, creating what industry organizations have described as a building boom. Yet if cables continue to be important, and have certainly been modernized in terms of design, the cable provides an apt image for a conventional form of connective power. The cable is thick and heavy, with armored plating at points. The construction and laying of it required immense capital investment, often through consortiums of up to a dozen stakeholders.[10] And its hardwired signals run between capitals, connecting the central points of (cloud) empires, while ignoring the hinterlands.

In contrast, edge connectivity—particularly toward its margins—will be provided primarily by microwaves. The infrastructure to support this radio network is only just emerging, as cities begin deploying 5G-based hardware like cellular base stations and switches across urban space. The protocols for such radio connectivity are also nascent.[11] Indeed, one of the key delays for rolling out edge-supporting technologies like 5G has been decisions around the radio spectrum. Yet if the details are still being worked out, the overall premise, drawing upon previous standards like 3G, is clear. Edge-based devices will connect with a cascading set of radio links: from the 15 kilometer radius of the macrocell, down to the single kilometer radius of the microcell, then the 250 meter zone of the picocell that supports 100 users, and finally the femtocell that might support only a handful of users.[12]

While these details may be technical, they also suggest an entirely different concept of connectivity—an alternative diagram of how spatial power is to be enacted and maintained. Here, the thick line of the subsea cable, rammed with as much electricity as possible in order to traverse points A and B, is replaced. Instead, the edge suggests an architecture more like a Russian doll, a set of nested rings that users join and leave as they move through space. As Adrian Mackenzie observed early on, "the problem for wireless communication is not to blaze some high-wattage transatlantic path, but to micro-differentiate many paths and to allow them to interweave and entwine with each other."[13] In this diagram, mobility is assumed, tracking the person or thing throughout a bounded area. And in this diagram, connectivity is not one-size-fits-all, but is ratcheted up and down in order to reach those smaller pockets of space. If this "promise of airy, weightless mobility of wireless communication"[14] has yet to be fully realized at an infrastructural level, the imaginary is firmly in place.

Hyperscale vs. Subscale. Cloud giants like Microsoft Azure, Alibaba Cloud, and Amazon Web Services all operate at the hyperscale. In the hyperscale model, surges in demand can be met by a network of data centers in major cities, each with thousands of physical servers and millions of virtual machines. "Each Azure region is comprised of multiple data centers (up to 16)—each roughly the size of a football field—that houses up to 600,000 servers per region," explains one journalist.[15] The 290,000 square feet of Facebook's hyperscale Lumea facility forms a "massive expanse," asserts another reporter.[16] Hyperscale computing "consists of thousands of individual computing nodes with their corresponding networking and storage subsystems, power distribution and conditioning equipment, and extensive cooling systems."[17] Here, computational power is measured in megawatts and new facilities only register when they hit hundreds of thousands of square feet.

Yet scale is not the only distinguishing characteristic of these systems. What characterizes these warehouse-scale forms of computing is that they "belong to a single organization, use a relatively homogeneous hardware and system software platform, and share a common systems management layer."[18] In order to achieve hyperscale, companies must standardize. As one industry whitepaper noted, the key insight from cloud giants is that "hardware standardization and simplification sets the stage for operations at scale."[19] Custom components are replaced with commodity hardware, proprietary setups are substituted with a modular approach. In this sense, hyperscale data centers conform to a broader trend identified by Keller Easterling in which buildings become "reproducible products set within similar urban arrangements"; these are "repeatable phenomena engineered around logistics and the bottom line."[20] If every switch, rack, and process can be rationalized into a universal standard, then scaling up can be accomplished by repeating the same thing, in the same way, at a different location.

If the edge exposes some of the weaknesses of the cloud model, the trend to hyperscale is no exception. As already discussed, connected devices, with their high data outputs and low-latency requirements, can no longer be served by a cloud model. "Is building hyperscale data centers enough?" asked one presenter in a Microsoft Research presentation, immediately responding with a definitive no; the smarter approach is to "build an extensive infrastructure of micro DCs [data centers]."[21] The edge embodies a trend toward a highly distributed model of computation, a layer of intelligence underpinned by a constellation of devices. Diffused throughout regions and neighborhoods, these cell towers, servlets, and microprocessors operate at a fundamentally different scale.

There is a move from a hyperscale model to a subscale model, explains tech CEO Jacob Smith; while the former was about making "a lot of the same things appear in a few places," the latter will be about making "a lot of different things appear in a lot of different places."[22] Rather than thousands of identical racks, Smith's edge infrastructure company will gladly provide clients with a half rack in Hong Kong, for example, that is close to a particular customer base and features custom silicon supporting a particular application. In the place of the homogeneous and the universal that characterizes hyperscale, the subscale stresses the heterogenous and local. It follows Foucault's formula for a new technology of power: "Shift the object and change the scale. Define new tactics in order to reach a target that is now more subtle but also more widely spread in the social body."[23] Rather than expanding to massive proportions, the edge shrinks down, placing itself in proximity to individuals.

Fortress vs. Frontier. The cloud model is one predicted on security and stability. "Data centers," media scholar Tung-Hui Hu suggested, should be "understood as a form of infrastructure designed to sustain itself at all costs."[24] The vision is of an indestructible fortress. Indeed, much of the rhetoric around data centers is based around maintaining an unwavering vigilance against attacks of all kinds, whether stemming from natural disaster, mechanical failure, or human sabotage. "Such threats include excessive server intake temperatures, water leaks, and unauthorized human access to the data center or inappropriate actions by personnel in the data center," warns one industry report.[25] Fire and flood can be shaken off. Wave upon wave of cyberattacks will not break it. This is an architecture of anxiety, characterized by shields and safeguards.

In response to these concerns, cloud provider Iron Mountain has built data centers 200 feet below ground, providing an "additional physical security layer specific to the subterranean nature of our facilities."[26] Recently, Iron Mountain purchased a new facility in Serangoon, Singapore, from financial services stalwart Credit Suisse. SIN-1, as it's known, now features a perimeter fence with a two meter concrete base, topped with anticlimb metal mesh. Similarly, at Equinix's Singapore data center, external measures like hydraulic bollards, security guards, and crash-proof barriers are designed to thwart vehicle attacks on the building itself, while internally, mantraps, antitailgating devices, and 2-factor authentication attempt to secure server rooms from unauthorized entry.[27] While these data center security features may blend into a contemporary aesthetic of white rooms and clean lines, they nevertheless uphold long-standing military imperatives to barricade and defend.

In this sense, cloud computing represents a model of power that is highly secure yet highly situated. Bunkered down and hedged in, the data centers of cloud computing form a hermetically sealed environment that cannot be penetrated by attack. Yet, from the perspective of power, it is precisely this sealed quality that prevented cloud computing from spreading out into the world and attaining the necessary ubiquity. If the fortress of the data center is secure, it is also locked at the center points of cloud empires, limiting its reach.

The edge, by contrast, might be conceived of as the frontier—forward deployed units at the outskirts of existing computational territories. "Giant, centralized server farms that take up 19 city blocks of power are just not going to work everywhere," stated the CEO of one company, which aims at "seeding the landscape with smaller server outposts" to form edge networks.[28] Given this frontier mentality, legacy telecommunication providers like AT&T are repositioning themselves as edge providers, drawing on their scattered network of hundreds of thousands of cell towers and distribution points as potential "candidates for compute."[29]

The edge is thus envisioned as a layer of intelligence spread across space, infusing itself into city infrastructure,[30] permeating into the smart home,[31] and even colonizing the body in the form of wearable and medical devices in order to conduct "pervasive monitoring."[32] As a range of connected devices increasingly comes on the market, the edge stretches into the workroom and the bathroom, the bedroom and the living room. In fact, this is by design. In the industry imaginary, edge-based architectures must be introduced at every locational and scalar juncture where typical data center infrastructures become thin. With this goal in mind, the edge's territory should be everywhere where the cloud is not—those locations or applications where the cloud based model has proved unfeasible technically or unviable economically. The edge begins precisely at the point where the cloud ends.

However, this dynamic frontier of the edge constitutes a far more vulnerable territory. In comparison to the data center, with its list of known clients and known hardware, the edge is distinctly ad hoc, composed of hundreds or thousands of devices dynamically joining and leaving the network. This lack of a global perimeter makes the edge more susceptible to rogue gateway attacks, in which an antagonistic node coaxes users to share data with it.[33] As the prolific literature from computer science attests,[34] the edge—with its high number of heterogeneous devices, consumer-grade hardware, and general lack of authorization and encryption capabilities—presents an array of significant security concerns. If the edge outstrips the cloud in terms of mobility and ubiquity, it trails far behind in terms of security.

Beast vs. Bantam. Intensive processing is integral to the cloud. In a recent industry conference, the CTO of Microsoft Azure laid out the rapid evolution of the processor chips used in their servers, moving from smaller Gen 2 to increasingly larger, faster Gen 3 chips and then through to a board dubbed Godzilla; as client workloads increased, even this was not enough, and the cloud company developed "the Beast" chip with 12 terabytes of memory.[35] The data centers of the cloud are being increasingly filled with high-density compute architectures. Indeed, the extremely high temperatures generated by this high-intensity processing mean that traditional fan cooling is no longer sufficient, initiating a shift where cloud providers like Google are moving to liquid cooling.[36]

If the data centers of the cloud feature monstrous processing power, the edge must rely on a far more meager set of resources. Such hardware may be battery powered, with a small microprocessor, limited storage, and a reduced memory. Edge-based devices are constrained by limited computation resources, requiring a "thrifty" approach.[37] Mobile devices in particular are forced to compromise due to their "resource-poor hardware, insecure connections and energy-driven computing tasks."[38] Moreover, the connectivity of such devices may be uneven, with devices going offline or being powered down entirely. These constraints are proving to be technically challenging, with research exploring ways to offload tasks or reduce the processing required.

These distinctions are embodied beautifully in two images. The first displays Google's Cloud TPU, or tensor processing unit, a variation of the central processing unit (CPU) that has been custom designed for machine learning and other AI-specific applications. Google claims that the monstrous chip, armed with 128 GB of high bandwidth memory, has 420 teraflops of computing power.[39] Snaking through its metal substrate are a series of gray rubber tubes, indicating the chip is liquid cooled.

The second image is Google's Edge TPU. While this is also a tensor pro-

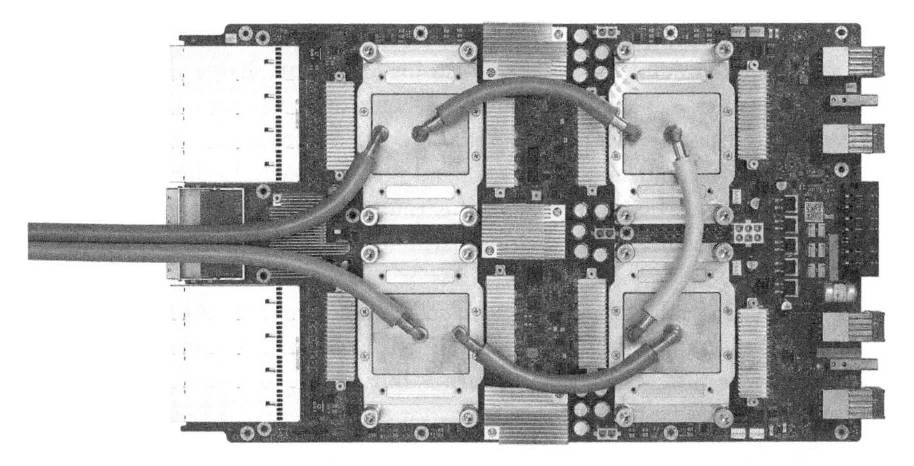

Fig. 5. Google's Cloud TPU

Fig. 6. Google's Edge TPU

cessing unit, designed to run machine learning applications, it is almost diametrically opposed to the first. The Edge TPU is presented on a US one cent coin, stressing its microscopic size. Rather than the raw computational power stressed in the first image, Google notes that the Edge TPU is "tiny," "lightweight," and "low power."[40] The reduced footprint and power requirements means that it can be embedded in a wide variety of connected devices, infusing everyday environments with an additional layer of computation.

Archived vs. Improvised. If the types of data captured differ between the edge and the cloud, so does the processing of this data. If one phrase sums up the imperative of cloud computing, it is the drive to capture it all. The cloud is predicated on the model of an information repository, a databank that is slowly accumulated, organized, and sifted through. In this sense, the cloud model could be considered a rather traditional paradigm, slotting into a longer historical lineage of institutional archives[41] and catalogue systems.[42] This data typically concerns populations or, translated into start-up terminology, user bases. Here, too, the cloud echoes older formations of sovereign power linked to the state, which "maintained an effective monopoly on data regimes concerning whole populations."[43] Indeed, popular platforms often feature user bases far larger than most nation-states.

Deriving insights from the cloud is a matter of assembling as much information as possible at a single point, combining this data into a comprehensive system, and then incessantly combing through this data, whether via human analysis or algorithmic processing. The epistemology of such power is an incessant process of aggregating as much knowledge as possible, and then meditating or reflecting on it, whether through data mining or machine learning. "This is a world where massive amounts of data and applied mathematics replace every other tool that might be brought to bear," claimed a *Wired* editor in a now infamous article, "with enough data, the numbers speak for themselves."[44] Such a form of knowledge production is not about understanding the data, nor about being selective, but aims to "accumulate and mine spectacularly large amounts of data for useful patterns."[45]

The edge, by contrast, carries out processing in a far more immediate and individuated way. A typical edge device, such a camera or sensor, is responding to the gestures of the body facing it, or reacting to temperature changes in the environment around it. Rather than the consolidation of knowledge witnessed in the cloud, a tiny edge device only "knows" about the people and things in its immediate vicinity. This means that, in contrast to the population-level aggregations of the cloud, edge devices are focused predominantly on a person or persons. From smart health to the smart home, the edge model offers the possibility of fixating on an individual to a degree that the cloud never could. Moreover, this processing of data is not slowly assembled over time, but is responded to in the moment. As numerous computer science articles attest,[46] some of the greatest promises of edge computing swirl around its real-time capabilities, with one paper describing real-time video analysis as the edge's "killer app."[47] If this responsiveness is certainly a technical feature produced by reducing latency, it is also an epistemological trait, where knowledge is not held or stored so much as reacted to. In doing

Table 3. Cloud versus Edge Architectures

	Cloud	Edge
POWER	Megawatts	Volts
STORAGE	Terabytes	Kilobytes
CONNECTIVITY	Cable/Fiber	Millimeter/Radio waves
INFORMATION	Abstracted	"Real-World"
PROTOCOLS	HTTP, TCP/IP	5G, SD-WAN
RESOURCES	Concentrated	Reduced, "resource-poor"
PROCESSING	Intensive, accelerated	Low-power, limited
LATENCY	High	Low
LOCATION	Centralized	Decentralized
ARCHITECTURE	Physical (Cables/DCs)	Virtual (Software Defined)
SCALE	Hyperscale	Subscale

so, the edge embodies a kind of active expertise—an immediacy and performativity that directly runs counter to the cloud model's slow churning over its massive repositories of knowledge.

By way of summarizing this comparison section, table 3 (above) outlines key distinctions between the cloud and the edge. While many of these are relatively simple observations about technical architectures, the previous discussion should demonstrate how these specifications combine to form two distinct modalities of power. The cloud and the edge exist in different spheres, they operate in different ways, and they each pursue a different set of imperatives. These specificities mean that each architecture possesses certain strengths and weaknesses when it comes to questions of subjectivation, governance, and control. Clearly, then, the goal becomes to construct a form of power that combines these two modalities. The next section explores what kinds of benefits a cloud-edge nexus offers.

Cloud-Edge Synergies

If the edge was spurred by the crisis of cloud computing, it does not replace it. The edge should be understood as an additional layer, an augmentation to cloud-based affordances. The discussion above laid out the strengths and weaknesses of the cloud and the edge. If the cloud is secure but situated, the edge is vulnerable but mobile. If the cloud is resource rich, capable of high intensity processing, the edge is resource poor, yet able to be embedded anywhere. If the cloud seeks to archive information and exhaustively process it, the edge responds to real-world information in real time. How do these particular affordances dovetail together in terms of power?

One way into this question is by examining how cloud-edge circuits are already being deployed—in machine learning. Here, data is collected from edge-based devices and collated by the closest edge node, processed to select desired values (only license plate numbers, for example), and then passed on to a centralized cloud facility, where it is assembled into a training set of machine learning. High intensity processing in the cloud is used to train a model based on this dataset, gradually becoming better over time. Once completed, the machine learning model is then compressed into a lightweight version and distributed back out to edge devices, where it can function autonomously. This closed loop—taking data from the edge, learning from it in the cloud, and spinning it back out to the edge—presents a nascent but already compelling form of power. Indeed, new divisions like "Greengrass" have been created at Amazon Web Services, and whole new companies like Foghorn have emerged based on leveraging this iterative circuit of "embedding edge intelligence as close to the source of streaming sensor data as possible."[48]

Here, the cloud and the edge work together. Machine learning requires huge sample sets to train on. Generally in the field of machine learning, the more samples and the more fine-grained the data, the more accurate the inferences of a model can be. In this regard, the edge provides an invaluable new frontier for data capture. Edge-based devices produce vast amounts of data from the environments they are situated in. Indeed, from video to audio and lidar, edge-based devices create far too much data for cloud architectures to handle, as already discussed. Yet this raw data can be parsed at the edge in order to pinpoint valuable nuggets of information that are sent back to the cloud. As one industry analyst suggested, this "data thinning" process will be used to "create smaller sets of actionable data as bits make their way from the edge to the cloud."[49] The cloud is supplemented with a constellation of small devices, gathering untapped data from the pockets of territory that it has so far failed to penetrate.

Yet if the cloud requires the edge, the edge also requires the cloud. With its low-power microprocessors and resource-poor devices, the edge cannot produce machine learning models itself. The "intelligence" of this intelligent layer has to come from somewhere else. Machine learning, as suggested above, requires the high volume storage and high intensity processing only available in the cloud. If the edge facilitates "the combination and integration of huge volumes of machine-generated sensor data" at a "level of detail that was not possible before," this big data is "rendered useless without analytics power."[50] Indeed, processing chips like the Google TPU discussed above suggest a potential clarification of this analytic role. While the cloud will certainly continue to distribute data, the design of some data centers—AI accelerated, liquid-cooled chips, designed for parallel processing—signal a possible shift in function. As one presentation noted, there are already "early signs of data center specialization" with new facilities that are "purpose-built data centers comprising large arrays of accelerators."[51] Will the emergence of the edge mean that the cloud becomes less about generic connectivity and more about dedicated computation? Regardless of their precise future roles, machine learning demonstrates the dependence of the edge on the cloud. If the edge represents the dream of highly distributed, ubiquitous computation, then it still requires the cloud's massive storage and intensive processing to generate intelligence.

The cloud and the edge thus form a synergistic coupling, a twinned architecture that functions together. As a spokesperson from EdgeConnex observed: "customers are asking for both more proximate deployments at the Edge, but also more dense deployments requiring greater power requirements per rack that can easily exceed 15kW to 20kW to even more than 30+kW/rack in some instances."[52] In other words, corporations want to distribute their applications into the edge layer, to place them nearer to the user—but, at the same time, they also want to increase the processing power they can draw on in the cloud, ramping up their hardware requirements in order to do so. These kind of requests, though phrased in the technical vernacular of the data center industry, suggest a "both/and" form of power, a formation that draws together the unique affordances of the cloud and the edge in order to establish a new set of operations.

This cloud-edge formation allows the apprehension of new forms of information. In order for computation to swallow the world, it needs to understand the world. In this sense, notes venture capital analyst Benedict Evans, the last 30 years of computing have focused mainly on doing what he terms the "simple stuff"—collecting, organizing, and commodifying information that had already been abstracted.[53] Evans points to examples such as Google Search, which organized web pages by using their text-based content and links, or Amazon, which organized products based on their text-based stock keeping unit (SKU) identifiers. In contrast, Evans predicts that the next 30 years will be driven by understanding the messier environments and unlabeled actors of the surrounding world.

In this pursuit of better apprehending the world, the edge and the cloud dovetail. This synergy, again, is easiest demonstrated by looking at how cloud-trained machine learning models have been spun out into the surrounding world of the edge. Here "real world" inference might include a model correctly classifying an object from a camera feed as an apple, for example. Yet if the functionalities of such models are by now generally understood, edge architectures offer a new set of affordances. One of these affordances, already noted above, is that the edge supports low-latency processing on high-volume data, allowing for a more reactive, real-time form of intervention. In a recent Google demo of edge-based facial analysis, for example, the presenter was delighted to announce that the computational model could detect "what their orientation is, what their attention is looking at . . . these glances last only a moment."[54] The goal here is to incisively penetrate into the surrounding world to capture aspects formerly overlooked or impossible to notice.

Impersonal Extraction

To demonstrate the high stakes of such abilities, this section delves into one possibility unlocked by edge-based architectures: surveillance in the form of ethnic filtering. In 2018, Cunrui Wang and his coauthors, funded by both the National Natural Science Foundation of China and the China Education & Research Network Innovation Project, published "Facial Feature Discovery for Ethnicity Recognition."[55] While this paper was not explicitly posited as an edge application, speculating about its deployment in this domain is hardly a leap. Indeed, despite the implications for privacy intrusions and personal freedoms, a slew of recent technical papers show that researchers are already embracing the new possibilities that edge computing offers for facial detection in urban areas,[56] crowd monitoring,[57] and intelligent surveillance.[58]

Such enthusiastic responses demonstrate that in many ways it was technics, rather than ethics, that limited the extent of previous intrusions into personal data. Network speeds, bandwidth capacities, and physical distance were hard restrictions. Edge computing removes or at least reduces many of these hurdles, allowing both public and private actors to delve further into individuals and their lives. These capabilities mean that the question of data collection will hinge less on technical and economic concerns (cost to transfer gigabytes back to the cloud) and more on company culture, ethical values, and policy stipulations—if these are even in place. With technical constraints lifted, companies will be under increased pressure to collect more, and more intrusive, data, which could provide key business insights. Yet individual companies are not entirely free in navigating this ethical terrain. Companies do not operate in isolation, but within competitive industries, particularly the highly contested technology field. Given these conditions, companies are subject to the "coercion of competition."[59] If one company chooses not to push the ethical boundaries of data capture, others will.[60] At a time when comprehensive data has become highly valuable, this decision grants one company strategic advantage over its competitors.

Returning to the paper, Wang and his coauthors begin by noting that "the analysis of race, nation, and ethnical groups based on facial images is a popular topic recently in face recognition community."[61] Bypassing even the barest consideration of ethics, the authors suggest that this new field would naturally be beneficial for state actors wishing to enforce certain restrictions on their citizens. "With rapid advance of people globalization [*sic*]," state the researchers, "face recognition has great application potential in border control, customs check, and public security."[62] Yet, frustratingly for the authors, ethnicity can often be difficult to detect, either because the morphologies of race are too subtle or because the individual contains traces of multiple ethnicities. The problem, from an engineering perspective, is that "the gene of one ethnical group is hardly unique and it may include various gene fragments from some other ethnical groups."[63] Fortunately, facial aspects can be analyzed in a far more fine-grained manner through computational technologies in order to reveal their ethnicities.

With this goal in mind, the authors set about identifying three ethnic groups: Uighur, Tibetan, and Korean. The paper, like many in machine learning, essentially lays out the steps used to produce the model and quantitatively measures its effectiveness against competing models. Their model is trained on an image set of university students, and gradually learns to identify the three ethnic groups with more success, displaying progressively lower levels of uncertainty.

Key for the authors' model is the extraction of a "T" feature from the center of each photograph containing the lips and nose. While the T varies with each ethnic group, these morphological features are considered to be the telltale markings that distinguish whether an individual is within the targeted ethnicity. Indeed, the extraction of the T, while obviously deleting key facial information, amplifies the model's ability to detect ethnicity. As the authors note, "Actually, the facial features extracted from the 'T' regions are more suitable for ethnicity recognition since the unrelated information has been filtered out."[64] In this application, the full photograph of the individual is unnecessary or even a distraction. The model does not need to do the computationally intensive work of facial identification—who exactly an individual is—but rather the simpler task of determining whether an individual is "ethnic" or not.

Such a technology would seem tailor-made for the edge. As more cameras are connected to networks, the possibilities of surveillance grow. However, video data itself is massive, becoming both economically expensive and technically infeasible to send back to the cloud. As the authors of one study suggested, processing raw video from widely distributed "CCTV cameras and mobile cameras not only incurs uncertainty in data transfer and timing but also poses significant overhead and delay to the communication networks."[65] In the cloud model, images need to be sent from all the cameras to a data center facility via the network, be processed in this centralized facility, and then the result delivered to a client or end user. This lengthy process not only introduces significant latency, but makes some surveillance applications essentially unviable from a technical perspective.

Instead, the edge allows processing to be conducted at the source. No identifying image needs to be sent back to the cloud and compared against an exhaustive database of citizens. No personal data is "collected" by the agency in the sense of being transmitted to a data center where it will be held indefinitely in a database or stored on a hard disk. Instead, this machine-learned model could be compressed and loaded onto a small edge-based device with a camera. Such a device would then process its image feed in real time, rapidly determining whether an individual is "ethnic" or not. Once determined, these highly consequential pieces of information might be used in any number of ways. In border security, for instance, one could imagine a green light turning red and a passenger selected for additional screening. In a "smart" (read: surveillance) city scenario, this data might be paired with a camera's location and uploaded to form an aggregated portrait of ethnic populations over time.

The edge thus introduces an additional layer of mediation between users and the cloud, forming a site for processing data after it has been captured, but before it is stored and centralized. This interposition creates new possibilities for data processing, capturing and responding immediately to the individual, while filtering out or generalizing data deemed to be personal. The edge can respond to these inputs in the moment, without storing the names and identifiers typically associated with "personal data." In a sense, such data is based on an individual but rendered impersonal, providing insights for governance while sidestepping the harder restrictions around personal data. Edge affordances underpin new forms of less governed control, avoiding direct confrontation with a stricter regulatory apparatus.

Rich, highly detailed data can be captured by edge devices and then processed by an edge hub in order to extract nuggets of valuable information, which is then passed back to a centralized cloud facility. Abstraction becomes a key term within this process. How will data be treated in order to remove identifying information? How will highly personal data be transformed into impersonal, anonymized data? Here edge computing can draw on a number of existing technologies, from k-anonymity[66] to micro-aggregation.[67] These established techniques, broadly applicable to any information set, include substitution, in which identifying values are randomly replaced; shuffling, so that associations between variables are lost; sampling, in which a partial set from the whole is transmitted; and variance, in which numerical values are perturbed or altered.[68]

Yet if such technologies provide established means of handling particular data types, they can also become a way of arriving too quickly at an ostensible privacy "solution." Instead, the task is to keep the question of data extraction in the foreground: How is data mediated at the edge and what is lost or gained in this intermediation? Highly specific location data, for instance, might be captured at the edge, but then generalized into a district or combined with other user locations. A gender field might be used in an edge calculation, but then dropped, something users may or may not want. An individual's race might be clumped into a parent category, imposing a statistical system and erasing specific origins. In every permutation, a slightly different "data subject" is rendered.[69] These examples stress that the technical transformation of information also has political and social implications.

As a site of preprocessing, the edge is able to draw upon single bodies and personal lives, yet immediately erase this data, abstract it, or aggregate it into a depersonalized mass. In this sense, the edge resonates with Antoinette Rouvroy's observation that algorithmic governance strives to never confront the person in her entirety, to never directly call her up as a political subject. "The only subject" such governmentality needs, Rouvroy stresses, is a "unique, supra-individual, constantly reconfigurated 'statistical body' made of the infra-individual digital traces of impersonal, disparate, heterogeneous, dividualized facets of daily life and interactions."[70] A subject is apprehended and individuated, but not necessarily identified.

Indeed, running through edge scenarios is the sense that the former key question—whether or not a user can be identified—may be subsumed by a far more fundamental question: What forms of life are being extracted from the user *even though* they are not identified? The de-facto framing of privacy proper ushered in by the GDPR has privileged personal data. Yet this entire legal edifice of protections only apply once this definition is reached. Perhaps data never needed to be personal to be valuable. Perhaps control may be enacted and maintained without identifying a unique individual. In fact, recent work on "group privacy"[71] responds precisely to this realization. Even without explicit identification, the new spaces enabled by edge computing present a verdant territory for extractive regimes,[72] a rich zone of markers and moments to capture and respond to. While this extractivist logic deals with each person in turn—capturing moods and faces, responding to bodies and individual inputs, identifying movements and work performances—its value is only obtained by aggregating this data, by assembling and mining it en masse. This is why Tiziana Terranova stresses that the "extractivism of data capital" siphons off the energetic behaviors and activities of the broader social body.[73] The edge enables a new form of extraction that is individualized but not personalized.

The edge thus provides a new intermediary layer of intelligence where data can be captured, derived from, and then discarded or fundamentally transformed before it is stored. Through this affordance, the edge establishes a new frontier site for processing, a gray zone seemingly sparsely covered by existing legislation, which has so far focused heavily on a centralized cloud model. The technology industry is all too aware of this possibility, even if it is framed as law abiding. "To avoid breaking the new law and thus being fined, companies should keep most of the data collected out of the cloud and process it at the edge," recommends one tech pundit.[74] Far more effective than eroding privacy is never confronting privacy proper to begin with.

If the shift to edge computing holds enticing promise for both public and private actors, it should also be understood as a set of technologies with the possibility to further impinge on the freedoms of individuals and the rights of communities. In this sense, edge computing forms the latest incarnation of a broader vector of what Shoshana Zuboff has described as surveillance capitalism. For Zuboff, surveillance capitalism accumulates "not only surveillance assets and capital, but also rights" through "processes that operate outside the auspices of legitimate democratic mechanisms."[75] Yet counter to Zuboff, rather than acquiring rights, these technical processes seek to never invoke rights. If big data accomplishes an "end run around procedural privacy protections,"[76] then edge computing also carries out an "end run" of its own. The goal is to enact a series of operations that extract information and provide strategic advantage, while never venturing into the legal and ethical minefield of privacy proper.

Cloud-Edge Intensities

In *Discipline and Punish*, Foucault traces the genealogy of a shift in power, a historical transformation from one modality of governance to another.

At the beginning of this narrative arc, power took the form of spectacular acts, scenes of brutal torture and bloody execution staged by the state in order to caution the populace against even attempting crime. If such power was spectacular, it was highly situated, constrained to a particular location, often the center of the empire. Moreover, as Foucault observes, it was highly expensive, an extravagant logistical exercise, drawing on significant amounts of time and capital, that was all poured into the punishment of a single body.

What was required, Foucault stresses, was a more economic mode of power. Foucault charts the gradual evolution in power over time, from punishments inflected directly on the body to a more supple yet pervasive form of power, where time and space, for example, could be structured by a comparatively modest instrument like the timetable. This diffusion of power finds its culmination in Foucault's well known chapter on the panopticon. In this prison design, the angles of the cells and the arrangement of the tower ensured that prisoners would never know when they were being watched. The notional architecture provided a new blueprint for power based not on brick and steel, nor blood and violence, but on the pressure of an ever-present gaze, a set of forces that are at once highly diffused yet highly personal. "The panopticon schema makes any apparatus of power more intense," Foucault asserted, "it assures economy (in material, in personnel, in time); it assures its efficacy by its preventative character, its continuous functioning and its automatic mechanisms."[77]

For Foucault, the historical trajectory of power was one characterized by casting off that which was heavy and clumsy, a vector that constantly moved toward more lighter and efficient modes. "The heaviness of the old 'houses of security,' with their fortress-like architecture, could be replaced by the simple, economic geometry of a 'house of certainty'" he observes, in a statement that echoes the cloud to edge shift: "By this very fact, the external power may throw off its physical weight; it tends to the non-corporal; and, the more it approaches this limit, the more constant, profound and permanent are its effects."[78] This progressive evolution of power toward that which is light, economic and efficient is what Jeffrey Nealon describes as its intensification. As Nealon argues, "Power's mutation over time exists alongside the parallel emergence of power's economic viability: producing the desired effects with fewer costs, less expenditure of time and effort; better results with less economic and political resistance."[79] What power wants, he suggests, is to achieve greater control, over a wider field, in a more efficient fashion.

For Nealon, "Power's intensity most specifically names its increasing *efficiency* within a system, coupled with increasing *saturation*."[80] The edge resonates strongly with both of these aspects. Its efficiency can be viewed rather literally, of course, as a constellation of tiny, low-powered devices that are always on and always connected. Yet if we consider a smart city scenario, with sensors embedded throughout the environment transmitting information back to a city council, it is also possible to see how this technical efficiency might translate into a more efficient governmentality, providing the state with an expansive vision and a high degree of control without requiring thousands of employees on the ground.

In a similar fashion, if intensity "names a 'lateral' or 'centrifugal' smearing or saturation of effects over a wide field,"[81] as Nealon suggests, then the edge accomplishes the same. Indeed, one of the key drivers behind the edge, as discussed previously, was that the cloud did not extend far enough over the "field"—whether that field took the form of regional towns, more local neighborhoods and homes, or the hyperlocal field of the body itself. Edge architectures allow for a smearing or saturation of control across the broader field of the every day. In this regard, the edge casts a somewhat tragic light on earlier attempts at decentralization as emancipation. An article like "Flawed Cloud Architectures and the Rise of Decentral Alternatives"[82] might now be read in a very cynical sense. Cloud architectures were indeed flawed, hamstrung by numerous weaknesses, and decentralized architectures did rise—but the current state of the edge suggests that these will not be "alternatives" forged by civil society that challenge asymmetries of power, but rather augmentations designed by corporate giants that further reinforce existing hegemonies.

However, if the edge slots rather neatly into a lineage of intensification, its coupling with the cloud complicates this dynamic. The cloud, as suggested above, resonates in many ways with older or more traditional forms of power: a centralized site, underpinned by formidable resources, where information is collected and processed, with the results being distributed throughout the cloud empire to individual subjects. Set against the lightness and mobility of the edge, the cloud appears in many ways to be clumsy and inflexible. Yet as the example of machine learning above stressed, the edge relies heavily on the concentration of technical power available in the cloud. It is only at these centralized sites of dense, dedicated processing that learning—an immensely computationally expensive task—can be achieved.

Thus, even though the cloud might resemble older forms of power with a Foucauldian framework, it is critical to retain it. Despite attention-grabbing claims of the "end of the cloud,"[83] commentators do not in fact foresee a wholesale replacement of technical architectures back to a decentralized, peer-to-peer model, but a new type of synthesis. This suggests a formation of power that bridges and builds on the juxtapositions between the two modes.

The result, in a way, seems paradoxical. As a product manager for Amazon Web Services stressed in an industry presentation, the cloud-edge "is both centralized and decentralized."[84]

In this sense, the cloud-edge territory resembles a lesser known section in *Discipline and Punish* on police power. On an immediate level, police power embodied the absolutism of the sovereign, the very conventional mode of power particular to the state. Characteristic of this mode was its centralization. "All the radiations of force and information that spread from the circumference culminate in the magistrate-general," Foucault noted, a network nexus that operated as a "single, strict, administrative machine."[85] However, he also realized that this power had to move beyond this centralized form of territory. Although this power "was certainly linked directly to the centre of political sovereignty," it must now extend, becoming "coextensive with the entire social body."[86]

This power would need to supplement itself, shifting its scale from the overarching eye of the state to a far more diffused form of vision. This vision would shrink down to the individual level, it would keep tabs on those quotidian details, it would remain vigilant to the everyday encounter. Such power must bear over everything. Yet rather than the top-down totality, this meant "the dust of events, actions, behavior, opinions—'everything that happens'; the police are concerned with 'those things of every moment', those 'unimportant things.'"[87] The phase could almost describe the edge and its imaginary, a diffused form of computation, spread across a broader number of scales and spaces, concerned with registering, capturing, and parsing the digital dust of everyday activity. "The traditional way of delivering analytics is no longer efficient or, in some cases, even possible," admits one industry specification document, "as we look deeper into business and technical processes, more granular data elements will be needed to create actionable business knowledge from information."[88]

The result is a territory that combines lightness and heaviness, drawing together the fortress and the frontier, the situated and the mobile, the resource rich with the resource poor. In doing so, the cloud-edge formation of power does not so much undermine the principle of intensity as enrich it. While the edge and the cloud operate completely differently—functioning in ways that are often diametrically opposed—these internal oppositions augment one another, coming together to form a coherent system of control. Decentralization suggests a "loss of control," began a promo text for one industry conference, "but in the world of cloud and infrastructure . . . it is a good bet that it will actually further enhance and add value to the hyperscale platforms at the centre of this new world order. It is good news for all involved."[89]

7 • Unmaking and Remaking Territory

"Are geographic isolation, poor connectivity, data sovereignty, and privacy laws holding your business back?" a recent ad in my social feed asked. The accompanying image, a smiling white male in a business suit alongside a crisp blue logo, was typical of the clean, conservative aesthetic that pervades the industry. The ad promoted an infrastructure product that would "solve all my cloud problems" and stressed that the time to act was now. Here the locatedness of data is presented as a purely economic problem. Regulations that hinder the flows of data also hinder the flows of capital. Business growth instead requires a borderless world where data can be freely transmitted, pooled, and mined for maximum value creation. The ad's "solution" implies that data infrastructures can deeply remake the world through technical means while carefully bracketing out the social, cultural, and political fallout.

This book has aimed to undermine that apolitical imaginary, using the concept of territory to stress the political stakes of data infrastructures in our present. Territories are contested, emerging from the antagonisms of disparate actors, who each have their own imperatives, their own strategies, their own overarching visions. Territories are not simply assumed, but must be maintained through a constant performance of practices and operations. And territories, once established, confer a distinct set of advantages, advancing certain interests in the political and geopolitical arena. Territory today is both enacted and contested through technical infrastructures.

These "technical territories" increasingly shape the world around us, structuring labor, funneling capital, and unlocking new modes of governance. Such territories are highly influential but often imperceptible, obfuscated by the banality of infrastructure and the complexity of technology. Rather than argue in the abstract, this book stepped through specific scenarios throughout Asia, demonstrating how these technical territories operate and what advantages they promise. Under the ocean, Huawei's subsea cables extend its network far beyond its operating base, while its standards dominance establishes its architectures and ideas over its rivals. In Hong Kong, surveillance infrastructures threaten to capture the face of a protestor and transmit it to the Mainland, where it can be assembled, identified, and weaponized against dissidents. In Singapore, data collection provides new ways to frame the nation, constructing a Smart Nation that includes some and excludes others. And on Christmas Island, technical territories function as a kind of filter, striving to incorporate the villager into the future "Australia" while erasing the migrant and any possibility of her future life in the Commonwealth. Technical territories matter.

If anything, COVID-19 only crystallized this power and the stakes involved. On the one hand, the global pandemic seemed to signal the return of that ancient power, the state. Borders were closed, lockdown measures were put in place, and masking and vaccine mandates established. In the name of security, public health, and the all-important economy, extraordinary powers were invoked. The everyday routines of millions of people were halted and their bodies constrained to the tightly circumscribed space of their home. During this crisis, there was a withdrawal and buttressing, a kind of defensive posture that carefully defined who and what was in the scope of protection. Hard lines between countries and regions, between "our" jurisdiction and "their" jurisdiction, were enforced. Similarly, the line between citizen and noncitizen—one that can exert a devastating impact on lives and livelihoods—was carefully delineated. These moves were backed by swiftly passed legislation and by physical force or the threat of physical force. No wonder, then, that some commentators argued that coronavirus had effectively reterritorialized the state.[1] What we are witnessing, exclaimed one article published in the midst of the pandemic, "is the most dramatic extension of state power since the second world war."[2]

Yet, on the other hand, these regimes were deeply dependent on the new capabilities offered by technical infrastructures explored throughout this book. Border crossings were screened by police with mobile devices that tapped into centralized databases, bringing together edge and cloud technologies. In South Korea, technical systems designed to monitor and manage new "smart" cities were quickly repurposed for epidemiology. Contact tracers could track an individual's cell-phone location data, credit card use, and movement over time, developing a highly detailed account of their journeys and activities.[3] Singapore and China soon followed South Korea's lead, rolling out similar systems. Such systems spliced together AI technologies, large networks of CCTV cameras, and facial recognition algorithms to form powerful new forms of surveillance.[4]

The infrastructure had already been in place, but previously such a use would be considered an overreach of power. Combining these invasive capabilities and openly deploying them on an entire population was off the table. Now, in the context of a pandemic, it was suddenly defensible and even seen as desirable. Indeed, technology companies pounced on this pivotal moment, quickly spinning out an array of systems and infrastructures designed for our new normal. In the United States and Europe, for example, health providers teamed up with private tech companies such as Palantir, which provide software, servers, and bespoke tools for clients in law enforcement, intelligence agencies, and immigration agencies. In this sense, tech providers adopted the well-known game plan of "disaster capitalism" in which every crisis is reframed as a potential opportunity.[5] Approached in the right way, a state of emergency is a perfect chance for record quarterly earnings.

While the accumulation of profit is certainly a key driver here, crisis also provides a wedge for deregulation and privatization, a new opening for companies to insert themselves as mediators, service providers, and gatekeepers. Private companies develop, maintain, and "optimize" the information infrastructure that increasingly constitutes the new territory of governance, providing health services, business services, communication services, securitization services, and other services that contribute to sustaining, defending, and administering the life of the population.[6]

So if such systems are ostensibly put to work for the state, these technical infrastructures also provide a distinct advantage to whoever owns and maintains them. Those who can spin up and maintain technical territories, as we saw with Huawei, become the standard setters, the first movers, the ones with backdoor access to critical infrastructure. Data is one obvious form this advantage may take. Today, data is a key commodity: the collection, centralization, and organization of vast amounts of data and metadata is foundational for tomorrow's "innovative" (and often exploitative) technologies. Companies that can achieve this, whether through operating cables, data centers, networked systems, platforms, or some other infrastructure, will have an edge. This brings us full circle to the key point stressed in the book's opening pages: technical infrastructures have become new mechanisms for territorialization.

Grappling with Territory

What implications do these technically driven shifts have? First, I've suggested we need to update the way we understand territoriality today. Here, conceptualizations tend to fall into two camps. On the one hand, there are those who suggest that technical systems and networked media have remade the world and annihilated spatial boundaries. When data blazes across borders at the speed of light, the argument goes, then those dusty dotted lines of the state no longer hold sway. Isolation becomes connection; the local becomes global. In the strongest versions of this vision, digital connectivity and information infrastructures render the state form largely obsolete. On the other hand, there are those who see territory as a bounded space indelibly linked to the state and its long-standing history. In this view, new technologies may provide new opportunities for communications or transactions, but are essentially faster or more efficient ways to carry out the same tasks. They add a new wrinkle or set of capabilities to the state but do not fundamentally alter the status quo.

Instead, I argued for another approach, asserting that technical infrastructures become a key new site of political and geopolitical power, exerting influence at scale through their processes and protocols—and yet as the portraits of Christmas Island, Singapore, and Hong Kong showed, these technical territories often draw on aspects of that ancient form of power, the nation-state, whether in their funding, interconnections, overall aims, or legal authority. These ties connect with the deep-seated imperative to secure the state's existence and maintain the well-being of some people over others. Such forms of spatial power draw upon the historical, political, and jurisdictional but extend it in particular ways through the technical and operational.

These operations are often imperceptible. While these processes and performances emerge from material infrastructures, they often take place silently and invisibly, away from the public's view. This suggests that what can be seen or represented, like the tip of an iceberg, may only supply a partial understanding of territory. The map, as Storey reminds us, has long been a powerful symbol of territory when defined as the state.[7] Yet if the map offers solidity and stability, a form that can be pointed to and believed in, it is one that increasingly seems misleading. Technical territories present a far more fluid picture, drawing on the power of this imagined community[8] while partially escaping it. Technical territories arc outward from the shoreline, extend upward into the stratosphere, or bury their way underneath established borders. They often operate far beyond the bounds of a particular jurisdiction or slide silently through existing zones. Overlooked or framed as supposedly apolitical, they nevertheless offer those who control them new opportunities for sensing and acting. In doing so, they represent a shift from representation to operation, challenging our conception of what power "looks like" in the present. Technical territories productively complicate purely legal or theoretical framings of territory, suggesting that researchers must attend to the ways in which state power becomes mediated and extended through contemporary technologies.

For governments and policy makers, technical territories must be grappled with. These infrastructural technologies should not be handed off lightly to tech companies to manage or sidelined as a set of arcane technical questions best handled by the "experts." Today, questions of technology have become questions of governmentality. These decisions alter who can capture, store, and commodify the personal information of citizens. They determine who owns and accesses the material networks—the cables, servers, fibers, and radio waves—that have increasingly become the conduits through which trade, education, and entertainment takes place. And they intersect deeply with issues of inclusion and exclusion—which groups are connected and supported and which are ignored or expelled. Certainly these technologies can be complex. They may pose a steep learning curve or present a fast-moving target. Yet the stakes are too high to ignore such questions or cede them to others. Investing time, resources, and finances to navigate these issues would allow a government to actively shape how these infrastructural capabilities are put to work in the future, embracing potential while mitigating problems.

To carry out this task, public agencies need figures who can bridge the technical and the governmental. These people would be able to grasp the consequences of funding a particular set of data infrastructures or modeling the population based on certain parameters. Without descending into minutia, they could understand the implications of selecting one provider or platform over another. And then—critically—they would have the communication and relational skills to distill these trade-offs and consequences down and convey them to others. By translating between these two spheres, such figures would allow stakeholders in public office to make sense of contemporary technologies and make informed choices that benefit those they represent. In a few corners of the world, we're already starting to see this hybrid role come to the fore when it comes to buzzword topics: AI, automation, digitalization. The goal would be to generalize this approach and make it sustainable by wrapping resources and funding around it. These are not just short-lived trends that require a five-year commitment, but long-term dynamics that will shape the lives of those in a city, region, or nation for decades to come.

For citizens and civic groups, technical territories introduce a new site where contemporary power plays out. From Hong Kong to Christmas Island, many of the portraits of technical territories in this book have stressed their role as asymmetric power formations. While new infrastructures, architectures, and affordances are theoretically open ended, available for a wide variety of uses, the instances here showed how they are often deployed to reinforce existing hegemonies. Software, hardware, sensors, and networks become the latest tool to perpetuate long-standing forms of settler-colonialism or xenophobic nationalism. Authoritarian regimes are handed more pervasive tools. Immigration enforcement expands its scope of operations. Edge architectures grant corporations and state agencies dangerous new capabilities. In these instances and others, technical territories intensify inequality, buttressing incumbents while undermining the already marginal.

For this reason, technical territories should be watched, understood, and actively contested by communities when necessary. Some groups are already recognizing the stakes here and taking up this challenge. In my own home country, for instance, the Aotearoa Māori Internet Organization was established early on, responding to the urgent need to "begin defining what the Internet is to Māori, how are and will Māori be affected, and Māori culture and identity impacted by this."[9] Even in these early days, it was clear that these technologies were designed in ways that ignored the needs of their particular community. The "modes of communication and dissemination of information" in these technical infrastructures were "inadequate to encompass and promote future dynamic growth of Māori culture, values, and discourse."[10] The group suggested that these technologies needed to be modified and altered. In that sense, digital inclusion initiatives seeking to give more Māori network access were not enough. Instead of merely being passive users, Māori should also be able to direct and shape these technical systems in meaningful ways. As the group stressed, there was a dire need for "authors and creators of web functions and web structures more conducive to Māori modus operandi."[11]

While the group has now disbanded, it was prescient in recognizing the power at the heart of infrastructures, protocols, and platforms. Left unchecked, technical territories may silently operationalize concepts of knowledge, culture, and private property that ignore or erode indigenous values. The same kinds of dangers may confront other communities in other forms, emerging as threats to racial justice, migrant rights, community autonomy, and so on. Such threats are often quiet rather than spectacular, taking the form of "apolitical" infrastructures, default settings, or "universal" design. Yet for precisely this reason, such technical infrastructures need to be exposed and evaluated. What are the needs of a particular community? How might technical infrastructures recognize or reflect a certain people, their identity and culture, their visions and values? And how might these aspirations get operationalized, translated into design features, developer road maps, and program objectives? These are difficult questions that will take vigilance and persistence to work through. Yet the value of discussing these issues, developing a consensus, and pursuing that vision is increasingly apparent for those who aim to uphold a community and defend their stake in the future.

Unbuilding and Remaking

New imaginations are needed to counteract these dynamics, to use and "abuse" these technical territories, experimenting with alternative structures, injecting them with different values, and splicing in other imperatives. If infrastructural operations tend to prop up hegemonic interests, then what would it look like to intervene in these territories? How might asymmetric power be taken apart and rebalanced in small but significant ways? These are technical questions, to be sure, but also experiential and ontological ones that ask how power may be confronted and critiqued by individuals and communities. For this reason, in these final few pages, I look beyond the often narrow world of the computational and draw insights from art, architecture, gender studies, and other disciplines.

In his essay "Unbuilding Gender Trans," Jack Halberstam investigates these kinds of questions by turning to the work of artist Gordon Matta-Clark. Matta-Clark was best known for his large scale sculptural work that involved cutting into buildings to create new forms. Breaking down a space's structural integrity through ruptures, voids, and fractures was core to a broader practice he referred to as "anarchitecture." "The adherents of anarchitecture," explains Halberstam, "create holes, gaps, fissures, and crevices within the built environment."[12]

These slices often chipped away facades, broke open enclosures, and peeled back layers to reveal previously hidden features of a space. Such practices, Halberstam writes, "insist on attention to what is not there, what has been removed, what is lacking—what has been destroyed, erased, or blacked out in order for what remains present to look permanent."[13] These buildings were often abandoned and condemned, slated for demolition to make way for new apartments and new shopping centers. Such developments were inevitably attended by gentrification for the upwardly mobile and eviction for those unable to make rising rents. This is why, for Halberstam, Matta-Clark's work "implicitly emphasized the absence of some bodies (the disabled and the sick), the suppression or incarceration of others (the poor and those deemed criminal), and the segregation of neighborhoods by race and class."[14]

In its own modest way, this book has attempted to do the same, to show how these territories are always already political in their inclusion of some bodies and exclusion or suppression of others. From protestors in Hong Kong to asylum-seekers on Christmas Island and Uighurs under surveillance, the scenarios here have tried to retain their focus on those who are disempowered, excluded, or ignored. These individuals are not included in the sovereign imaginary of the nation. They are absent from the infrastructural empires constructed by tech titans—or else rendered hypervisible only in order to be targeted and excluded. If it is important to scrutinize the grand march of technically driven power and the advantages it promises, it is equally necessary to linger, attending to the people and things left in its wake. Who is abandoned on the way toward global cable connections, hyperscale data centers, and the securing of an environment friendly to business and state?

"Nothing works," reads one notecard from Matta-Clark. The phrase aptly summarizes the state of New York City infrastructure in the mid-1960s, a crumbling, decaying system in need of repair. On the surface, such an image seems a world away from the global cities examined here like Hong Kong and Singapore, with their gleaming systems and hypermodern services. And yet, as the book has aimed to show, this incredible utility is always selective by design—these operations work for some and against others. Infrastructures establish zones of compatibility that operate according to certain standards, that uphold certain rules, and that privilege certain actors. For owners and operators, these technical territories function as intended, extending their influence, shoring up security, and accumulating capital. For those they exclude, the same systems and structures are irrelevant or even dysfunctional, ignoring a critical array of urgent social, political, and financial needs. Surrounded on all sides by seamless designs and smooth operations, the excluded inhabit a broken world, a world of antagonistic systems designed to bracket out their demands and impede their progress—a world stacked against them. For the asylum-seeker, the elderly shut-in, or the domestic worker in these contemporary territories, the same phrase could be applied: nothing works.

Of course, this is not to claim that emancipatory territories and alternative infrastructures do not exist. Lighting up a high-speed cable will not suddenly erase long-standing social formations in an area. Similarly, launching a data center does not delete the forms of community and solidarity that surround it. Despite Friedrich Kittler's warning, media do not entirely determine our situation.[15] Systems are never totalizing and no technical territory will ever completely shape a space and its inhabitants. Alternative forms of social and cultural life continue in the cracks between formal systems and structures. "While infrastructure sets lines of articulation and instantiates particular conceptions of space and time," stresses AbdouMaliq Simone, "it always engenders shadows, recesses, and occlusions that can be occupied as staging areas for unscripted incursions."[16] Pockets of agency can be found in the glitches and slippages that attend these systems, or even in small, ad-hoc actions that take place outside them. Within this "relational infrastructure" Simone suggests that the "marginalized, weakened or threatened" work out their own "operational spaces"—however temporary.[17]

How are these alternative "operational spaces" made? Drawing again from anarchitecture, we might note on an immediate level its emphasis on disruption and destruction. These practices literally take a sledgehammer to the brick-and-mortar of a building, slicing into these spaces and hacking through their seeming stability. If the territories explored here, like the infrastructures that Halberstam focuses on, "are a structural grammar for organizing space and situating bodies in it, then anarchitecture is premised on the exposure of those logics, and their destruction."[18] The aim is to chip away at the facade of these structures until the inherent contingency of their existence is revealed. But along with destruction, anarchitectural practice also seems to have a constructive dimension, moving beyond an annihilation of the established order to offer something of its own. In ripping through a wall, a new vista is created. In tearing down a column, a corridor is constructed. Anarchitecture breaks down a building in order to open it up and out. In this sense, anarchitecture provides broader inspiration for intervening within the less "concrete" sociotechnical infrastructures discussed throughout these pages, gesturing to ways that default configurations might be taken apart, reassembled, and taken up toward a different purpose.

The practices of Hong Kong antiextradition protestors display both these destructive and constructive components. For protestors, the state's ability to control the territory of the streets is directly tied to key information infrastructure. As we saw in chapter 3, protestors have literally torn down "smart" lampposts in the city. A short viral video showed activists wrapping several ropes around the pole and yanking downward, sending it crashing to the ground. Panels were popped open and the post's electronic innards were inspected, revealing multiple cameras and a network card licensed for mainland China. Alongside these spectacular moments of overt destruction are long term but no less effective techniques of blocking, breaking, or simple refusal. Electronic ticketing systems capable of tracking individuals are boycotted. Cameras linked to facial recognition systems are inhibited with masks or disrupted with a sea of swirling laser pointers. These techniques are all designed to thwart, to damage, or even to destroy.

Yet, like the cutting and reconfiguring of anarchitectures, destructions are always closely followed by constructions. In a sense, the antiextradition protestors have forged their own technical territory, underpinned by a sophisticated array of customized infrastructures. For example, groups have been set up on encrypted messaging apps and online forums, some with tens of thousands of subscribers. These have facilitated a rich form of crowd-sourced knowledge from locals, knowledge that is used to organize marches, to warn others of police presence, and to offer supplies such as masks.[19] The same groups have been used to share legal and medical advice to those in need. And in their commitment to more democratic modes of governance, protestors have frequently used real-time voting on these platforms, allowing participants to have their say on when and where the next protest should be.

Together, these measures alter the space of protest, whether the web forum or the city street. Weaving together the destructive—such as ripping down lampposts or "breaking" facial recognition with a mask—and the constructive—such as pooling together knowledge from protestors about police, supplies, and dangers—they correct, even if slightly, the formidable information asymmetry enjoyed by the state. They start to build a new territory over the old one, a space that is safer for the protestor, more sensitive to communal struggle, and more open to democratic modes of governance. "The demand for infrastructure is the demand for a certain kind of inhabitable ground," Judith Butler once stated.[20] The interventions and infrastructures put to work in Hong Kong, though inevitably temporary, attempt to carve out this inhabitable ground, to support what Butler calls a "livable life." While the territories explored in these pages inevitably required delving into technical details and geopolitical scales, they have always aimed to stress these personal stakes. At their base, technical territories are a contest over the possession of information, the contours of labor, the forms of governance, and the distribution of capital. Who gets to administer these operations and under what conditions? This question points to the stakes of technical territories, which increasingly delineate the boundaries between livable and unlivable life.

Notes

Chapter 1

1. Easterling, *Extrastatecraft*, 13.
2. Kobrin, "Safe Harbours Are Hard to Find," 113.
3. Elden, *Birth of Territory*, 431.
4. Peters, Steinberg, and Stratford, *Territory beyond Terra*, 4.
5. Peters, Steinberg, and Stratford, *Territory beyond Terra*, 4.
6. Neilson, Rossiter, and Samaddar, *Logistical Asia*, 12.
7. Bratton, *The Stack*, 33.
8. Storey, *Research Agenda for Territory and Territoriality*, 18.
9. Brighenti, "On Territorology," 56.

Chapter 2

1. Lawder and Heavey, "U.S. Blacklists China's Huawei as Trade Dispute Clouds Global Outlook."

2. Dupont, "Crackdown on Chinese Tech Giant Huawei Has Global Ramifications"; Laskai, "Why Blacklisting Huawei Could Backfire"; Zakaria, "Blacklisting of Huawei Might Be China's Sputnik Moment."

3. Hillman, "Influence and Infrastructure," 2.

4. Gillespie, "Politics of 'Platforms'"; Ruppert, Isin, and Bigo, "Data Politics"; Gray, "Three Aspects of Data Worlds."

5. Shen, "Building a Digital Silk Road?," 2692.

6. Sum, "Intertwined Geopolitics and Geoeconomics of Hopes/Fears."

7. Rolland, "China's 'Belt and Road Initiative.'"

8. Agnew, *Globalization and Sovereignty*, 9.

9. Krasner, *Problematic Sovereignty*. This is a distinction drawn out explicitly by Douglas Howland: "Krasner differentiates 'rules of sovereignty' that exist in textbooks or casebooks of international law from the 'script of sovereignty,' which involves the acting out of rules or principles and thus creates space for the pursuit of legitimate alternatives." Howland, *International Law and Japanese Sovereignty*.

10. Mayer and Acuto, "Global Governance of Large Technical Systems," 663.
11. Nielsen, "SubTel Forum's Annual Industry Report," 12.
12. Starosielski, "Fixed Flow."
13. Starosielski, *Undersea Network*, 93.
14. Starosielski, *Undersea Network*, 93.
15. Headrick, *Tentacles of Progress, 1850–1940*, 98.
16. Nielsen, "SubTel Forum's Annual Industry Report."
17. Partington, "Huawei Marine Networks."
18. Huawei Marine, "Experience."
19. CAICT, "White Paper on China International Optical Cable Interconnection."
20. Lee, "Cybersecurity Implications of Chinese Undersea Cable Investment."
21. Malecki and Wei, "Wired World."
22. Cohen, *Between Truth and Power*, 226.
23. Wong, "Google and Facebook Are Doubling Down on Internet Infrastructure with a New Pacific Cable."
24. Quigley, "New Undersea Cable Expands Capacity for Google APAC Customers and Users."
25. Roberts, Secor, and Zook, "Critical Infrastructure," 8.
26. Page, O'Keeffe, and Taylor, "America's Undersea Battle with China for Control of the Global Internet Grid."
27. Page, O'Keeffe, and Taylor, "America's Undersea Battle with China for Control of the Global Internet Grid."
28. Lightwave, "Huawei Marine to Build Hibernia Altantic's [*sic*] Project Express."
29. U.S. House Permanent Select Committee on Intelligence, "Investigation of the Security Threat Posed by Chinese Telecommunications Companies Huawei and ZTE."
30. Buckley, "Hibernia Halts Cable Build with Huawei Due to US-China Cybersecurity Issues."
31. Easterling, *Extrastatecraft*, 59.
32. Submarine Networks, "APG."
33. Carse, Cons, and Middleton, "Chokepoints"; Starosielski, "Strangling the Internet."
34. Khazan, "Creepy, Long-Standing Practice of Undersea Cable Tapping."
35. Cowie, "Geopolitics of Internet Infrastructure."
36. MacAskill and Rushe, "Snowden Document Reveals Key Role of Companies in NSA Data Collection."
37. Winseck, "Internet Infrastructure and the Persistent Myth of U.S. Hegemony."
38. Winseck, "Geopolitical Economy of the Global Internet Infrastructure," 255.
39. Maxwell and Miller, *Greening the Media*; Holt and Vonderau, "'Where the Internet Lives.'"
40. SUNeVision Holdings, "AWS Direct Connect."
41. Ye, "UK-Based Global Switch Opens HK$5b Data Centre in Hong Kong."
42. Jacob, "Global Switch Launches State-of-Art HK$5BN Hong Kong Data Centre Services with China Telecom and Daily-Tech."
43. Huawei, "TGT Built Next-Generation Data Centers with Huawei Servers."
44. Perez, "Mainland Internet Giants Lift Hong Kong's Data Centre Market."
45. Perez, "Mainland Internet Giants Lift Hong Kong's Data Centre Market."
46. Acuto and Curtis, "Assemblage Thinking and International Relations."

47. Hong, *Networking China*; Block and Keller, *State of Innovation*.
48. Rossiter, *Software, Infrastructure, Labor*, 415.
49. Seta, "Into the Red Stack."
50. Ragland et al., "Red Cloud Rising," 53.
51. Rossiter, "Imperial Infrastructures and Asia beyond Asia," 153.
52. Rossiter, "Imperial Infrastructures and Asia beyond Asia," 153.
53. In general, space in Hong Kong is scarce. The data center industry and the government have both expressed anxieties in the past that there is too little land available for the construction of new data centers, a disadvantage that will see them slipping behind competitors like Indonesia or Singapore, for example. Indeed, the designation of the industrial estate to data centers emerged precisely from this pressure. Yet the estate has now become overcrowded, a condition that meant SUNeVision paid a record price for the last block of auctioned land. "The winning price was 45 per cent higher than the upper limit of the land's valuation and four times more than that of a similar site in the area." Ka-sing, "High Data Centre Rents Let Three Firms Dominate US$883 Million Sector."
54. Sverdlik, "Hong Kong, China's Data Center Gateway to the World."
55. Amoore, "Cloud Geographies," 13.
56. Amoore, "Cloud Geographies," 12.
57. HK does have a Hong Kong Personal Data (Privacy) Ordinance, with a number of key principles, such as ensuring that personal data is not captured excessively, ensuring it is accurate, ensuring it is stored securely, and so on. This ordinance also includes a restriction on cross-border data transfer, but that section has never been made operational. "The cross border data transfer restriction in Hong Kong (Section 33 of the PDPO) was passed into law in 1995 at the time the PDPO was first introduced. However, as of December 2017 the section has not been brought into operation." Here law is code that is never triggered or made operational, but rather lies dormant as nonfunctional lines within a functional piece of legislation. Kennedy and Lee, "Change It Up."
58. Sassen, "Embedded Borderings," 8.
59. Sassen, "Embedded Borderings," 9.
60. ETSI, "5G Specs."
61. Hu, "Huawei Is Still Winning 5G Contracts around the World despite the U.S. Ban."
62. Huawei, "Huawei Launches Full Range of 5G End-to-End Product Solutions."
63. Easterling, *Extrastatecraft*, 9.
64. Bowker and Star, "Invisible Mediators of Action."
65. Lampland and Star, *Standards and Their Stories*.
66. Dourish and Mainwaring, "Ubicomp's Colonial Impulse," 134.
67. ETSI, "5G Specs."
68. Cohen, *Between Truth and Power*, 220.
69. Leiponen, "Competing through Cooperation."
70. Scott, "Telcogeopolitics."
71. Qin, "From Follower to Leader."
72. Purnell and Woo, "China's Huawei Is Determined to Lead the Way on 5G Despite U.S. Concerns."
73. Strumpf, "Where China Dominates in 5G Technology"; Lerner and Tirole, "Standard-Essential Patents."
74. Strumpf, "Where China Dominates in 5G Technology."

75. Cantero Gamito, "Europeanization through Standardization."

76. Cohen, *Between Truth and Power*, 226.

77. Kania, "China's Play for Global 5G Dominance—Standards and the 'Digital Silk Road'"; Bryan-Low et al., "Special Report—Hobbling Huawei."

78. Cai, "Understanding China's Belt and Road Initiative," 11.

79. Munn, *Ferocious Logics*.

80. Sassen, "Embedded Borderings," 8.

81. Fang, "Huawei's Expansion in Africa Comes under Scrutiny."

82. Huawei, "Video Surveillance as the Foundation of 'Safe City' in Kenya."

83. Huawei, "Video Surveillance as the Foundation of 'Safe City' in Kenya."

84. Mutambo, "Huawei Poised to Fuel China Foreign Policy in Kenya."

85. Mutambo, "Huawei Poised to Fuel China Foreign Policy in Kenya."

86. Cave, "African Union Headquarters Hack and Australia's 5G Network."

87. Huawei, "Desktop Cloud Draws Praise in Africa."

88. Tilouine and Kadiri, "A Addis-Abeba, le siège de l'Union africaine espionné par Pékin."

89. Bhaya, "China, African Leaders Slam French Report on AU Headquarters Hacking as 'Ridiculous,' 'Nonsense.'"

90. Shahbaz, "Freedom on the Net 2018."

91. Rossiter, *Software, Infrastructure, Labor*, 178.

92. Mozur, Kessel, and Chan, "Made in China, Exported to the World."

93. Akita, "China Is Exporting AI-Driven Authoritarianism"; Abramowitz and Chertoff, "Global Threat of China's Digital Authoritarianism."

94. Rossiter, *Software, Infrastructure, Labor*, 345.

95. Abramowitz and Chertoff, "Global Threat of China's Digital Authoritarianism."

96. Ho, "Algorithmic Authoritarianism."

Chapter 3

1. Lee, Fugitive Offenders and Mutual Legal Assistance in Criminal Matters Legislation (Amendment) Bill.

2. Luoji, "Human Rights Critique of the Chinese Legal System."

3. Noakes, "Disappearing Act."

4. Dahlin, "Can You Get a Fair Trial in China?"

5. ABC News, "Hong Kong Protesters Cut Down Data-Collecting Lamppost."

6. Mahtani, "Hong Kong Protesters Coordinate to Beat Chinese Surveillance."

7. Flowerdew, Feng, and Manley, "Constructing Data Zones for Scottish Neighbourhood Statistics."

8. Schafran and Wegmann, "Restructuring, Race, and Real Estate."

9. Tomlinson, "Geographic Information System for Regional Planning"; Pickles, *Ground Truth*; Crampton, *Mapping*.

10. Crampton, "Cartography: Maps 2.0"; Leszczynski and Elwood, "Feminist Geographies of New Spatial Media."

11. Bates, Lin, and Goodale, "Data Journeys."

12. Steyerl, "In Defense of the Poor Image."

13. Ash, Kitchin, and Leszczynski, "Digital Turn, Digital Geographies?"

14. Girot, *Regulation of Cross-Border Transfers of Personal Data in Asia*.

15. Kuner et al., "Internet Balkanization Gathers Pace."

16. Goldsmith, "Sovereign Difference and Sovereign Deference on the Internet."

17. Amoore, "Cloud Geographies," 11.

18. Chan and Pun, "Economic Power of the Political Powerless in the 2019 Hong Kong Pro-Democracy Movement"; Lee, "Solidarity in the Anti-Extradition Bill Movement in Hong Kong."

19. Lee, So, and Leung, "Social Media and Umbrella Movement"; Lee and Chan, "Digital Media Activities and Mode of Participation in a Protest Campaign"; Lee, Chen, and Chan, "Social Media Use and University Students' Participation in a Large-Scale Protest Campaign."

20. Kwong, "Dynamics of Mainstream and Internet Alternative Media in Hong Kong."

21. Fernandez, "Policing Protest Spaces"; Wood, *Crisis and Control*; Garrett, *Counter-Hegemonic Resistance in China's Hong Kong*.

22. Hui, "Why Hong Kong's Protesters Were Afraid to Use Their Metro Cards."

23. SCMP Reporter, "Octopus Sold Personal Data of Customers for HK$44m."

24. SCMP Reporter, "Octopus Escapes Penalty for Selling Data."

25. Kaltheuner, "What Hong Kong's Protesters Can Teach Us about the Future of Privacy."

26. ZWF0cHVzc3k, "R/HongKong—[8.3] Clothes, Drinks and One-Way Ticket Left on Ticket Machines."

27. Wakefield, "Hong Kong Protesters Using Bluetooth App."

28. Wakefield, "Hong Kong Protesters Using Bluetooth App."

29. Ng, "Umbrella Movement in Hong Kong."

30. Lee and Chan, "Digital Media Activities and Connective Actions."

31. Freedom Hongkonger, "香港被送中誓要成G20話題 眾籌《金融時報》及日德法英等各國報章頭版公開信 Hong Kong G20 Open Letter Initiative."

32. Yu, "'It Would Become Like Xinjiang.'"

33. Mahtani, "Masks, Cash and Apps."

34. Han, *Psychopolitics*, 21.

35. Harcourt, *Exposed*, 19.

36. Mozur, "In Hong Kong Protests, Faces Become Weapons."

37. Hollingsworth, "Why Protests Are Becoming Increasingly Faceless."

38. Ruiz, "Revealing PowerMasked Protest and the Blank Figure," 267.

39. Zhang, "Hong Kong Protester Lasers Are Frying Photographers' Cameras."

40. Cheng, "Hong Kong Activists Complain Police Failed to Display ID Numbers."

41. Hikvision, *Hikvision Brand Video*.

42. Chan, "China-Made Cameras Focus on HK Protesters."

43. Mozur, "Biometric Data Becomes New Weapon in Hong Kong Protests."

44. ABC News, "Hong Kong Protesters Cut down Data-Collecting Lamppost."

45. Gates, *Our Biometric Future*; Magnet, *When Biometrics Fail*; Ajana, *Governing through Biometrics*.

46. Pugliese, *Biometrics*, 1.

47. Blas, "Escaping the Face."

48. Ajana, *Governing through Biometrics*, 3.

49. Demosistō, "香港眾志 Demosistō."

50. Kirschenbaum, *Mechanisms*; Parikka, *Medianatures*; Kittler, *Truth of the Technological World*.
51. Harper, "Data."
52. Wagner, "What China's Cybersecurity Law Says about the Future."
53. Collins, *CLOUD Act*.
54. Zhou, "DJI May Hand Over Drone Data in Hong Kong to Chinese Government."
55. Watts, "Brazil Demands Explanation from US over NSA Spying"; Lam, "Exclusive: NSA Targeted China's Tsinghua University."
56. Khazan, "Creepy, Long-Standing Practice of Undersea Cable Tapping."
57. Office of the Communications Authority, "Landing of Submarine Cables in Hong Kong."
58. TeleGeography, "EAC-C2C."
59. Dataplugs, "High Speed and Stable Global Network with Direct China."
60. Pirie, "Advancing the ASEAN Economic Community," 17.
61. Yang, "HK Well-Positioned as Data Hub."
62. Fong, "Asia Pacific Gateway (APG)—Tseung Kwan O."
63. Ranjan, "Streaming Big Data Processing in Datacenter Clouds."
64. Edwards, *Vast Machine*, 84.
65. Legislative Council, Personal Data (Privacy) Ordinance.
66. Girot, *Regulation of Cross-Border Transfers of Personal Data in Asia*.
67. Hughes and Sutherland, "Impact of 'BREXIT' on Australia's Cross-Border Data Transfer Laws."
68. Kennedy and Lee, "Change It Up."
69. Kuo, "Hong Kong's Digital Battle."
70. Parsons, "Hong Kong SAR (China)," 98.
71. Parsons, "Hong Kong SAR (China)," 96.
72. Mozur and Qiqing, "Hong Kong Takes Symbolic Stand against China's High-Tech Controls."
73. Sassen, "Embedded Borderings: Making New Geographies of Centrality," 8.
74. Zuboff, *Age of Surveillance Capitalism*, 103.
75. Cohen, "Review of Zuboff's The Age of Surveillance Capitalism," 240.
76. Cohen, "Review of Zuboff's The Age of Surveillance Capitalism," 242.
77. Layne and Lee, "Developing Fully Functional E-Government"; Gil-Garcia, "Towards a Smart State?"
78. Kim, Trimi, and Chung, "Big-Data Applications in the Government Sector."
79. Rossiter, *Software, Infrastructure, Labor*, 346.
80. Mozur, "One Month, 500,000 Face Scans"; Mozur, "In Hong Kong Protests, Faces Become Weapons."
81. Lovink, *Sad by Design*, 90.
82. Legislative Council Panel on Security, "Replacing and Upgrading the Information Technology Infrastructure," 8.
83. Mozur, "One Month, 500,000 Face Scans."
84. Megvii, "Face++ AI Open Platform."
85. AFP, "'They Have No Clue about Network Security.'"
86. Kitchin, *Data Revolution*, 70.
87. Boyajian and Cook, "Democratic Crisis in Hong Kong."

88. Chan and Blundy, "'Bulletproof' China-Backed Doxxing Site Attacks Hong Kong's Democracy Activists."
89. Laskai and Sacks, "China Is Having an Unexpected Privacy Awakening."
90. Ruan, "Big Data in China and the Battle for Privacy."
91. Yu, "'It Would Become like Xinjiang.'"
92. Zenz, "'Thoroughly Reforming Them towards a Healthy Heart Attitude'"; Raza, "China's 'Political Re-Education' Camps of Xinjiang's Uyghur Muslims."
93. Chin, "Life Inside China's Total Surveillance State"; Leibold, "Surveillance in China's Xinjiang Region."
94. Buckley and Mozur, "How China Uses High-Tech Surveillance to Subdue Minorities."
95. Hogan, "Data Is Airborne; Data Is Inborn."
96. Bates, "The Politics of Data Friction."
97. Rossiter, *Software, Infrastructure, Labor*; Toscano, "Lineaments of the Logistical State."
98. Rossiter, *Software, Infrastructure, Labor*, 479.
99. Polyakova and Meserole, "Exporting Digital Authoritarianism," 6.
100. Wagner, "What China's Cybersecurity Law Says about the Future."
101. Collins, *CLOUD Act*.
102. Munn, *Ferocious Logics*.
103. Kaye, "Epsilon and Others Scramble for Alexa Data from Amazon."
104. Gold, "This European Court Case against Facebook Could Have Implications Far beyond Tech."
105. Morozov, "Socialize the Data Centres!"; Morozov, "After the Facebook Scandal It's Time to Base the Digital Economy on Public v Private Ownership of Data."
106. Sadowski, "When Data Is Capital."

Chapter 4

1. Elden, "Missing the Point," 10.
2. Painter, "Rethinking Territory," 1097.
3. Storey, *Territories*, 1.
4. Cowen and Gilbert, "Politics of War, Citizenship, Territory," 16.
5. Agnew, "Territorial Trap"; Agnew, *Globalization and Sovereignty*.
6. Agnew, *Globalization and Sovereignty*, 3.
7. Caporaso, "Changes in the Westphalian Order," 2.
8. Caporaso, "Changes in the Westphalian Order," 6.
9. Cowen and Gilbert, "Politics of War, Citizenship, Territory," 1.
10. Kolers, *Land, Conflict, and Justice*, 69.
11. Herb, "National Identity and Territory," 10.
12. Parker, "State, Citizenship, and Territory," 586.
13. Bodin, *Six Books of the Commonwealth*; Schmitt, *Political Theology*; Schmitt, *Nomos of the Earth*.
14. Opitz and Tellmann, "Global Territories."
15. Andrews, *Monograph of Christmas Island (Indian Ocean)*, ix.
16. Rintoul, "Pre-Election Surge Pushes Island Centres Far beyond Capacity."

17. Anderson and Ferng, "No Boat," 216.
18. Australian Government, "Detention and Community Statistics Summary," 11.
19. Allain, "Jus Cogens Nature of Non-Refoulement"; Goodwin-Gill, "Right to Seek Asylum."
20. Evans to Minister for Immigration and Citizenship, "Joint Letter Re Christmas Island Immigration Detention Centre."
21. Australian Human Rights Commission, "Immigration Detention on Christmas Island," 31.
22. Australian Human Rights Commission, "Immigration Detention on Christmas Island," 8.
23. Jai, "My Last Hours on Christmas Island."
24. Johnson, *Borders, Asylum and Global Non-Citizenship*, 210.
25. Pugliese, "Transnational Carceral Archipelagos," 587.
26. Pugliese, "Transnational Carceral Archipelagos."
27. SMH, "Nauru Child Detainees Running on Empty."
28. Mathew, "Australian Refugee Protection in the Wake of the Tampa"; Fox, "International Asylum and Boat People"; Perera, *Australia and the Insular Imagination*; Giannacopoulos, "Tampa."
29. Australian Government, Migration Amendment (Excision from Migration Zone) Act 2001.
30. Johnson et al., "Interventions on Rethinking 'the Border' in Border Studies," 62.
31. Budz, "Heterotopian Analysis of Maritime Refugee Incidents," 22.
32. Opitz and Tellmann, "Global Territories."
33. Australian Government, Migration Amendment (Unauthorised Maritime Arrivals and Other Measures) Act 2013.
34. Perera, *Australia and the Insular Imagination*, 54.
35. Weber, "Shifting Frontiers of Migration Control," 28.
36. Palmer and Matthews, "Excising Democracy," 29.
37. Mountz, "Enforcement Archipelago," 126.
38. Coddington et al., "Embodied Possibilities, Sovereign Geographies, and Island Detention," 27.
39. Harari, "Life on Christmas Island."
40. Joint Standing Committee on the National Capital and External Territories, "Inquiry into the Changing Economic Environment in the Indian Ocean Territories," iii.
41. Rose, "Governing the Enterprising Self"; Foucault, *The Birth of Biopolitics*; McNay, "Self as Enterprise"; Kelly, *Self as Enterprise*.
42. Joint Standing Committee on the National Capital and External Territories, "Inquiry into the Changing Economic Environment in the Indian Ocean Territories," 48.
43. Joint Standing Committee on the National Capital and External Territories, "Inquiry into the Changing Economic Environment in the Indian Ocean Territories," 112.
44. Joint Standing Committee on the National Capital and External Territories, "Inquiry into the Changing Economic Environment in the Indian Ocean Territories," 112.
45. Vocus Communications, "Australia Singapore Cable."
46. Bleine et al., "Surfing the Data Wave."

47. Pirie, "Advancing the ASEAN Economic Community."
48. Pearce, "Vocus Touts 60Tbps Capacity on Australia Singapore Cable."
49. Joyner, "Undersea Cable Delivering Internet to Transform Christmas Island."
50. Joyner, "Undersea Cable Delivering Internet to Transform Christmas Island."
51. Nott, "INDIGO West Cable Lands at Perth Beach."
52. Telstra Global, "INDIGO Subsea Cable System between Australia and South East Asia Now Commissioned."
53. Vocus Communications, "Data and Secure Networks."
54. The World Economic Forum, "Data Policy in the Fourth Industrial Revolution," 7.
55. Opitz and Tellmann, "Global Territories."
56. Neilson, "Currency of Migration."
57. Perera, "Line in the Sea," 14.
58. Harari, "Life on Christmas Island."
59. Boochani, *No Friend but the Mountains*, 169.
60. Mieville, *The City & The City*.
61. Mieville, *The City & The City*, 44.
62. Mountz, "Where Asylum-Seekers Wait," 386.
63. Opitz and Tellmann, "Global Territories," 274.
64. Delaney, *Territory*, 19.
65. Nail, *Figure of the Migrant*, 2.
66. Sassen, *Expulsions*, 13.
67. Sassen, Interview with Saskia Sassen on Expulsions; Sassen, "At the Systemic Edge."
68. Sassen, *Expulsions*, 404.
69. Foucault, *Society Must Be Defended*, 255.
70. Foucault, *Society Must Be Defended*, 256.
71. Melamed, "Racial Capitalism," 77.
72. Melamed, "Racial Capitalism," 79.
73. Chambers, "Society Has Been Defended," 18.
74. El-Enany and Keenan, "From Pacific to Traffic Islands," 34.
75. Chambers, "Offshore Is a Form, Not a Place," 4.
76. Chambers, "Imagining the Political Transformation of Australia's Christmas Island," 117.
77. Neilson, "Borderscape"; Casas-Cortes, Cobarrubias, and Pickles, "Riding Routes and Itinerant Borders"; Watkins, "Australia's Irregular Migration Information Campaigns."
78. Casas-Cortes, Cobarrubias, and Pickles, "'Good Neighbours Make Good Fences,'" 246.
79. Chambers, "Imagining the Political Transformation of Australia's Christmas Island," 131.
80. Morrison, "Transcript of Press Conference."

Chapter 5

1. Storey, *Territories*, 1.
2. Cowen and Gilbert, "Politics of War, Citizenship, Territory," 16.

3. Elden, *Birth of Territory*, 432.
4. Painter, "Rethinking Territory."
5. Sassen, "When Territory Deborders Territoriality."
6. Rossiter, "Imperial Infrastructures and Asia beyond Asia"; Neilson, Rossiter, and Samaddar, *Logistical Asia*.
7. Peters, Steinberg, and Stratford, *Territory beyond Terra*.
8. Harvey, "'New' Imperialism," 2004; Harvey, *New Imperialism*, 2005.
9. Moore, *Capitalism in the Web of Life*.
10. Gillespie, "Politics of 'Platforms'"; Ruppert, Isin, and Bigo, "Data Politics"; Gray, "Three Aspects of Data Worlds."
11. Peduzzi, "Sand, Rarer Than One Thinks"; Anderson and Heifetz, "Hong Kong's Government Is Spending Billions Taking Land from the Sea."
12. Huang, "China's Cable Strategy"; Page, O'Keeffe, and Taylor, "America's Undersea Battle With China for Control of the Global Internet Grid."
13. Kar et al., "Moving beyond Smart Cities."
14. Olds and Yeung, "Pathways to Global City Formation." 508.
15. Bratton, *The Stack*, 14.
16. Peduzzi, "Sand, Rarer Than One Thinks."
17. Hoe, "Defining a Smart Nation," 326.
18. Elden, *Birth of Territory*, 432.
19. King, *Singapore Miracle*.
20. Peduzzi, "Sand, Rarer Than One Thinks."
21. De Koninck, *Singapore's Permanent Territorial Revolution*.
22. Jamieson, "There's Sand in My Infinity Pool."
23. Royal BAM, "Large Land Reclamation Contract for HAM in Singapore."
24. New York Times, "Indonesia's Islands Are Buried Treasure for Gravel Pirates."
25. Milton, "Sand Smugglers."
26. Guerin, "Shifting Sands of Time—and Singapore," 200.
27. New York Times, "Indonesia's Islands Are Buried Treasure for Gravel Pirates."
28. Henderson, "Singapore Accused of Launching 'Sand Wars.'"
29. Strangio and Sokheng, "Sand Mining Spikes in Koh Kong Estuaries."
30. Gavriletea, "Environmental Impacts of Sand Exploitation."
31. Beiser, "Sand Mining." While several of the sources in these paragraphs are journalistic and focus on very specific impacts, the broader environmental impacts of land reclamation, such as the loss of coral reefs and other marine habitats along with their flora and fauna, have been well documented by scholars and scientists for a number of decades. See, for example, Tay et al., "Land Reclamation and the Consequent Loss of Marine Habitats around the Ayer Islands, Singapore," as well as Lai et al., "Effects of Urbanisation on Coastal Habitats and the Potential for Ecological Engineering."
32. Strangio and Sokheng, "Sand Mining Spikes in Koh Kong Estuaries."
33. Tan, "Two Rivers Dry up in Johor, Allegedly from Sand-Mining."
34. Beiser, "He Who Controls the Sand."
35. Dwyer and Nettelbeck, *Violence, Colonialism and Empire in the Modern World*.
36. Schmitt, *Nomos of the Earth*, 45.
37. Schmitt, *Nomos of the Earth*, 46.
38. Schmitt, *Nomos of the Earth*, 46.
39. Schmitt, *Nomos of the Earth*, 46.

40. Schmitt, *Nomos of the Earth*, 37.

41. Bratton, *The Stack*, 33.

42. Rossiter, *Software, Infrastructure, Labor*, 314.

43. Baharudin, "Undersea Superhighway."

44. Duckett, "Indigo Subsea Cable Made Ready for Use."

45. Raffles, *Memoir of the Life and Public Services of Sir Thomas Stamford Raffles*, 25.

46. "A Vision of an Intelligent Island: The IT2000 Report" (Singapore: National Computer Board, 1992), quoted in Murray, *Singapore*, 152.

47. Info-communications Media Development Authority, "Guidelines on Deployment of Submarine Cables into Singapore."

48. Chua, "Singapore the Most Connected Country in the World."

49. Bushell-Embling, "Southeast Asia-Japan 2 Cable to Link 9 Markets."

50. Rossiter, *Software, Infrastructure, Labor*, 402.

51. Bratton, *The Stack*, 29.

52. Allen, *Topologies of Power*, 43.

53. Allen, *Topologies of Power*, 2.

54. Schmitt, *Political Theology*, 18.

55. Rodan, "Internet and Political Control in Singapore"; Lee, "Internet Control and Auto-Regulation in Singapore"; Reyes, "Social Media Networks and Tactical Globalization."

56. Gibson, "Disneyland with the Death Penalty."

57. Ibrahim, "Everyday Authoritarianism," 219.

58. Intel, "From Sand to Silicon."

59. Ong, "Intelligent Island, Baroque Ecology," 176.

60. Bhunia, "Towards Smart Nation Singapore."

61. DataSpark, *Mobility Genome*.

62. Rossiter, *Software, Infrastructure, Labor*, 407.

63. Kong and Woods, "Ideological Alignment of Smart Urbanism in Singapore."

64. An, "Crisis and Contingency at the Dashboard." The invisibility of these subjects within a data-driven territory is reiterated in a recent interview. "There are almost a million work permit holders in Singapore, laboring in a range of low-wage, stigmatized professions: construction, manufacturing, domestic work. But many face physical and social segregation, and are excluded from data on Singapore's resident population." Fordyce and Chok, "Political Agenda."

65. Kong and Woods, "Ideological Alignment of Smart Urbanism in Singapore," 693.

66. Hoe, "Defining a Smart Nation."

67. Delaney, *Territory*, 3.

68. Tay, "Intelligent 'Island.'"

69. Sack, *Human Territoriality*, 76.

70. Tan, *Does Class Matter?*, 85.

71. Marx, *Capital*; Harvey, *New Imperialism*; Moore, *Capitalism in the Web of Life*.

72. Gillespie, "Politics of 'Platforms'"; Kitchin, *Data Revolution*; Gray, "Three Aspects of Data Worlds."

73. Raffestin, "Space, Territory, and Territoriality," 130.

74. Parikka, "*Medianatures* Introduction: The Materiality of Media and Waste"; Parikka, *Geology of Media*.

75. Cubitt, *Finite Media*.

76. Harvey, "'New' Imperialism," 2004, 74.
77. Beller, *Message Is Murder*, 2.
78. Morozov, *To Save Everything, Click Here.*
79. Kitiarsa, *"Bare Life" of Thai Migrant Workmen in Singapore.*
80. Rosenberg, "Virtual Reality Check Digital Daydreams, Cyberspace Nightmares."
81. Mezzadra and Neilson, "On the Multiple Frontiers of Extraction."
82. Tay, "Intelligent Island."

Chapter 6

1. Stack, "Internet of Things (IoT) Data Continues to Explode Exponentially. Who Is Using That Data and How?"
2. Shi and Dustdar, "Promise of Edge Computing."
3. Cisco Systems, "Fog Computing and the Internet of Things," 1.
4. Zhang et al., "The Cloud Is Not Enough."
5. Luan et al., "Fog Computing."
6. Bonomi et al., "Fog Computing and Its Role in the Internet of Things."
7. Headrick, *Tentacles of Progress*, 98.
8. Starosielski, *Undersea Network*, 93.
9. Carter, United Nations Environment Programme, and World Conservation Monitoring Centre, *Submarine Cables and the Oceans.*
10. Green, "Submarine Cable Industry."
11. ETSI, "5G Specs."
12. Grover and Garimella, "Optimization in Edge Computing and Small-Cell Networks," 19.
13. Mackenzie, "Intensive Movement in Wireless Digital Signal Processing," 1299.
14. Mackenzie, "Intensive Movement in Wireless Digital Signal Processing," 1303.
15. Hernandez, "Microsoft Expands Its Hyperscale Cloud Footprint."
16. Miller, "Hyper-Scale Cloud Data Center, Seen from the Clouds."
17. Barroso, Clidaras, and Hölzle, *Datacenter as a Computer*, 2.
18. Barroso, Clidaras, and Hölzle, *Datacenter as a Computer*, 2.
19. Fichera and Staten, "Five Data Center and IT Infrastructure Lessons from the Cloud Giants," 4.
20. Easterling, *Extrastatecraft*, 1.
21. Bahl, "Emergence of Micro Datacenter (Cloudlets/Edges) for Mobile Computing."
22. Smith, "Finding Packet."
23. Foucault, *Discipline and Punish*, 89.
24. Hu, "Black Boxes and Green Lights," 85.
25. Cowan and Gaskins, "Monitoring Physical Threats in the Data Center."
26. Iron Mountain, "Underground Data Centers."
27. Equinix, *IBX® Singapore 3 (SG3) Data Center Tour.*
28. Hsu, "It's Time to Think beyond Cloud Computing."
29. Hsu, "It's Time to Think beyond Cloud Computing."
30. Dautov et al., "Metropolitan Intelligent Surveillance Systems for Urban Areas."

31. Verma and Sood, "Fog Assisted-IoT Enabled Patient Health Monitoring in Smart Homes."

32. Cao et al., "Distributed Analytics and Edge Intelligence."

33. Roman, Lopez, and Mambo, "Mobile Edge Computing," 13.

34. Alrawais et al., "Fog Computing for the Internet of Things"; Mukherjee et al., "Security and Privacy in Fog Computing."

35. Russinovich, "Inside Azure Datacenter Architecture."

36. Sverdlik, "When Air No Longer Cuts It."

37. Chen et al., "ThriftyEdge."

38. Abbas et al., "Mobile Edge Computing."

39. Google, "Cloud TPU."

40. Google, "Edge TPU."

41. Ernst, *Digital Memory and the Archive*.

42. Krajewski, *Paper Machines*.

43. Ruppert, Isin, and Bigo, "Data Politics," 3.

44. Anderson, "End of Theory."

45. Andrejevic and Gates, "Big Data Surveillance," 190.

46. Nastic et al., "Serverless Real-Time Data Analytics Platform for Edge Computing." Bailas et al., "Performance of Video Processing at the Edge for Crowd-Monitoring Applications." Ning, Huang, and Wang, "Vehicular Fog Computing."

47. Ananthanarayanan et al., "Real-Time Video Analytics."

48. FogHorn, "FogHorn Lightning."

49. Miller, "Eight Trends That Will Shape the Data Center Industry in 2019."

50. Ahmed et al., "Role of Big Data Analytics in Internet of Things."

51. Magaki et al., "ASIC Clouds."

52. Miller, "How Powerful New AI Hardware Will Impact Data Center Design."

53. Evans, "Ten-Year Futures."

54. Holmes, "IoT at the Edge."

55. Wang et al., "Facial Feature Discovery for Ethnicity Recognition."

56. Dautov et al., "Metropolitan Intelligent Surveillance Systems for Urban Areas."

57. Bailas et al., "Performance of Video Processing at the Edge for Crowd-Monitoring Applications."

58. Hu et al., "Intelligent Video Surveillance Based on Mobile Edge Networks."

59. Marx, *Capital*, 675.

60. Kokalitcheva, "Wave of Tech Companies Have Pushed Ethical Boundaries to Maximize Profit."

61. Wang et al., "Facial Feature Discovery for Ethnicity Recognition."

62. Wang et al., "Facial Feature Discovery for Ethnicity Recognition."

63. Wang et al., "Facial Feature Discovery for Ethnicity Recognition."

64. Wang et al., "Facial Feature Discovery for Ethnicity Recognition."

65. Nikouei, Chen, and Faughnan, "Smart Surveillance as an Edge Service."

66. Sweeney, "K-Anonymity: A Model for Protecting Privacy."

67. Domingo-Ferrer, Sánchez, and Soria-Comas, "Database Anonymization: Privacy Models, Data Utility, and Microaggregation-Based Inter-Model Connections."

68. Curzon, Almehmadi, and El-Khatib, "Survey of Privacy Enhancing Technologies for Smart Cities."

69. Cheney-Lippold, *We Are Data*; Koopman, *How We Became Our Data*.

70. Rouvroy, "End(s) of Critique," 154.

71. Floridi, "Open Data, Data Protection, and Group Privacy"; Taylor, Floridi, and Van der Sloot, *Group Privacy*; Mittelstadt, "From Individual to Group Privacy in Big Data Analytics."

72. Mezzadra and Neilson, *Politics of Operations.*

73. Terranova, "Data Mining the Body of the Socius," 1.

74. Valerio, "To Comply with GDPR, Most Data Should Remain at the Edge."

75. Zuboff, "Big Other," 83.

76. Barocas and Nissenbaum, "Big Data's End Run around Procedural Privacy Protections."

77. Foucault, *Discipline and Punish*, 206.

78. Foucault, *Discipline and Punish*, 203.

79. Nealon, *Foucault beyond Foucault,* 31.

80. Nealon, *Foucault beyond Foucault,* 32.

81. Nealon, *Foucault beyond Foucault,* 147.

82. Filippi, "Flawed Cloud Architectures and the Rise of Decentral Alternatives."

83. Levine, "End of Cloud Computing."

84. Prahlad, "Computing at the Edge with AWS Greengrass & Amazon FreeRTOS."

85. Foucault, *Discipline and Punish*, 213.

86. Foucault, *Discipline and Punish*, 213.

87. Foucault, *Discipline and Punish*, 213.

88. OpenFog Consortium Architecture Working Group, "Reference Architecture for Fog Computing," 54.

89. Shih, "Infra // STRUCTURE."

Chapter 7

1. Moisio, "State Power and the COVID-19 Pandemic," 600.

2. Economist, "State in the Time of COVID-19."

3. Kim, "Who's Watching?"

4. Cha, "S. Korea to Test AI-Powered Facial Recognition to Track COVID-19 Cases."

5. Klein, *Shock Doctrine.*

6. The terminology of sustaining, defending, and administering life here draws from Foucault's well-known notion of biopower as the new way in which governance and political power is framed, rationalized, and conducted. Foucault, *History of Sexuality*, 214.

7. Storey, "Research Agenda for Territory and Territoriality," 17.

8. Anderson, *Imagined Communities.*

9. Taiuru, "Aotearoa Māori Internet Organisation."

10. Taiuru, "Aotearoa Māori Internet Organisation."

11. Taiuru, "Aotearoa Māori Internet Organisation."

12. Halberstam, "Unbuilding Gender."

13. Halberstam, "Unbuilding Gender."

14. Halberstam, "Unbuilding Gender."
15. Kittler, *Gramophone, Film, Typewriter*, xxxix.
16. Simone, "Relational Infrastructures in Postcolonial Urban Worlds," 120.
17. Simone, "Relational Infrastructures in Postcolonial Urban Worlds," 84.
18. Halberstam, "Unbuilding Gender."
19. Vincent, "How Apps Power Hong Kong's Leaderless Protests."
20. Butler, *Notes toward a Performative Theory of Assembly*, 127.

References

Abbas, N., Y. Zhang, A. Taherkordi, and T. Skeie. 2018. "Mobile Edge Computing: A Survey." *IEEE Internet of Things Journal* 5 (1): 450–65. https://doi.org/10.1109/JIOT.2017.2750180

ABC News. 2019. "Hong Kong Protesters Cut Down Data-Collecting Lamppost." ABC News, August 24. https://www.abc.net.au/news/2019-08-24/hong-kong-protests-smart-lampposts-cut-down-surveillance-fears/11445606

Abramowitz, Michael, and Michael Chertoff. 2018. "The Global Threat of China's Digital Authoritarianism." *Washington Post*, November 1. https://www.washingtonpost.com/opinions/the-global-threat-of-chinas-digital-authoritarianism/2018/11/01/46d6d99c-dd40-11e8-b3f0-62607289efee_story.html

Acuto, Michele, and Simon Curtis. 2014. "Assemblage Thinking and International Relations." In *Reassembling International Theory*, 1–15. Cham, Switzerland: Springer.

AFP. 2019. "'They Have No Clue about Network Security': China Data Leak Exposes Mass Surveillance across Muslim Xinjiang." *Hong Kong Free Press*, February 20. https://hongkongfp.com/2019/02/20/no-clue-network-security-china-data-leak-exposes-mass-surveillance-across-muslim-xinjiang/

Agnew, John. 1994. "The Territorial Trap: The Geographical Assumptions of International Relations Theory." *Review of International Political Economy* 1 (1): 53–80.

Agnew, John. 2017. *Globalization and Sovereignty: Beyond the Territorial Trap*. London: Rowman & Littlefield.

Ahmed, Ejaz, Ibrar Yaqoob, Ibrahim Abaker Targio Hashem, Imran Khan, Abdelmuttlib Ibrahim Abdalla Ahmed, Muhammad Imran, and Athanasios V. Vasilakos. 2017. "The Role of Big Data Analytics in Internet of Things." Special issue, "5G Wireless Networks for IoT and Body Sensors," *Computer Networks* 129 (December): 459–71. https://doi.org/10.1016/j.comnet.2017.06.013

Ajana, Btihaj. 2013. *Governing through Biometrics: The Biopolitics of Identity*. New York: Springer.

Akita, Hiroyuki. 2019. "China Is Exporting AI-Driven Authoritarianism." *Nikkei Asian Review*, June 14. https://asia.nikkei.com/Spotlight/Comment/China-is-exporting-AI-driven-authoritarianism

Allain, Jean. 2001. "The Jus Cogens Nature of Non-Refoulement." *International Journal of Refugee Law* 13 (4): 533–58.

Allen, John. 2016. *Topologies of Power: Beyond Territory and Networks*. New York: Routledge.

Alrawais, Arwa, Abdulrahman Alhothaily, Chunqiang Hu, and Xiuzhen Cheng. 2017. "Fog Computing for the Internet of Things: Security and Privacy Issues." *IEEE Internet Computing* 21 (2): 34–42. https://doi.org/10.1109/MIC.2017.37

Amoore, Louise. 2018. "Cloud Geographies: Computing, Data, Sovereignty." *Progress in Human Geography* 42 (1): 4–24. https://doi.org/10.1177/0309132516662147

Ananthanarayanan, G., P. Bahl, P. Bodík, K. Chintalapudi, M. Philipose, L. Ravindranath, and S. Sinha. 2017. "Real-Time Video Analytics: The Killer App for Edge Computing." *Computer* 50 (10): 58–67. https://doi.org/10.1109/MC.2017.3641638

Anderson, Benedict. 2016. *Imagined Communities*. London: Verso.

Anderson, Brian, and Justin Heifetz. 2017. "Hong Kong's Government Is Spending Billions Taking Land from the Sea." *Vice* (blog), November 10. https://www.vice.com/en_us/article/wjgpm9/hong-kong-spending-billions-taking-land-from-sea

Anderson, Chris. 2008. "The End of Theory: The Data Deluge Makes the Scientific Method Obsolete." *Wired*, June 23. https://www.wired.com/2008/06/pb-theory/

Anderson, Sean, and Jennifer Ferng. 2013. "No Boat: Christmas Island and the Architecture of Detention." *Architectural Theory Review* 18 (2): 212–26.

Andrejevic, Mark, and Kelly Gates. 2014. "Big Data Surveillance: Introduction." *Surveillance & Society* 12 (2): 185–96.

Andrews, Charles William. 1900. *A Monograph of Christmas Island (Indian Ocean): Physical Features and Geography*. London: British Museum.

Aouragh, Miriyam, and Paula Chakravartty. 2016. "Infrastructures of Empire: Towards a Critical Geopolitics of Media and Information Studies." *Media, Culture & Society* 38 (4): 559–75. https://doi.org/10.1177/0163443716643007

Arabi, Karim. 2014. "Mobile Computing Opportunities, Challenges and Technology Drivers." Presented at the Design Automation Conference, San Francisco, June 4. http://www2.dac.com/events/videoarchive.aspx?confid=170&filter=keynote&id=170-103--0&#video

Ash, James, Rob Kitchin, and Agnieszka Leszczynski. 2016. "Digital Turn, Digital Geographies?" *Progress in Human Geography* 42 (1) (August). https://doi.org/10.1177/0309132516664800

Australian Government. 2001. Migration Amendment (Excision from Migration Zone) Act 2001. C2004A00887. https://www.legislation.gov.au/Details/C2004A00887/Html/Text

Australian Government. 2013. Migration Amendment (Unauthorised Maritime Arrivals and Other Measures) Act 2013. https://www.legislation.gov.au/Details/C2013A00035/Html/Text, http://www.legislation.gov.au/Details/C2013A00035

Australian Government. 2019. "Detention and Community Statistics Summary." Department of Home Affairs. https://reliefweb.int/sites/reliefweb.int/files/resources/immigration-detention-statistics-jan-2019.pdf

Australian Human Rights Commission. 2010. "Immigration Detention on Christmas Island." Sydney: Australian Human Rights Commission. https://www.humanrights.gov.au/sites/default/files/content/human_rights/immigration/idc2010_christmas_island.pdf

Baharudin, Hariz. 2018. "Undersea Superhighway: A New 4,600km Submarine Cable

Linking Perth to Singapore." *Straits Times*, October 15. https://www.straitstimes.com/singapore/undersea-superhighway-a-a-new-4600km-submarine-cable-linking-perth-to-singapore

Bahl, Victor. 2015. "Emergence of Micro Datacenter (Cloudlets/Edges) for Mobile Computing." Presented at Microsoft Research, Redmond, WA, May 13.

Bahnhof. 2019. "Pionen." Bahnhof. 2019. https://www.bahnhof.net/page/datacenter-pionen

Bailas, C., M. Marsden, D. Zhang, N. E. O'Connor, and S. Little. 2018. "Performance of Video Processing at the Edge for Crowd-Monitoring Applications." In *2018 IEEE 4th World Forum on Internet of Things (WF-IoT)*, edited by H. Mueller, Y. Rongshan, and A. Skarmeta, 482–87. New York: IEEE Computer Society. https://doi.org/10.1109/WF-IoT.2018.8355170

Balding, Christopher. 2019. "Huawei Technologies' Links to Chinese State Security Services." SSRN Scholarly Paper ID 3415726. Rochester, NY: Social Science Research Network. https://papers.ssrn.com/abstract=3415726

Baran, Paul. 1964. "On Distributed Communications Networks." *IEEE Transactions on Communications Systems* 12 (1): 1–9.

Barocas, Solon, and Helen Nissenbaum. 2014. "Big Data's End Run Around Procedural Privacy Protections." *Communications of the ACM* 57 (11): 31–33.

Barroso, Luiz André, Jimmy Clidaras, and Urs Hölzle. 2013. *The Datacenter as a Computer: An Introduction to the Design of Warehouse-Scale Machines, Second Edition.* San Rafael, CA: Morgan & Claypool.

Bates, Jo. 2018. "The Politics of Data Friction." *Journal of Documentation* 74 (2): 412–29. https://doi.org/10.1108/JD-05-2017-0080

Bates, Jo, Yu-Wei Lin, and Paula Goodale. 2016. "Data Journeys: Capturing the Socio-Material Constitution of Data Objects and Flows." *Big Data & Society* 3 (2): 1–12. https://doi.org/10.1177/2053951716654502

Beck, Michael Till, Martin Werner, Sebastian Feld, and S. Schimper. 2014. "Mobile Edge Computing: A Taxonomy." In *Proceedings of the Sixth International Conference on Advances in Future Internet*, 48–55. Lisbon: Citeseer.

Beiser, Vince. 2017a. "Sand Mining: The Global Environmental Crisis You've Never Heard Of." *Guardian*, February 27. https://www.theguardian.com/cities/2017/feb/27/sand-mining-global-environmental-crisis-never-heard

Beiser, Vince. 2017b. "He Who Controls the Sand: The Mining 'Mafias' Killing Each Other to Build Cities." *Guardian*, February 28. https://www.theguardian.com/cities/2017/feb/28/sand-mafias-killing-each-other-build-cities

Beller, Jonathan. 2018. *The Message Is Murder: Substrates of Computational Capital.* London: Pluto Press.

Bhaya, Abhishek. 2018. "China, African Leaders Slam French Report on AU Headquarters Hacking as 'Ridiculous', 'Nonsense.'" CGTN, January 31. https://news.cgtn.com/news/346b6a4e30677a6333566d54/share_p.html

Bhunia, Priyankar. 2017. "Towards Smart Nation Singapore—Developments in 2017 (Part 1 of 3)." *OpenGov Asia*. December 28. https://www.opengovasia.com/towards-smart-nation-singapore-developments-in-2017-part-1-of-3/

Blas, Zach. 2013. "Escaping the Face: Biometric Facial Recognition and the Facial Weaponization Suite." *Media-N*, July. http://median.newmediacaucus.org/caa-conference-edition-2013/escaping-the-face-biometric-facial-recognition-and-the-facial-weaponization-suite/

Bleine, Maxime, Jesline Teo, Oliver Wilkinson, and Ervin Jocson. 2017. "Surfing the Data Wave: The Surge in Asia Pacific's Data Centre Market." PricewaterhouseCoopers. https://www.pwc.com/sg/en/publications/assets/surfing-the-data-wave.pdf

Block, Fred L., and Matthew R. Keller. 2015. *State of Innovation: The U.S. Government's Role in Technology Development*. New York: Routledge.

Bodin, Jean. 1576. *Six Books of the Commonwealth*. Translated by M. J. Tooley. Oxford: Basil Blackwood Oxford.

Bonomi, Flavio, Rodolfo Milito, Jiang Zhu, and Sateesh Addepalli. 2012. "Fog Computing and Its Role in the Internet of Things." In *Proceedings of the First Edition of the MCC Workshop on Mobile Cloud Computing—MCC '12*, edited by Mario Gerla and Dijiang Huang, 13–16. Helsinki: ACM Press. https://doi.org/10.1145/2342509.2342513

Boochani, Behrouz. 2018. *No Friend but the Mountains: Writing from Manus Prison*. Sydney: Picador Australia.

Bowker, Geoffrey C., and Susan Leigh Star. 2000. "Invisible Mediators of Action: Classification and the Ubiquity of Standards." *Mind, Culture, and Activity* 7 (1–2): 147–63. https://doi.org/10.1080/10749039.2000.9677652

Boyajian, Annie, and Sarah Cook. 2019. "Democratic Crisis in Hong Kong." New York: Freedom House. https://freedomhouse.org/report/special-reports/democratic-crisis-hong-kong

Bradbury, Danny. 2016. "Super Cool: Arctic Data Centres Aren't Just for Facebook." The Register, May 12. https://www.theregister.co.uk/2016/05/12/power_in_a_cold_climate/

Bratton, Benjamin. 2016. *The Stack: On Software and Sovereignty*. Cambridge, MA: MIT Press.

Brighenti, Andrea. 2010. "On Territorology: Towards a General Science of Territory." *Theory Culture & Society* 27 (March): 52–72. https://doi.org/10.1177/0263276409350357

Bryan-Low, Cassell, Colin Packham, David Lague, Steve Stecklow, and Jack Stubbs. 2019. "Hobbling Huawei: Inside the U.S. War on China's Tech Giant." *Reuters*, May 21. https://www.reuters.com/article/us-huawei-usa-5g-specialreport-idUSKCN1SR1EU

Buckley, Chris, and Paul Mozur. 2019. "How China Uses High-Tech Surveillance to Subdue Minorities." *New York Times*, May 22. https://www.nytimes.com/2019/05/22/world/asia/china-surveillance-xinjiang.html

Buckley, Sean. 2013. "Hibernia Halts Cable Build with Huawei Due to US-China Cybersecurity Issues." FierceTelecom. February 11. https://www.fiercetelecom.com/telecom/hibernia-halts-cable-build-huawei-due-to-us-china-cybersecurity-issues

Budz, Michele. 2009. "A Heterotopian Analysis of Maritime Refugee Incidents." *International Political Sociology* 3 (1): 18–35.

Bushell-Embling, Dylan. 2018. "Southeast Asia-Japan 2 Cable to Link 9 Markets." Telecom Asia. March 16. https://www.telecomasia.net/content/southeast-asia-japan-2-cable-link-9-markets

Butler, Judith. 2015. *Notes toward a Performative Theory of Assembly*. Cambridge, MA: Harvard University Press.

Cai, Peter. 2017. "Understanding China's Belt and Road Initiative." Sydney: Lowy Institute for International Policy.

CAICT. 2018. "White Paper on China International Optical Cable Interconnection." Beijing: China Academy of Information and Communications Technology. http://www.caict.ac.cn/english/yjcg/bps/201808/P020180829385778461678.pdf

Cantero Gamito, Marta. 2018. "Europeanization through Standardization: ICT and Telecommunications." *Yearbook of European Law* 37 (January): 395–423. https://doi.org/10.1093/yel/yey018

Cao, Yu, Peng Hou, Donald Brown, Jie Wang, and Songqing Chen. 2015. "Distributed Analytics and Edge Intelligence: Pervasive Health Monitoring at the Era of Fog Computing." In *Proceedings of the 2015 Workshop on Mobile Big Data*, 43–48. Mobidata '15. New York: ACM. https://doi.org/10.1145/2757384.2757398

Caporaso, James A. 2000. "Changes in the Westphalian Order: Territory, Public Authority, and Sovereignty." *International Studies Review* 2 (2): 1–28.

Carse, Ashley, Jason Cons, and Townsend Middleton, eds. 2018. "Limn: Chokepoints." *Limn*, no. 10 (February). https://limn.it/issues/chokepoints/

Carter, L., United Nations Environment Programme, and World Conservation Monitoring Centre, eds. 2009. *Submarine Cables and the Oceans: Connecting the World.* UNEP-WCMC Biodiversity Series no. 31. Cambridge: UNEP World Conservation Monitoring System; Portsmouth, UK: International Cable Protection Committee.

Casas-Cortes, Maribel, Sebastian Cobarrubias, and John Pickles. 2015. "Riding Routes and Itinerant Borders: Autonomy of Migration and Border Externalization." *Antipode* 47 (4): 894–914.

Casas-Cortes, Maribel, Sebastian Cobarrubias, and John Pickles. 2016. "'Good Neighbours Make Good Fences': Seahorse Operations, Border Externalization and Extra-Territoriality." *European Urban and Regional Studies* 23 (3): 231–51.

Cave, Danielle. 2018. "The African Union Headquarters Hack and Australia's 5G Network." *The Strategist*, December 26. https://www.aspistrategist.org.au/editors-picks-for-2018-the-african-union-headquarters-hack-and-australias-5g-network/

Cha, Sangmi. 2021. "S. Korea to Test AI-Powered Facial Recognition to Track COVID-19 Cases." *Reuters*, December 13. https://www.reuters.com/world/asia-pacific/skorea-test-ai-powered-facial-recognition-track-covid-19-cases-2021-12-13/

Chambers, Peter. 2011. "Society Has Been Defended: Following the Shifting Shape of State through Australia's Christmas Island." *International Political Sociology* 5 (1): 18–34.

Chambers, Peter. 2012. "Imagining the Political Transformation of Australia's Christmas Island, from Sovereignty to Governance." *Shima: The International Journal of Research into Island Cultures* 6 (2): 22.

Chambers, Peter. 2018. "Offshore Is a Form, Not a Place: Paradoxes, Global Spaces and Global Classes in Offshoring Finance and Detention." *Distinktion: Scandinavian Journal of Social Theory* 19 (1): 1–27.

Chan, Debby Sze Wan, and Ngai Pun. 2020. "Economic Power of the Political Powerless in the 2019 Hong Kong Pro-Democracy Movement." *Critical Asian Studies* (January 6): 1–11. https://doi.org/10.1080/14672715.2019.1708019

Chan, Esther, and Rachel Blundy. 2019. "'Bulletproof' China-Backed Doxxing Site Attacks Hong Kong's Democracy Activists." *Hong Kong Free Press*, November 1. https://www.hongkongfp.com/2019/11/01/bulletproof-china-backed-doxxing-site-attacks-hong-kongs-democracy-activists/

Chan, K. G. 2019. "China-Made Cameras Focus on HK Protesters." *Asia Times*, July 23.

https://www.asiatimes.com/2019/07/article/china-made-cameras-focus-on-hk-protesters/

Chander, Anupam, and Uyen P. Le. 2015. "Data Nationalism." SSRN Scholarly Paper 2577947. Rochester, NY: Social Science Research Network. https://papers.ssrn.com/abstract=2577947

Cheney-Lippold, John. 2018. *We Are Data: Algorithms and the Making of Our Digital Selves*. New York: NYU Press.

Cheah, W. L. 2009. "Migrant Workers as Citizens within the ASEAN Landscape: International Law and the Singapore Experiment." *Chinese Journal of International Law* 8 (1): 205–31. https://doi.org/10.1093/chinesejil/jmn041

Chen, X., Q. Shi, L. Yang, and J. Xu. 2018. "ThriftyEdge: Resource-Efficient Edge Computing for Intelligent IoT Applications." *IEEE Network* 32 (1): 61–65. https://doi.org/10.1109/MNET.2018.1700145

Cheng, Kris. 2019. "Hong Kong Activists Complain Police Failed to Display ID Numbers, as Security Chief Says Uniform Has 'No Room.'" *Hong Kong Free Press*, June 21. https://www.hongkongfp.com/2019/06/21/hong-kong-activists-complain-police-failed-display-id-numbers-security-chief-says-uniform-no-room/

Chin, Josh. 2017. "Life Inside China's Total Surveillance State." *Wall Street Journal*, December 19. https://www.wsj.com/video/life-inside-chinas-total-surveillance-state/CE86DA19-D55D-4F12-AC6A-3B2A573492CF.html

Chua, Ernest. 2016. "Singapore the Most Connected Country in the World." TODAY-online. February 26. https://www.todayonline.com/singapore/singapore-most-connected-country-world

Cisco Systems. 2015. "Fog Computing and the Internet of Things: Extend the Cloud to Where the Things Are." San Jose, CA: Cisco Systems. https://www.cisco.com/c/dam/en_us/solutions/trends/iot/docs/computing-overview.pdf

Coddington, Kate, R. Tina Catania, Jenna Loyd, Emily Mitchell-Eaton, and Alison Mountz. 2012. "Embodied Possibilities, Sovereign Geographies, and Island Detention: Negotiating the 'Right to Have Rights' on Guam, Lampedusa, and Christmas Island." *Shima: The International Journal of Research into Island Cultures* 6 (2): 27–48.

Cohen, Julie. 2019a. "Review of Zuboff's The Age of Surveillance Capitalism: The Fight for a Human Future at the New Frontier of Power." *Surveillance & Society* 17 (1): 240–45.

Cohen, Julie E. 2019b. *Between Truth and Power: The Legal Constructions of Informational Capitalism*. Oxford: Oxford University Press.

Collins, Doug. 2018. *CLOUD Act*: *4943*. https://www.congress.gov/bill/115th-congress/house-bill/4943

Cowan, Christian, and Chris Gaskins. 2006. "Monitoring Physical Threats in the Data Center." West Kingston, RI: American Power Conversion.

Cowen, Deborah, and Emily Gilbert. 2008. "The Politics of War, Citizenship, Territory." In *War, Citizenship, Territory*, edited by Deborah Cowen and Emily Gilbert, 1–32. New York: Routledge. https://doi.org/10.4324/9780203938126-4

Cowie, James. 2011. "The Geopolitics of Internet Infrastructure." Berkman Klein Center for Internet & Society, November 8. https://www.youtube.com/watch?v=xx13GO2kJU0

Crampton, Jeremy W. 2009. "Cartography: Maps 2.0." *Progress in Human Geography* 33 (1): 91–100.

Crampton, Jeremy W. 2011. *Mapping: A Critical Introduction to Cartography and GIS*. Vol. 11. Hoboken, NJ: John Wiley & Sons.

Cubitt, Sean. 2016. *Finite Media: Environmental Implications of Digital Technologies*. Durham: Duke University Press.

Curzon, James, Abdulaziz Almehmadi, and Khalil El-Khatib. 2019. "A Survey of Privacy Enhancing Technologies for Smart Cities." *Pervasive and Mobile Computing* 55 (April): 76–95. https://doi.org/10.1016/j.pmcj.2019.03.001

Dahlin, Peter. 2019. "Can You Get a Fair Trial in China? The Extradition Row Reaches a Supreme Court in Europe." *Hong Kong Free Press*, June 18. https://www.hongkongfp.com/2019/06/18/can-get-fair-trial-china-extradition-row-reaches-supreme-court-europe/

Dataplugs. 2019. "High Speed and Stable Global Network with Direct China." Dataplugs. 2019. https://www.dataplugs.com/en/company/network/

DataSpark. 2017. *Mobility Genome—How It Works*. https://www.youtube.com/watch?time_continue=158&v=iAi9jjZJkrs

Dautov, Rustem, Salvatore Distefano, Dario Bruneo, Francesco Longo, Giovanni Merlino, Antonio Puliafito, and Rajkumar Buyya. 2018. "Metropolitan Intelligent Surveillance Systems for Urban Areas by Harnessing IoT and Edge Computing Paradigms." *Software: Practice and Experience* 48 (8): 1475–92. https://doi.org/10.1002/spe.2586

Davenport, Tara. 2015. "Submarine Cables, Cybersecurity and International Law: An Intersectional Analysis." *Catholic University Journal of Law and Technology* 24 (1): 54.

Davies, Alex. 2014. "Cisco Pushes IoT Analytics to the Extreme Edge with Mist Computing." Rethink, December 19. https://rethinkresearch.biz/articles/cisco-pushes-iot-analytics-extreme-edge-mist-computing-2/

De Koninck, Rodolphe. 2017. *Singapore's Permanent Territorial Revolution: Fifty Years in Fifty Maps*. Singapore: National University of Singapore Press.

Delaney, David. 2008. *Territory: A Short Introduction*. Hoboken, NJ: John Wiley & Sons.

Demosistō. 2019. "香港眾志 Demosistō." August 24. https://www.facebook.com/demosisto/posts/1180947455447408

Dixon, Lucas, Thomas Ristenpart, and Thomas Shrimpton. 2016. "Network Traffic Obfuscation and Automated Internet Censorship." *ArXiv:1605.04044*, May. http://arxiv.org/abs/1605.04044

Domingo-Ferrer, Josep, David Sánchez, and Jordi Soria-Comas. 2016. "Database Anonymization: Privacy Models, Data Utility, and Microaggregation-Based Inter-Model Connections." *Synthesis Lectures on Information Security, Privacy, & Trust* 8 (1): 1–136.

Dourish, Paul, and Scott Mainwaring. 2012. "Ubicomp's Colonial Impulse." In *Proceedings of the 2012 ACM Conference on Ubiquitous Computing*, 133–42. Pittsburgh. https://doi.org/10.1145/2370216.2370238

Duckett, Chris. 2019. "Indigo Subsea Cable Made Ready for Use." ZDNet. May 30. https://www.zdnet.com/article/indigo-subsea-cable-made-ready-for-use/

Dupont, Alan. 2019. "Crackdown on Chinese Tech Giant Huawei Has Global Ramifications." *Australian*, June 8.

Dwyer, Philip, and Amanda Nettelbeck, eds. 2018. *Violence, Colonialism and Empire in the Modern World*. London: Palgrave Macmillan.

Easterling, Keller. 2016. *Extrastatecraft: The Power of Infrastructure Space*. London: Verso.

Economist. 2020. "The State in the Time of Covid-19." *Economist*, March 26. https://www.economist.com/leaders/2020/03/26/the-state-in-the-time-of-covid-19

Edwards, Paul N. 2013. *A Vast Machine: Computer Models, Climate Data, and the Politics of Global Warming*. Cambridge, MA: MIT Press.

Elden, Stuart. 2005. "Missing the Point: Globalization, Deterritorialization and the Space of the World." *Transactions of the Institute of British Geographers* 30 (1): 8–19.

Elden, Stuart. 2013. *The Birth of Territory*. Chicago: University of Chicago Press.

El-Enany, Nadine, and Sarah Keenan. 2019. "From Pacific to Traffic Islands: Challenging Australia's Colonial Use of the Ocean through Creative Protest." *Acta Academica* 51 (1): 28–52. https://doi.org/10.18820/24150479/aa51i1.2

Equinix. 2015. *IBX® Singapore 3 (SG3) Data Center Tour*. https://www.youtube.com/watch?v=AnDz9Clzs8k

Ernst, Wolfgang. 2012. *Digital Memory and the Archive*. Minneapolis: University of Minnesota Press.

ETSI. 2019. "5G Specs." ETSI. June. https://www.etsi.org/technologies/5g

Evans, Benedict. 2019. *Ten-Year Futures: How Will Tech Change the World?* https://www.youtube.com/watch?v=-cxby9Nff2w

Evans, Chris. 2008. "Joint Letter Re Christmas Island Immigration Detention Centre." Letter to Minister for Immigration and Citizenship. August 15.

Fang, Frank. 2019. "Huawei's Expansion in Africa Comes under Scrutiny." *Epoch Times*, January 20. https://www.theepochtimes.com/huaweis-expansion-in-africa-comes-under-scrutiny_2772269.html

Fernandez, Luis Alberto. 2005. "Policing Protest Spaces: Social Control in the Anti-Globalization Movement." PhD diss., Arizona State University. http://search.proquest.com/docview/305031766/abstract/43F470A756E649F7PQ/1

Fichera, Richard, and James Staten. 2013. "Five Data Center and IT Infrastructure Lessons from the Cloud Giants." Cambridge, MA: Forrester Research.

Filippi, Primavera De. 2013. "Flawed Cloud Architectures and the Rise of Decentral Alternatives." *Internet Policy Review* 2 (4). https://policyreview.info/articles/analysis/flawed-cloud-architectures-and-rise-decentral-alternatives

Floridi, Luciano. 2014. "Open Data, Data Protection, and Group Privacy." *Philosophy & Technology* 27 (1): 1–3. https://doi.org/10.1007/s13347-014-0157-8

Flowerdew, Robin, Zhiqiang Feng, and David Manley. 2007. "Constructing Data Zones for Scottish Neighbourhood Statistics." *Computers, Environment and Urban Systems* 31 (1): 76–90. https://doi.org/10.1016/j.compenvurbsys.2005.07.008

FogHorn. 2019. "FogHorn Lightning." *FogHorn Systems* (blog). July 1. https://www.foghorn.io/lightning-iot-edge-computing/

Fong, Terence. 2014. "Asia Pacific Gateway (APG)—Tseung Kwan O." Hong Kong: Environmental Resources Management. https://www.epd.gov.hk/eia/register/english/permit/ep4852014/documents/emar201401/pdf/emar201401.pdf

Fordyce, Debbie, and Stephanie Chok. 2018. "Singapore's Invisible Population." Interview by Kirsten Han. https://newnaratif.com/podcast/political-agenda-singapores-invisible-population/

Foucault, Michel. 1978. *The History of Sexuality*. Translated by Robert Hurley. Vol. 1. New York: Pantheon Books.

Foucault, Michel. 1995. *Discipline and Punish: The Birth of the Prison*. Translated by Alan Sheridan. New York: Vintage.
Foucault, Michel. 2003. *Society Must Be Defended: Lectures at the Collège de France, 1975–76*. London: Picador.
Foucault, Michel. 2008. *The Birth of Biopolitics: Lectures at the Collège de France, 1978–1979*. London: Palgrave Macmillan.
Fox, Peter. 2010. "International Asylum and Boat People: The Tampa Affair and Australia's 'Pacific Solution.'" *Maryland Journal of International Law* 25 (1): 356–73.
Fraser, Erica. 2016. "Data Localisation and the Balkanisation of the Internet." *SCRIPTed: A Journal of Law, Technology and Society* 13: 359–73.
Freedom Hongkonger. 2019. "香港被送中誓要成G20話題 眾籌《金融時報》及日德法英等各國報章頭版公開信 Hong Kong G20 Open Letter Initiative: Make the Anti-Extradition Bill an Issue for the G20 Summit! Crowdfunding Campaign for a Front-Page Open Letter Advertisement on the Financial Times and Other International Newspapers." GoGetFunding. June. https://gogetfunding.com/香港被送中誓要成g20話題-眾籌《金融時報》及日德
Garrett, Daniel. 2015. *Counter-Hegemonic Resistance in China's Hong Kong: Visualizing Protest in the City*. London: Springer.
Gates, Kelly. 2011. *Our Biometric Future: Facial Recognition Technology and the Culture of Surveillance*. New York: New York University Press.
Gavriletea, Marius Dan. 2017. "Environmental Impacts of Sand Exploitation: Analysis of Sand Market." *Sustainability* 9 (7): 1–26. https://doi.org/10.3390/su9071118
Ghoshal, Abhimanyu. 2019. "Telegram CEO: China Disrupted the App to Sabotage Hong Kong Protesters." The Next Web. June 13. https://thenextweb.com/asia/2019/06/13/telegram-founder-claims-china-hacked-the-app-to-disrupt-hong-kong-protesters/
Giannacopoulos, Maria. 2005. "Tampa: Violence at the Border." *Social Semiotics* 15 (1): 29–42. https://doi.org/10.1080/10350330500059098
Gibson, William. 1993. "Disneyland with the Death Penalty." *Wired*, April. https://www.wired.com/1993/04/gibson-2/
Gil-Garcia, J. Ramon. 2012. "Towards a Smart State? Inter-Agency Collaboration, Information Integration, and Beyond." *Information Polity* 17 (3–4): 269–80. https://doi.org/10.3233/IP-2012-000287
Gillespie, Tarleton. 2010. "The Politics of 'Platforms.'" *New Media & Society* 12 (3): 347–64. https://doi.org/10.1177/1461444809342738
Girot, Clarissa, ed. 2018. *Regulation of Cross-Border Transfers of Personal Data in Asia*. Singapore: Asian Business Law Institute. https://abli.asia/UploadPDF/DP_Compendium_May_2018.pdf
Gold, Hadas. 2019. "This European Court Case against Facebook Could Have Implications Far beyond Tech." CNN Business, July 9. https://www.cnn.com/2019/07/09/tech/facebook-data-privacy-max-schrems/index.html
Goldsmith, Jack. 2019. "Sovereign Difference and Sovereign Deference on the Internet." *Yale Law Journal Forum* 128 (March): 818–26.
Goodwin-Gill, Guy S. 2011. "The Right to Seek Asylum: Interception at Sea and the Principle of Non-Refoulement." *International Journal of Refugee Law* 23 (3): 443–57. https://doi.org/10.1093/ijrl/eer018
Google. 2019a. "Cloud TPU." Google Cloud. https://cloud.google.com/tpu/

Google. 2019b. "Edge TPU." Google Cloud. https://cloud.google.com/edge-tpu/

Gray, Jonathan. 2018. "Three Aspects of Data Worlds." *Krisis*, no. 1. https://krisis.eu/three-aspects-of-data-worlds/

Green, Mick. 2013. "The Submarine Cable Industry: How Does It Work?" In *Submarine Cables*, edited by Douglas R. Burnett, Robert Beckman, and Tara M. Davenport, 41–60. Leiden: Brill. https://brill.com/view/title/22898

Grover, Jitender, and Ram Murthy Garimella. 2018. "Optimization in Edge Computing and Small-Cell Networks." In *Edge Computing: From Hype to Reality*, edited by Fadi Al-Turjman. Cham, Switzerland: Springer Nature.

Guerin, Bill. 2003. "The Shifting Sands of Time—and Singapore." *Asia Times*, July 31. http://www.wildsingapore.com/news/2004/030731-1.htm

Gupta, Rohan. 2019. "Breaking Down Facial Recognition: The Viola-Jones Algorithm." Medium. August 9. https://medium.com/swlh/the-intuition-behind-facial-detection-the-viola-jones-algorithm-29d9106b6999

Halberstam, Jack. 2018. "Unbuilding Gender: Trans* Anarchitectures in and beyond the Work of Gordon Matta-Clark." *Places Journal*, October. https://doi.org/10.22269/181003

Han, Byung-Chul. 2017. *Psychopolitics: Neoliberalism and New Technologies of Power*. London: Verso.

Harari, Fiona. 2014. "Life on Christmas Island." *Sydney Morning Herald*, September 11. https://www.smh.com.au/lifestyle/life-on-christmas-island-20140828-109dpf.html

Harcourt, Bernard. 2015. *Exposed: Desire and Disobedience in the Digital Age*. Cambridge, MA: Harvard University Press.

Harper, Douglas. 2019. "Data." In *Etymology Dictionary*. https://www.etymonline.com/word/data

Harvey, David. 2004. "The 'New' Imperialism: Accumulation by Dispossession." *Socialist Register* 40. https://socialistregister.com/index.php/srv/article/view/5811

Harvey, David. 2005. *The New Imperialism*. Oxford: Oxford University Press.

Headrick, Daniel R. 1988. *The Tentacles of Progress: Technology Transfer in the Age of Imperialism, 1850–1940*. Oxford: Oxford University Press.

Henderson, Barney. 2010. "Singapore Accused of Launching 'Sand Wars.'" *Telegraph*, February 12. https://www.telegraph.co.uk/news/worldnews/asia/singapore/7221987/Singapore-accused-of-launching-Sand-Wars.html

Herb, Guntram Henrik. 1999. "National Identity and Territory." In *Nested Identities: Nationalism, Territory, and Scale*, edited by David H. Kaplan and Guntram Henrik Herb. London: Rowman & Littlefield.

Hernandez, Pedro. 2014. "Microsoft Expands Its Hyperscale Cloud Footprint." EWEEK, October 20. https://www.eweek.com/cloud/microsoft-expands-its-hyperscale-cloud-footprint

Hikvision. 2017. *Hikvision Brand Video: See Far, Go Further*. https://www.youtube.com/watch?v=cap3fzXGHcU

Hillman, Jonathan. 2019. *Influence and Infrastructure: The Strategic Stakes of Foreign Projects*. Washington, DC: Center for Strategic and International Studies.

Ho, Estella. 2018. "Algorithmic Authoritarianism: China's Ideological Export for the Digital Age." *Journal of International and Public Affairs* 1 (1). https://www.jipasg.org/posts/2018/9/11/algorithmic-authoritarianism-chinas-ideological-export-for-the-digital-age

Hoe, Siu Loon. 2016. "Defining a Smart Nation: The Case of Singapore." *Journal of Information, Communication and Ethics in Society*, November. https://doi.org/10.1108/JICES-02-2016-0005

Hogan, Mél. 2015. "Data Flows and Water Woes: The Utah Data Center." *Big Data & Society* 2 (2). https://doi.org/10.1177/2053951715592429

Hogan, Mél. 2018. "Data Is Airborne; Data Is Inborn: The Labor of the Body in Technoecologies." *First Monday* 23 (3). https://doi.org/10.5210/fm.v23i3.8285

Hollingsworth, Julia. 2019. "Why Protests Are Becoming Increasingly Faceless." CNN Style, August 25. https://www.cnn.com/style/article/protest-design-future-intl-hnk/index.html

Holmes, Preston. 2018. "IoT at the Edge: Bringing Intelligence to the Edge Using Cloud IoT." Presented at the Cloud Next '18, San Francisco, August 17. https://www.youtube.com/watch?v=-T9MNR-Bl8I

Holt, Jennifer, and Patrick Vonderau. 2015. "'Where the Internet Lives': Data Centers as Cloud Infrastructure." In *Signal Traffic: Critical Studies of Media Infrastructures*, edited by Lisa Parks and Nicole Starosielski, 175–229. Chicago: University of Illinois Press.

Hong, Yu. 2017. *Networking China: The Digital Transformation of the Chinese Economy*. Chicago: University of Illinois Press.

Howard, Bill. 2018. "Fatal Arizona Crash: Uber Car Saw Woman, Called It a False Positive." ExtremeTech. May 7. https://www.extremetech.com/extreme/268915-fatal-arizona-crash-ubercar-saw-woman-called-it-a-false-positive

Howland, Douglas. 2016. *International Law and Japanese Sovereignty: The Emerging Global Order in the 19th Century*. New York: Palgrave Macmillan.

Hsu, Jeremy. 2017. "It's Time to Think beyond Cloud Computing." *Wired*, August 23. https://www.wired.com/story/its-time-to-think-beyond-cloud-computing/

Hu, H., H. Shan, Z. Zheng, Z. Huang, C. Cai, C. Wang, X. Zhen, L. Yu, Z. Zhang, and T. Q. S. Quek. 2018. "Intelligent Video Surveillance Based on Mobile Edge Networks." In *2018 IEEE International Conference on Communication Systems (ICCS)*, edited by Shaoqian Li, 286–91. IEEE. https://doi.org/10.1109/ICCS.2018.8689194

Hu, Krystal. 2019. "Huawei Is Still Winning 5G Contracts around the World despite the U.S. Ban." Yahoo Finance, April 18. https://finance.yahoo.com/news/huawei-is-still-winning-5-g-contracts-around-the-world-despite-the-us-ban-193456655.html

Hu, Tung-Hui. 2015. *A Prehistory of the Cloud*. Cambridge, MA: MIT Press.

Hu, Tung-Hui. 2017. "Black Boxes and Green Lights: Media, Infrastructure, and the Future at Any Cost." *English Language Notes* 55 (1–2): 81–88. https://doi.org/10.1215/00138282-55.1-2.81

Huang, Eli. 2017. "China's Cable Strategy: Exploring Global Undersea Dominance." *The Strategist*, December 4. https://www.aspistrategist.org.au/chinas-cable-strategy-exploring-global-undersea-dominance/

Huawei. 2013. "Desktop Cloud Draws Praise in Africa." Huawei Enterprise, July 25. https://e.huawei.com/au/case-studies/global/older/hw_201214

Huawei 2015. "TGT Built Next-Generation Data Centers with Huawei Servers." http://e.huawei.com/~/media/EBG/Download_Files/Cases/en/TGT%20Built%20Next-Generation%20Data%20Centers%20with%20Huawei%20Servers.pdf

Huawei. 2017. "Huawei Creates a Smart City Nervous System for More Than 100 Cities with Leading New ICT." Huawei Press Center, November 14. https://www.huawei.com/en/press-events/news/2017/11/Huawei-Smart-City-Nervous-System-SCEWC2017

Huawei. 2018. "Huawei Launches Full Range of 5G End-to-End Product Solutions." Huawei, February 26. https://www.huawei.com/en/press-events/news/2018/2/Huawei-Launches-Full-Range-of-5G-End-to-End-Product-Solutions

Huawei. 2019. "Video Surveillance as the Foundation of 'Safe City' in Kenya." https://www.huawei.com/nz/industry-insights/technology/digital-transformation/video/video-surveillance-as-the-foundation-of-safe-city-in-kenya

Huawei Marine. 2019. "Experience." Huawei Marine. 2019. http://www.huaweimarine.com/en/Experience

Hughes, Gordon, and Andrew Sutherland. 2016. "Impact of 'BREXIT' on Australia's Cross-Border Data Transfer Laws." Davies Collison Cave. August 11. https://dcc.com/services/privacy-data-protection/impact-of-brexit-on-australias-cross-border-data-transfer-laws/

Hui, Mary. 2019. "Why Hong Kong's Protesters Were Afraid to Use Their Metro Cards." Quartz. June 13. https://qz.com/1642441/extradition-law-why-hong-kong-protesters-didnt-use-own-metro-cards/

Ibrahim, Nur Amali. 2018. "Everyday Authoritarianism: A Political Anthropology of Singapore." *Critical Asian Studies* 50 (2): 219–31. https://doi.org/10.1080/14672715.2018.1445538

Info-communications Media Development Authority. 2016. "Guidelines on Deployment of Submarine Cables into Singapore." Singapore: Singapore Government. https://www2.imda.gov.sg/-/media/imda/files/regulation-licensing-and-consultations/codes-of-practice-and-guidelines/subcablelanding.pdf?la=en

Intel. 2009. *From Sand to Silicon: The Making of a Chip*. https://www.youtube.com/watch?time_continue=116&v=Q5paWn7bFg4

Iron Mountain. 2019. "Underground Data Centers." Iron Mountain. 2019. https://www.ironmountain.com/digital-transformation/data-centers/about/underground-data-centers

Jacob, Marc. 2017. "Global Switch Launches State-of-Art HK$5BN Hong Kong Data Centre Services with China Telecom and Daily-Tech." *Global Security Magazine*, December. http://www.globalsecuritymag.com/Global-Switch-launches-State-of,20171213,75709.html

Jai, Leo. 2018. "My Last Hours on Christmas Island." *Vice*, November 25. https://www.vice.com/en_au/article/ev3pxj/my-last-hours-on-christmas-island

Jamieson, William. 2017. "There's Sand in My Infinity Pool: Land Reclamation and the Rewriting of Singapore." *GeoHumanities* 3 (2): 396–413. https://doi.org/10.1080/2373566X.2017.1279021

Johnson, Corey, Reece Jones, Anssi Paasi, Louise Amoore, Alison Mountz, Mark Salter, and Chris Rumford. 2011. "Interventions on Rethinking 'the Border' in Border Studies." *Political Geography* 30 (2): 61–69.

Johnson, Heather L. 2014. *Borders, Asylum and Global Non-Citizenship: The Other Side of the Fence*. Cambridge: Cambridge University Press.

Joint Standing Committee on the National Capital and External Territories. 2010. "Inquiry into the Changing Economic Environment in the Indian Ocean Territories." Canberra. https://www.aph.gov.au/Parliamentary_Business/Committees/Ho

use_of_Representatives_Committees?url=/ncet/economicenvironment/report/full%20report.pdf

Joyner, Tom. 2019. "Undersea Cable Delivering Internet to Transform Christmas Island." ABC Radio, February 8. https://www.abc.net.au/radio/programs/pm/undersea-cable-delivering-internet-to-transform-christmas-island/10795396

Kaltheuner, Frederike. 2019. "What Hong Kong's Protesters Can Teach Us about the Future of Privacy." Gizmodo Australia. June 23. https://www.gizmodo.com.au/2019/06/what-hong-kongs-protesters-can-teach-us-about-the-future-of-privacy/

Kania, Elsa. 2018. "China's Play for Global 5G Dominance—Standards and the 'Digital Silk Road.'" *The Strategist*, June 27. https://www.aspistrategist.org.au/chinas-play-for-global-5g-dominance-standards-and-the-digital-silk-road/

Kar, Arpan Kumar, Vigneswara Ilavarasan, M. P. Gupta, Marijn Janssen, and Ravi Kothari. 2019. "Moving beyond Smart Cities: Digital Nations for Social Innovation and Sustainability." *Information Systems Frontiers* 21 (3): 495–501. https://doi.org/10.1007/s10796-019-09930-0

Ka-sing, Lam. 2019. "High Data Centre Rents Let Three Firms Dominate US$883 Million Sector." *South China Morning Post*, February 13. https://www.scmp.com/property/hong-kong-china/article/2185881/high-data-centre-rents-have-allowed-three-firms-dominate

Kaye, Kate. 2017. "Epsilon and Others Scramble for Alexa Data from Amazon." *Advertising Age*, February 7. http://adage.com/article/datadriven-marketing/epsilon-scramble-alexa-data-amazon/307843/

Kelly, Peter. 2016. *The Self as Enterprise: Foucault and the Spirit of 21st Century Capitalism*. London: Routledge. https://doi.org/10.4324/9781315553030

Kennedy, Gabriela, and Karen Lee. 2019. "Change It Up: Amendments to the Hong Kong Personal Data (Privacy) Ordinance Being Considered." Mondaq. January 9. http://www.mondaq.com/hongkong/x/769550/Data+Protection+Privacy/Change+It+Up+Amendments+To+The+Hong+Kong+Personal+Data+Privacy+Ordinance+Being+Considered

Khazan, Olga. 2013. "The Creepy, Long-Standing Practice of Undersea Cable Tapping." *Atlantic*, July 16. https://www.theatlantic.com/international/archive/2013/07/the-creepy-long-standing-practice-of-undersea-cable-tapping/277855/

Kim, Gang-Hoon, Silvana Trimi, and Ji-Hyong Chung. 2014. "Big-Data Applications in the Government Sector." *Communications of the ACM* 57 (3): 78–85. https://doi.org/10.1145/2500873

Kim, Victoria. 2021. "Who's Watching? How Governments Used the Pandemic to Normalize Surveillance." *Los Angeles Times*, December 9. https://www.latimes.com/world-nation/story/2021-12-09/the-pandemic-brought-heightened-surveillance-to-save-lives-is-it-here-to-stay

King, Rodney. 2006. *The Singapore Miracle: Myth and Reality*. Inglewood, WA: Insight Press.

Kirschenbaum, Matthew. 2008. *Mechanisms: New Media and the Forensic Imagination*. Cambridge, MA: MIT Press.

Kitchin, Rob. 2013. "Big Data and Human Geography: Opportunities, Challenges and Risks." *Dialogues in Human Geography* 3 (3): 262–67.

Kitchin, Rob. 2014. *The Data Revolution: Big Data, Open Data, Data Infrastructures and Their Consequences*. London: Sage.

Kitchin, Rob. 2015. "The Promise and Perils of Smart Cities." *Computers and Law* 26 (2).

Kitiarsa, Pattana. 2014. *The "Bare Life" of Thai Migrant Workmen in Singapore*. Chiang Mai, Thailand: Silkworm Books.

Kittler, Friedrich. 1999. *Gramophone, Film, Typewriter*. Stanford, CA: Stanford University Press.

Kittler, Friedrich. 2014. *The Truth of the Technological World: Essays on the Genealogy of Presence*. Translated by Erik Butler. Stanford: Stanford University Press.

Klein, Naomi. 2007. *The Shock Doctrine: The Rise of Disaster Capitalism*. New York: Macmillan.

Kobrin, Stephen J. 2004. "Safe Harbours Are Hard to Find: The Trans-Atlantic Data Privacy Dispute, Territorial Jurisdiction and Global Governance." *Review of International Studies* 30 (1): 111–31. https://doi.org/10.1017/S0260210504005856

Kokalitcheva, Kia. 2019. "A Wave of Tech Companies Have Pushed Ethical Boundaries to Maximize Profit." Axios. July 2. https://www.axios.com/big-tech-companies-ethics-facebook-doordash-59abf670-078d-4e15-9033-c0e6e6d75127.html

Kolers, Avery. 2009. *Land, Conflict, and Justice: A Political Theory of Territory*. Cambridge: Cambridge University Press.

Kong, Lily, and Orlando Woods. 2018. "The Ideological Alignment of Smart Urbanism in Singapore: Critical Reflections on a Political Paradox." *Urban Studies* 55 (4): 679–701. https://doi.org/10.1177/0042098017746528

Krajewski, Markus. 2011. *Paper Machines: About Cards and Catalogs, 1548–1929*. Translated by Peter Krapp. Cambridge, MA: MIT Press.

Krasner, Stephen, ed. 2001. *Problematic Sovereignty: Contested Rules, and Political Possibilities*. New York: Columbia University Press.

Kuner, Christopher, Fred H. Cate, Christopher Millard, Dan Jerker B. Svantesson, and Orla Lynskey. 2015. "Internet Balkanization Gathers Pace: Is Privacy the Real Driver?" *International Data Privacy Law* 5 (1): 1–2. https://doi.org/10.1093/idpl/ipu032

Kuo, Lily. 2019. "Hong Kong's Digital Battle: Tech That Helped Protesters Now Used against Them." *Guardian*, June 14. https://www.theguardian.com/world/2019/jun/14/hong-kongs-digital-battle-technology-that-helped-protesters-now-used-against-them

Kwong, Ying-Ho. 2015. "The Dynamics of Mainstream and Internet Alternative Media in Hong Kong: A Case Study of the Umbrella Movement." *International Journal of China Studies; Kuala Lumpur* 6 (3): 273–95.

Lai, Samantha, Lynette H. L. Loke, Michael J. Hilton, Tjeerd J. Bouma, and Peter A. Todd. 2015. "The Effects of Urbanisation on Coastal Habitats and the Potential for Ecological Engineering: A Singapore Case Study." *Ocean & Coastal Management* 103 (January): 78–85. https://doi.org/10.1016/j.ocecoaman.2014.11.006

Lam, Lana. 2013. "Exclusive: NSA Targeted China's Tsinghua University in Extensive Hacking Attacks, Says Snowden." *South China Morning Post*, June 22. https://www.scmp.com/news/china/article/1266892/exclusive-nsa-targeted-chinas-tsinghua-university-extensive-hacking

Lampland, Martha, and Susan Leigh Star, eds. 2009. *Standards and Their Stories: How Quantifying, Classifying, and Formalizing Practices Shape Everyday Life*. Ithaca, NY: Cornell University Press.

Larson, Christina. 2018a. "China's AI Imperative." *Science* 359 (6376): 628–30. https://doi.org/10.1126/science.359.6376.628

Larson, Christina. 2018b. "Asia's Hunger for Sand Takes Toll on Ecology." *Science* 359 (6379): 964–65. https://doi.org/10.1126/science.359.6379.964

Laskai, Lorand. 2019. "Why Blacklisting Huawei Could Backfire." *Foreign Affairs*, June 21. https://www.foreignaffairs.com/articles/china/2019-06-19/why-blacklisting-huawei-could-backfire

Laskai, Lorand, and Samm Sacks. 2019. "China Is Having an Unexpected Privacy Awakening." *Slate*, February 7. https://slate.com/technology/2019/02/china-consumer-data-protection-privacy-surveillance.html

Lawder, David, and Susan Heavey. 2019. "U.S. Blacklists China's Huawei as Trade Dispute Clouds Global Outlook." *Reuters*, May 16. https://www.reuters.com/article/us-usa-trade-china-idUSKCN1SL2DI

Layne, Karen, and Jungwoo Lee. 2001. "Developing Fully Functional E-Government: A Four Stage Model." *Government Information Quarterly* 18 (2): 122–36. https://doi.org/10.1016/S0740-624X(01)00066-1

Lee, Alex. 2018. "Google Is Laying Even More Subsea Cables—One in Completely Unclaimed Territory." Alphr. January 17. https://www.alphr.com/go/1008223

Lee, Francis. 2019. "Solidarity in the Anti-Extradition Bill Movement in Hong Kong." *Critical Asian Studies* (December 15): 1–15. https://doi.org/10.1080/14672715.2020.1700629

Lee, Francis L. F., and Joseph M. Chan. 2018. "Digital Media Activities and Connective Actions." In *Digital Media Activities and Connective Actions*. Oxford: Oxford University Press. http://www.oxfordscholarship.com/view/10.1093/oso/9780190856779.001.0001/oso-9780190856779-chapter-5

Lee, Francis L. F., and Joseph Man Chan. 2016. "Digital Media Activities and Mode of Participation in a Protest Campaign: A Study of the Umbrella Movement." *Information, Communication & Society* 19 (1): 4–22. https://doi.org/10.1080/1369118X.2015.1093530

Lee, Francis L. F., Hsuan-Ting Chen, and Michael Chan. 2017. "Social Media Use and University Students' Participation in a Large-Scale Protest Campaign: The Case of Hong Kong's Umbrella Movement." *Telematics and Informatics* 34 (2): 457–69. https://doi.org/10.1016/j.tele.2016.08.005

Lee, John. 2019. Fugitive Offenders and Mutual Legal Assistance in Criminal Matters Legislation (Amendment) Bill. https://www.legco.gov.hk/yr18-19/english/bills/b201903291.pdf

Lee, Paul S. N., Clement Y. K. So, and Louis Leung. 2015. "Social Media and Umbrella Movement: Insurgent Public Sphere in Formation." *Chinese Journal of Communication* 8 (4): 356–75. https://doi.org/10.1080/17544750.2015.1088874

Lee, Stacia. 2017. "The Cybersecurity Implications of Chinese Undersea Cable Investment." East Asia Center. February 6. https://jsis.washington.edu/eacenter/2017/02/06/cybersecurity-implications-chinese-undersea-cable-investment/

Lee, T. 2005. "Internet Control and Auto-Regulation in Singapore." *Surveillance & Society* 3 (1): 74–95.

Legislative Council. 1995. Personal Data (Privacy) Ordinance. Vol. 614. https://www.elegislation.gov.hk/hk/cap486!en-zh-Hant-HK.pdf?FROMCAPINDEX=Y.

Legislative Council Panel on Security. 2016. "Replacing and Upgrading the Information

Technology Infrastructure and Applications of the Hong Kong Police Force and Replacement of the Command and Control Communications System of the Hong Kong Police Force." https://www.legco.gov.hk/yr15-16/english/panels/se/papers/se20160301cb2-949-5-e.pdf

Leibold, James. 2020. "Surveillance in China's Xinjiang Region: Ethnic Sorting, Coercion, and Inducement." *Journal of Contemporary China* 29 (121): 46–60. https://doi.org/10.1080/10670564.2019.1621529

Leiponen, Aija Elina. 2008. "Competing through Cooperation: The Organization of Standard Setting in Wireless Telecommunications." *Management Science* 54 (11): 1904–19. https://doi.org/10.1287/mnsc.1080.0912

Lerner, Josh, and Jean Tirole. 2015. "Standard-Essential Patents." *Journal of Political Economy* 123 (3): 547–86. https://doi.org/10.1086/680995

Leszczynski, Agnieszka, and Sarah Elwood. 2015. "Feminist Geographies of New Spatial Media." *Canadian Geographer/Le Géographe Canadien* 59 (1): 12–28. https://doi.org/10.1111/cag.12093

Levine, Peter. 2019. "The End of Cloud Computing." Presented at the CloudSummitX, San Diego, March 22. https://www.youtube.com/watch?v=74tKg06Jfpo

Lightwave. 2012. "Huawei Marine to Build Hibernia Altantic's [*sic*] Project Express." Lightwave. January 17, 2012. https://www.lightwaveonline.com/network-design/article/16664889/huawei-marine-to-build-hibernia-altantics-project-express

Lovink, Geert. 2019. *Sad by Design: On Platform Nihilism*. London: Pluto Press.

Luan, Tom H., Longxiang Gao, Zhi Li, Yang Xiang, Guiyi Wei, and Limin Sun. 2015. "Fog Computing: Focusing on Mobile Users at the Edge." *ArXiv:1502.01815 [Cs]*, February. http://arxiv.org/abs/1502.01815

Luoji, Guo. 1996. "A Human Rights Critique of the Chinese Legal System." *Harvard Human Rights Journal* 9 (1): 1–14.

MacAskill, Ewen, and Dominic Rushe. 2013. "Snowden Document Reveals Key Role of Companies in NSA Data Collection." *Guardian*, November 1. https://www.theguardian.com/world/2013/nov/01/nsa-data-collection-tech-firms

Mackenzie, Adrian. 2009. "Intensive Movement in Wireless Digital Signal Processing: From Calculation to Envelopment." *Environment and Planning A: Economy and Space* 41 (6): 1294–1308. https://doi.org/10.1068/a40351

Magaki, Ikuo, Moein Khazraee, Luis Vega Gutierrez, and Michael Bedford Taylor. 2016. "ASIC Clouds: Specializing the Datacenter." In *2016 ACM/IEEE 43rd Annual International Symposium on Computer Architecture (ISCA)*, 178–90. Seoul: IEEE.

Magnet, Shoshana. 2011. *When Biometrics Fail: Gender, Race, and the Technology of Identity*. Durham: Duke University Press.

Mahtani, Shibani. 2019a. "Hong Kong Protesters Coordinate to Beat Chinese Surveillance." *The Independent*, June 16. https://www.independent.co.uk/news/world/asia/hong-kong-protests-china-surveillance-tech-telegram-extradition-bill-a8960911.html

Mahtani, Shibani. 2019b. "Masks, Cash and Apps: How Hong Kong's Protesters Find Ways to Outwit the Surveillance State." *Washington Post*, June 16. https://www.washingtonpost.com/world/asia_pacific/masks-cash-and-apps-how-hong-kongs-protesters-find-ways-to-outwit-the-surveillance-state/2019/06/15/8229169c-8ea0-11e9-b6f4-033356502dce_story.html

Malecki, Edward, and Hu Wei. 2009. "A Wired World: The Evolving Geography of Submarine Cables and the Shift to Asia." *Annals of the Association of American Geographers* 99 (2): 360–82. https://doi.org/10.1080/00045600802686216

Marx, Karl. 2004. *Capital: A Critique of Political Economy*. Translated by Ben Fowkes. London: Penguin Books.

Mathew, Penelope. 2002. "Australian Refugee Protection in the Wake of the Tampa." *American Journal of International Law* 96 (3): 661–76.

Maxwell, Richard, and Toby Miller. 2012. *Greening the Media*. Oxford: Oxford University Press.

Mayer, Maximilian, and Michele Acuto. 2015. "The Global Governance of Large Technical Systems." *Millennium* 43 (2): 660–83.

McNay, Lois. 2009. "Self as Enterprise: Dilemmas of Control and Resistance in Foucault's The Birth of Biopolitics." *Theory, Culture & Society* 26 (6): 55–77.

Megvii. 2019. "Face++ AI Open Platform." 2019. https://www.faceplusplus.com/

Melamed, Jodi. 2015. "Racial Capitalism." *Critical Ethnic Studies* 1 (1): 76–85.

Mezzadra, Sandro, and Brett Neilson. 2017. "On the Multiple Frontiers of Extraction: Excavating Contemporary Capitalism." *Cultural Studies* 31 (2–3): 185–204. https://doi.org/10.1080/09502386.2017.1303425

Mezzadra, Sandro, and Brett Neilson. 2019. *The Politics of Operations: Excavating Contemporary Capitalism*. Durham: Duke University Press.

Mieville, China. 2009. *The City & The City*. New York: Del Rey.

Miller, Rich. 2012. "A Hyper-Scale Cloud Data Center, Seen from the Clouds." Data Center Knowledge. November 6. https://www.datacenterknowledge.com/archives/2012/11/06/facebook-lulea-aerial-view

Miller, Rich. 2019a. "The Eight Trends That Will Shape the Data Center Industry in 2019." *Data Center Frontier* (blog), January 4. https://datacenterfrontier.com/the-eight-trends-that-will-shape-the-data-center-industry-in-2019/

Miller, Rich. 2019b. "How Powerful New AI Hardware Will Impact Data Center Design." *Data Center Frontier* (blog), June 20. https://datacenterfrontier.com/how-powerful-new-ai-hardware-will-impact-data-center-design/

Milton, Chris. 2010. "The Sand Smugglers." *Foreign Policy*, August 4. https://foreignpolicy.com/2010/08/04/the-sand-smugglers/

Mittelstadt, Brent. 2017. "From Individual to Group Privacy in Big Data Analytics." *Philosophy & Technology* 30 (4): 475–94. https://doi.org/10.1007/s13347-017-0253-7

Moisio, Sami. 2020. "State Power and the COVID-19 Pandemic: The Case of Finland." *Eurasian Geography and Economics* 61 (4–5): 598–605. https://doi.org/10.1080/15387216.2020.1782241

Moore, Jason. 2015. *Capitalism in the Web of Life: Ecology and the Accumulation of Capital*. London: Verso.

Moore, Margaret. 2015. *A Political Theory of Territory*. Oxford: Oxford University Press.

Morozov, Evgeny. 2013. *To Save Everything, Click Here: Technology, Solutionism, and the Urge to Fix Problems That Don't Exist*. London: Penguin.

Morozov, Evgeny. 2015. "Socialize the Data Centres!" *New Left Review* 91 (1): 45–66.

Morozov, Evgeny. 2018. "After the Facebook Scandal It's Time to Base the Digital Economy on Public v Private Ownership of Data." *The Observer*, March 31. https://www.theguardian.com/technology/2018/mar/31/big-data-lie-exposed-simply-blaming-facebook-wont-fix-reclaim-private-information

Morrison, Scott. 2019. "Transcript of Press Conference." Parliament of Australia. February 13. https://parlinfo.aph.gov.au/parlInfo/search/display/display.w3p;query=Id%3A%22media%2Fpressrel%2F6495465%22

Mountz, Alison. 2011a. "The Enforcement Archipelago: Detention, Haunting, and Asylum on Islands." *Political Geography* 30 (3): 118–28.

Mountz, Alison. 2011b. "Where Asylum-Seekers Wait: Feminist Counter-Topographies of Sites between States." *Gender, Place & Culture* 18 (3): 381–99.

Mozur, Paul. 2019a. "One Month, 500,000 Face Scans: How China Is Using A.I. to Profile a Minority." *New York Times*, April 14. https://www.nytimes.com/2019/04/14/technology/china-surveillance-artificial-intelligence-racial-profiling.html

Mozur, Paul. 2019b. "In Hong Kong Protests, Faces Become Weapons." *New York Times*, July 26. https://www.nytimes.com/2019/07/26/technology/hong-kong-protests-facial-recognition-surveillance.html

Mozur, Paul. 2019c. "Biometric Data Becomes New Weapon in Hong Kong Protests." Interview by Hari Sreenivasan. *PBS News*, July 27. https://www.pbs.org/newshour/show/biometric-data-becomes-new-weapon-in-hong-kong-protests

Mozur, Paul, Jonah M. Kessel, and Melissa Chan. 2019. "Made in China, Exported to the World: The Surveillance State." *New York Times*, April 24. https://www.nytimes.com/2019/04/24/technology/ecuador-surveillance-cameras-police-government.html

Mozur, Paul, and Lin Qiqing. 2019. "Hong Kong Takes Symbolic Stand against China's High-Tech Controls." *New York Times*, October 3. https://www.nytimes.com/2019/10/03/technology/hong-kong-china-tech-surveillance.html

Mukherjee, M., R. Matam, L. Shu, L. Maglaras, M. A. Ferrag, N. Choudhury, and V. Kumar. 2017. "Security and Privacy in Fog Computing: Challenges." *IEEE Access* 5: 19293–304. https://doi.org/10.1109/ACCESS.2017.2749422

Munn, Luke. 2018. *Ferocious Logics: Unmaking the Algorithm*. Lüneburg: Meson Press.

Munn, Luke. 2020. "Staying at the Edge of Privacy: Edge Computing and Impersonal Extraction." *Media and Communication* 8 (2): 270–79. https://doi.org/10.17645/mac.v8i2.2761

Murray, Geoffrey. 1996. *Singapore: The Global City-State*. New York: St. Martin's Press.

Mutambo, Aggrey. 2019. "Huawei Poised to Fuel China Foreign Policy in Kenya." *Business Daily*, May 6, Africa edition. https://www.businessdailyafrica.com/corporate/companies/Huawei-fuel-China-foreign-policy-Kenya/4003102-5103174-ojagkpz/index.html

Myers, Steven Lee, and Paul Mozur. 2019. "China Is Waging a Disinformation War against Hong Kong Protesters." *New York Times*, August 13. https://www.nytimes.com/2019/08/13/world/asia/hong-kong-protests-china.html

Nail, Thomas. 2015. *The Figure of the Migrant*. Stanford: Stanford University Press.

Nastic, S., T. Rausch, O. Scekic, S. Dustdar, M. Gusev, B. Koteska, M. Kostoska, B. Jakimovski, S. Ristov, and R. Prodan. 2017. "A Serverless Real-Time Data Analytics Platform for Edge Computing." *IEEE Internet Computing* 21 (4): 64–71. https://doi.org/10.1109/MIC.2017.2911430

National Computer Board. 1992. "A Vision of an Intelligent Island: The IT2000 Report." Singapore: National Computer Board.

Nealon, Jeffrey. 2008. *Foucault beyond Foucault: Power and Its Intensifications since 1984*. Stanford: Stanford University Press.

Negash, Behailu, Tuan Nguyen Gia, Arman Anzanpour, Iman Azimi, Mingzhe Jiang, Tomi Westerlund, Amir M. Rahmani, Pasi Liljeberg, and Hannu Tenhunen. 2018. "Leveraging Fog Computing for Healthcare IoT." In *Fog Computing in the Internet of*

Things: Intelligence at the Edge, edited by Amir M. Rahmani, Pasi Liljeberg, Jürgo-Sören Preden, and Axel Jantsch, 145–69. Cham, Switzerland: Springer International. https://doi.org/10.1007/978-3-319-57639-8_8

Neilson, Brett. 2010. "Borderscape: Between Governance and Sovereignty—Remaking the Borderscape to Australia's North." *Local-Global: Identity, Security, Community* 8: 124–40.

Neilson, Brett. 2018. "The Currency of Migration." *South Atlantic Quarterly* 117 (2): 375–96.

Neilson, Brett, Ned Rossiter, and Ranabir Samaddar, eds. 2018. *Logistical Asia: The Labour of Making a World Region*. London: Palgrave Macmillan. https://doi.org/10.1007/978-981-10-8333-4

New York Times. 2010. "Indonesia's Islands Are Buried Treasure for Gravel Pirates." *New York Times*, March 27. https://www.nytimes.com/2010/03/28/weekinreview/28gr ist.html

Ng, Ho Chuen. 2016. "The Umbrella Movement in Hong Kong: Social Movements in the Digital Age." *Diggit Magazine*, March 13. https://www.diggitmagazine.com/pa pers/social-movements-digital-age

Nielsen, Kristian. 2019. "SubTel Forum's Annual Industry Report." Sterling, VA: Submarine Telecoms Industry. https://subtelforum.com/products/submarine-telecoms-in dustry-report/

Nikouei, S. Y., Y. Chen, and T. R. Faughnan. 2018. "Smart Surveillance as an Edge Service for Real-Time Human Detection and Tracking." In *2018 IEEE/ACM Symposium on Edge Computing (SEC)*, 336–37. https://doi.org/10.1109/SEC.2018 .00036

Ning, Z., J. Huang, and X. Wang. 2019. "Vehicular Fog Computing: Enabling Real-Time Traffic Management for Smart Cities." *IEEE Wireless Communications* 26 (1): 87–93. https://doi.org/10.1109/MWC.2019.1700441

Noakes, Stephen. 2018. "A Disappearing Act: The Evolution of China's Administrative Detention System." *Journal of Chinese Political Science* 23 (2): 199–216. https://doi .org/10.1007/s11366-016-9433-z

Nott, George. 2018. "INDIGO West Cable Lands at Perth Beach." CIO. September 19. https://www.cio.com.au/article/646976/indigo-west-cable-lands-perth-beach/

Office of the Communications Authority. 2019. "Landing of Submarine Cables in Hong Kong." February 11. https://www.ofca.gov.hk/en/industry_focus/telecommunicati ons/facility_based/infrastructures/submarine_cables/

Olds, Kris, and Henry Yeung. 2004. "Pathways to Global City Formation: A View from the Developmental City-State of Singapore." *Review of International Political Economy* 11 (3): 489–521. https://doi.org/10.1080/0969229042000252873

Ong, Aihwa. 2004. "Intelligent Island, Baroque Ecology." In *Beyond Description: Singapore Space Historicity*, edited by Ryan Bishop, John Phillips, and Wei-Wei Yeo, 176–89. London: Routledge.

OpenFog Consortium Architecture Working Group. 2017. "Reference Architecture for Fog Computing." Needham, MA: OpenFog Consortium. https://www.iiconsorti um.org/pdf/OpenFog_Reference_Architecture_2_09_17.pdf

Opitz, Sven, and Ute Tellmann. 2012. "Global Territories: Zones of Economic and Legal Dis/Connectivity." *Distinktion: Scandinavian Journal of Social Theory* 13 (December): 261–82.

Page, Jeremy, Kate O'Keeffe, and Rob Taylor. 2019. "America's Undersea Battle with China for Control of the Global Internet Grid." *Wall Street Journal*, March 12. https://www.wsj.com/articles/u-s-takes-on-chinas-huawei-in-undersea-battle-over-the-global-internet-grid-11552407466

Painter, Joe. 2010. "Rethinking Territory." *Antipode* 42 (5): 1090–1118.

Palmer, Victoria, and Julie Matthews. 2006. "Excising Democracy: Ethical Irresponsibility, Refugees and Migration Zones." *Social Alternatives* 25 (3): 26–31.

Parikka, Jussi. 2011. *Medianatures: The Materiality of Information Technology and Electronic Waste*. Ann Arbor: Open Humanities Press.

Parikka, Jussi. 2015. *A Geology of Media*. Minneapolis: University of Minnesota Press.

Parker, Kunal M. 2001. "State, Citizenship, and Territory: The Legal Construction of Immigrants in Antebellum Massachusetts." *Law and History Review* 19 (3): 583–643.

Parks, Lisa, and Nicole Starosielski, eds. 2017. *Signal Traffic: Critical Studies of Media Infrastructures*. Urbana: University of Illinois Press.

Parsons, Mark. 2018. "Hong Kong SAR (China)." In *Regulation of Cross-Border Transfers of Personal Data in Asia*, edited by Clarissa Girot, 95–116. Singapore: Asian Business Law Institute. https://abli.asia/UploadPDF/DP_Compendium_May_2018.pdf

Partington, Angela. 2012. "Huawei Marine Networks: Reinventing the Submarine Cable Industry." Capacity Media, March 1. https://www.capacitymedia.com/articles/2986303/huawei-marine-networks-reinventing-the-submarine-cable-industry

Pearce, Rohan. 2019. "Vocus Touts 60Tbps Capacity on Australia Singapore Cable." Computerworld, July 11. https://www2.computerworld.com.au/article/663902/vocus-touts-60tbps-capacity-australia-singapore-cable/

Peduzzi, Pascal. 2014. "Sand, Rarer Than One Thinks." Nairobi: United Nations Environment Programme. http://wedocs.unep.org/bitstream/handle/20.500.11822/8665/GEAS_Mar2014_Sand_Mining.pdf?sequence=3&isAllowed=y

Perera, Suvendrini. 2002. "A Line in the Sea." *Race & Class* 44 (2): 23–39.

Perera, Suvendrini. 2009. *Australia and the Insular Imagination: Beaches, Borders, Boats, and Bodies*. New York: Palgrave Macmillan.

Perez, Bien. 2017. "Mainland Internet Giants Lift Hong Kong's Data Centre Market." *South China Morning Post*, June 25. https://www.scmp.com/tech/enterprises/article/2099871/hong-kong-data-centres-booming-back-mainland-internet-giants

Peters, Kimberley, Philip Steinberg, and Elaine Stratford, eds. 2018. *Territory beyond Terra*. London: Rowman & Littlefield International.

Pickles, John. 1995. *Ground Truth: The Social Implications of Geographic Information Systems*. New York: Guilford Press.

Pirie, Jeff. 2017. "Advancing The ASEAN Economic Community—the Digital Economy and the Free Flow of Data." *Access Asia Magazine*, March 6.

Polyakova, Alina, and Chris Meserole. 2019. "Exporting Digital Authoritarianism." Washington, DC: Brooking Institution.

Prahlad, Prashant. 2018. "Computing at the Edge with AWS Greengrass & Amazon FreeRTOS." Presented at the AWS re:Invent 2018, San Francisco, November 28. https://www.youtube.com/watch?v=iKXzcRnIvWA

Pugliese, Joseph. 2010. "Transnational Carceral Archipelagos: Lampedusa and Christmas Island." In *Transmediterranean: Diaspora, Histories, Geopolitical Spaces*, 105–24. New York: Peter Lang.

Pugliese, Joseph. 2012. *Biometrics: Bodies, Technologies, Biopolitics*. London: Routledge.

Pugliese, Joseph. 2013. "Technologies of Extraterritorialisation, Statist Visuality and Irregular Migrants and Refugees." *Griffith Law Review* 22 (3): 571–97.

Purnell, Newley, and Stu Woo. 2018. "China's Huawei Is Determined to Lead the Way on 5G despite U.S. Concerns." *Wall Street Journal*, March 30. https://www.wsj.com/articles/washington-woes-aside-huawei-is-determined-to-lead-the-way-on-5g-1522402201

Qin, Hai. 2015. "From Follower to Leader: China and the Mobile Telecommunications Standards." In *World Scientific Reference on Globalisation in Eurasia and the Pacific Rim*, 117–34. Singapore: World Scientific. https://doi.org/10.1142/9789813140318_0007

Qui, Winston. 2012. "China Mobile to Build APG Cable Landing Station in Hong Kong." Submarine Networks, August 19. https://www.submarinenetworks.com/en/systems/intra-asia/apg/china-mobile-to-build-apg-cable-landing-station-in-hong-kong

Quigley, Brian. 2016. "New Undersea Cable Expands Capacity for Google APAC Customers and Users." *Google Cloud* (blog), October 13. https://cloud.google.com/blog/products/gcp/new-undersea-cable-expands-capacity-for-google-apac-customers-and-users/

Raffestin, Claude. 2012. "Space, Territory, and Territoriality." *Environment and Planning D: Society and Space* 30 (1): 121–41.

Raffles, Lady Sophia. 1835. *Memoir of the Life and Public Services of Sir Thomas Stamford Raffles*. London: John Murray.

Ragland, Leigh Ann, Joseph McReynolds, Matthew Southerland, and James Mulvenon. 2014. "Red Cloud Rising: Cloud Computing in China." Vienna, VA: Defense Group.

Ranjan, Rajiv. 2014. "Streaming Big Data Processing in Datacenter Clouds." *IEEE Cloud Computing* 1 (1): 78–83. https://doi.org/10.1109/MCC.2014.22

Raza, Zainab. 2019. "China's 'Political Re-Education' Camps of Xinjiang's Uyghur Muslims." *Asian Affairs* 50 (4): 488–501.

Reyes, Vicente Chua. 2013. "Social Media Networks and Tactical Globalization: An Exploratory Case Study of Contesting Political 'Space' in Singapore." *St Antony's International Review* 8 (2): 33–46.

Rintoul, Stuart. 2013. "Pre-Election Surge Pushes Island Centres Far beyond Capacity." *Australian*, June 20.

Roberts, Sue, Anna Secor, and Matthew Zook. 2012. "Critical Infrastructure: Mapping the Leaky Plumbing of US Hegemony." *Antipode* 44 (1): 5–9.

Rodan, Garry. 1998. "The Internet and Political Control in Singapore." *Political Science Quarterly* 113 (1): 63–89. https://doi.org/10.2307/2657651

Rolland, Nadège. 2017. "China's 'Belt and Road Initiative': Underwhelming or Game-Changer?" *Washington Quarterly* 40 (January): 127–42. https://doi.org/10.1080/0163660X.2017.1302743

Roman, Rodrigo, Javier Lopez, and Masahiro Mambo. 2018. "Mobile Edge Computing, Fog et al.: A Survey and Analysis of Security Threats and Challenges." *Future Generation Computer Systems* 78 (January): 680–98. https://doi.org/10.1016/j.future.2016.11.009

Rose, Nikolas. 1992. "Governing the Enterprising Self." In *The Values of the Enterprise*

Culture: The Moral Debate, edited by Paul Heelas and Paul Morris. London: Routledge.

Rosenberg, Scott. 1992. "Virtual Reality Check Digital Daydreams, Cyberspace Nightmares." *San Francisco Examiner*, April 19.

Rossiter, Ned. 2017a. *Software, Infrastructure, Labor: A Media Theory of Logistical Nightmares*. New York: Routledge.

Rossiter, Ned. 2017b. "Imperial Infrastructures and Asia beyond Asia: Data Centres, State Formation and the Territoriality of Logistical Media." *Fibreculture Journal*, no. 29 (June): 152–71.

Rouvroy, Antoinette. 2013. "The End(s) of Critique: Data Behaviourism versus Due Process." In *Privacy, Due Process and the Computational Turn*, edited by Mireille Hildebrandt and Katja De Vries, 143–67. New York: Routledge.

Royal BAM. 2000. "Large Land Reclamation Contract for HAM in Singapore." BAM International. June 18. https://www.baminternational.com/en/news/large-land-reclamation-contract-for-ham-in-singapore

Ruan, Lotus. 2018. "Big Data in China and the Battle for Privacy." Barton: Australian Strategic Policy Institute. https://www.aspi.org.au/report/big-data-china-and-battle-privacy

Ruiz, Pollyanna. 2013. "Revealing PowerMasked Protest and the Blank Figure." *Cultural Politics* 9 (3): 263–79. https://doi.org/10.1215/17432197-2346973

Ruppert, Evelyn, Engin Isin, and Didier Bigo. 2017. "Data Politics." *Big Data & Society* 4 (2): 1–7. https://doi.org/10.1177/2053951717717749

Russinovich, Mark. 2018. "Inside Azure Datacenter Architecture." Presented at Microsoft Ignite, Orlando, October 2. https://www.youtube.com/watch?v=D8hMu4jJAwo

Sack, Robert David. 1986. *Human Territoriality: Its Theory and History*. Cambridge: Cambridge University Press.

Sadowski, Jathan. 2019. "When Data Is Capital: Datafication, Accumulation, and Extraction." *Big Data & Society* 6 (1). https://doi.org/10.1177/2053951718820549

Sandfort, Sandy. 1993. "The Intelligent Island." *Wired*, April 1. https://www.wired.com/1993/04/sandfort/

Sassen, Saskia. 2009. *Territory, Authority, Rights: From Medieval to Global Assemblages*. Princeton: Princeton University Press.

Sassen, Saskia. 2013. "When Territory Deborders Territoriality." *Territory, Politics, Governance* 1 (1): 21–45.

Sassen, Saskia. 2014. *Expulsions: Brutality and Complexity in the Global Economy*. Cambridge, MA: Harvard University Press.

Sassen, Saskia. 2015a. "At the Systemic Edge." *Cultural Dynamics* 27 (1): 173–81. https://doi.org/10.1177/0921374014567395

Sassen, Saskia. 2015b. "An Interview with Saskia Sassen on Expulsions." Interview by School of Public Policy at Central European University. https://www.youtube.com/watch?v=FK8s3SK65hU

Sassen, Saskia. 2018. "Embedded Borderings: Making New Geographies of Centrality." *Territory, Politics, Governance* 6 (1): 5–15. https://doi.org/10.1080/21622671.2017.1290546

Satyanarayanan, M., P. Bahl, R. Caceres, and N. Davies. 2009. "The Case for VM-Based Cloudlets in Mobile Computing." *IEEE Pervasive Computing* 8 (4): 14–23. https://doi.org/10.1109/MPRV.2009.82

Schafran, Alex, and Jake Wegmann. 2012. "Restructuring, Race, and Real Estate: Changing Home Values and the New California Metropolis, 1989–2010." *Urban Geography* 33 (5): 630–54. https://doi.org/10.2747/0272-3638.33.5.630

Schmitt, Carl. 2005. *Political Theology: Four Chapters on the Concept of Sovereignty*. Chicago: University of Chicago Press.

Schmitt, Carl. 2006. *The Nomos of the Earth*. Translated by G. L. Ulmen. New York: Telos Press.

SCMP Reporter. 2010a. "Octopus Sold Personal Data of Customers for HK$44m." *South China Morning Post*, July 27. https://www.scmp.com/article/720620/octopus-sold-personal-data-customers-hk44m

SCMP Reporter. 2010b. "Octopus Escapes Penalty for Selling Data." *South China Morning Post*, October 19. https://www.scmp.com/article/727912/octopus-escapes-penalty-selling-data

SCMP Reporter. 2014. "The Masked Faces of Hong Kong's Occupy Protests." *South China Morning Post*, December 3. https://www.scmp.com/news/hong-kong/article/1654635/masked-faces-occupy-how-hong-kong-protesters-have-disguised-and

Scott, Mark. 2018. "Telcogeopolitics: West vs. China in 5G Race." *Politico*, July 1. https://www.politico.eu/article/5g-telecommunications-infrastructure-china-us-eu-qualcomm-nokia-ericsson-huawei/

Seng, Lim Tin. 2017. "Land From Sand: Singapore's Reclamation Story." *BiblioAsia* 13 (1). http://www.nlb.gov.sg/biblioasia/2017/04/04/land-from-sand-singapores-reclamation-story/

Seta, Gabriele de. 2018. "Into the Red Stack." *Hong Kong Review of Books* 香港書評, April 17. https://hkrbooks.com/2018/04/17/into-the-red-stack/

Shahbaz, Adrian. 2018. "Freedom on the Net 2018: The Rise of Digital Authoritarianism." New York: Freedom House. https://freedomhouse.org/report/freedom-net/freedom-net-2018/rise-digital-authoritarianism

Shen, Hong. 2018. "Building a Digital Silk Road? Situating the Internet in China's Belt and Road Initiative." *International Journal of Communication* 12: 19.

Shi, W., and S. Dustdar. 2016. "The Promise of Edge Computing." *Computer* 49 (5): 78–81. https://doi.org/10.1109/MC.2016.145

Shih, Philbert. 2019. "Infra // STRUCTURE." https://www.infrastructuresummit.io

Simone, AbdouMaliq. 2015. "Relational Infrastructures in Postcolonial Urban Worlds." In *Infrastructural Lives: Urban Infrastructure in Context*, edited by Stephen Graham and Colin McFarlane. London: Routledge.

SMH. 2005. "Nauru Child Detainees Running on Empty." *Sydney Morning Herald*, April 16. https://www.smh.com.au/world/nauru-child-detainees-running-on-empty-20050416-gdl52n.html

Smith, Jacob. 2019. "Finding Packet." Interview by Sean Tario. https://soundcloud.com/ilovedatacenters/packet-episode-035-jacob-smith

Soo, Zen. 2016. "Unicom Opens HK$3 Bn Data Center in Tseung Kwan O." *South China Morning Post*, August 18. https://www.scmp.com/business/companies/article/2005745/unicom-opens-hk3-bn-data-center-tseung-kwan-o

Stack, Tim. 2018. "Internet of Things (IoT) Data Continues to Explode Exponentially. Who Is Using That Data and How?" Cisco Blogs. February 5. https://blogs.cisco.com/datacenter/internet-of-things-iot-data-continues-to-explode-exponentially-who-is-using-that-data-and-how

Starosielski, Nicole. 2015a. "Fixed Flow: Undersea Cables as Media Infrastructure." In *Signal Traffic: Critical Studies of Media Infrastructures*, edited by Lisa Parks and Nicole Starosielski, 130–74. Chicago: University of Illinois Press.

Starosielski, Nicole. 2015b. *The Undersea Network*. Durham: Duke University Press.

Starosielski, Nicole. 2018. "Strangling the Internet." *Limn*, no. 10 (March). https://limn.it/articles/strangling-the-internet/

Steyerl, Hito. 2009. "In Defense of the Poor Image." *E-Flux Journal* 10 (11).

Storey, David. 2012. *Territories: The Claiming of Space*. London: Routledge.

Storey, David. 2020. *A Research Agenda for Territory and Territoriality*. Cheltenham, UK: Edward Elgar.

Strangio, Sebastian, and Vong Sokheng. 2009. "Sand Mining Spikes in Koh Kong Estuaries." *Phnom Penh Post*, March 10. https://www.phnompenhpost.com/national/sand-mining-spikes-koh-kong-estuaries

Strumpf, Dan. 2019. "Where China Dominates in 5G Technology." *Wall Street Journal*, February 27. https://www.wsj.com/articles/where-china-dominates-in-5g-technology-11551236701

Submarine Networks. 2019a. "APG." https://www.submarinenetworks.com/en/systems/intra-asia/apg

Submarine Networks. 2019b. "HK-G." https://www.submarinenetworks.com/en/systems/trans-pacific/hk-g

Submarine Networks. 2019c. "SJC." https://www.submarinenetworks.com/systems/intra-asia/sjc/sjc-cable-system

Sum, Ngai-Ling. 2018. "The Intertwined Geopolitics and Geoeconomics of Hopes/Fears: China's Triple Economic Bubbles and the 'One Belt One Road' Imaginary." *Territory, Politics, Governance* (October): 1–25. https://doi.org/10.1080/21622671.2018.1523746

SUNeVision Holdings. 2019. "AWS Direct Connect." IAdvantage. 2019. https://www.iadvantage.net/index.php/solutions-and-services/aws-direct-connect

Sverdlik, Yevgeniy. 2016. "Hong Kong, China's Data Center Gateway to the World." Data Center Knowledge. February 1. https://www.datacenterknowledge.com/archives/2016/02/01/hong-kong-data-center-market-growing-thanks-to-china-effect

Sverdlik, Yevgeniy. 2017. "Here Are the Submarine Cables Funded by Cloud Giants." Data Center Knowledge. March 3. https://www.datacenterknowledge.com/archives/2017/03/03/here-are-the-submarine-cables-funded-by-cloud-giants

Sverdlik, Yevgeniy. 2018. "When Air No Longer Cuts It: Inside Google's AI-Driven Shift to Liquid Cooling." Data Center Knowledge. July 31. https://www.datacenterknowledge.com/google-alphabet/when-air-no-longer-cuts-it-inside-google-s-ai-driven-shift-liquid-cooling

Sweeney, Latanya. 2002. "K-Anonymity: A Model for Protecting Privacy." *International Journal of Uncertainty, Fuzziness and Knowledge-Based Systems* 10 (5): 557–70.

Taiuru, Karaitiana. 2016. "Aotearoa Māori Internet Organisation." November 6. https://www.taiuru.maori.nz/publications/analysis-maori-ict-groups/aotearoa-maori-internet-organisaiton-amio/

Tan, Ben. 2018. "Two Rivers Dry Up in Johor, Allegedly from Sand-Mining." *Malay Mail*, November 4. https://www.malaymail.com/news/malaysia/2018/11/04/two-rivers-dry-up-in-johor-allegedly-from-sand-mining/1689811

Tan, Ern Ser. 2004. *Does Class Matter? Social Stratification and Orientations in Singapore*. Singapore: World Scientific.

Tay, Jessica Y. L., Shermaine K. M. Wong, L. M. Chou, and Peter A. Todd. 2018. "Land Reclamation and the Consequent Loss of Marine Habitats around the Ayer Islands, Singapore." *Nature in Singapore* 11: 1–5.

Tay, Kenneth. 2018. "Intelligent Island: A Media Theory of Singapore." Medium. April 5. https://medium.com/@kennethtaywh/intelligent-island-a-media-theory-of-singapore-1ab84a82bad

Tay, Kenneth. 2019. "Intelligent 'Island': Smart Nation and Its Liquid Futures." *So-Far*, February 2. https://www.so-far.online/issue-01-smart-cities/intelligent-island-smart-nation-and-its-liquid-futures

Taylor, Linnet, Luciano Floridi, and Bart Van der Sloot. 2016. *Group Privacy: New Challenges of Data Technologies*. Cham, Switzerland: Springer.

TeleGeography. 2019. "EAC-C2C." Submarine Cable Map. August 29. https://www.submarinecablemap.com/#/submarine-cable/eac-c2c

Telstra Global. 2019. "INDIGO Subsea Cable System between Australia and South East Asia Now Commissioned and Is Ready for Use." May 30. https://www.telstraglobal.com/insights/news/newsitem/indigo-subsea-cable-system-between-australia-and-south-east-asia-now-commissioned-and-is-ready-for-use

Terranova, Tizziana. 2018. "Data Mining the Body of the Socius." Staatliche Museen Zu Berlin. https://smart.smb.museum/export/downloadPM.php?id=5349

Tilouine, Joan, and Ghalia Kadiri. 2018. "A Addis-Abeba, le siège de l'Union africaine espionné par Pékin." *Le Monde*, January 26. https://www.lemonde.fr/afrique/article/2018/01/26/a-addis-abeba-le-siege-de-l-union-africaine-espionne-par-les-chinois_5247521_3212.html

Tomlinson, R. 1968. "A Geographic Information System for Regional Planning." Department of Forestry and Rural Development, Government of Canada.

Topolovic, Milica, Martin Knuessel, and Marcel Jaeggi. 2013. "Construction of Territory: Singapore's Expansion into the Sea." ETH Zurich. http://topalovic.arch.ethz.ch/wp-content/uploads/2014/04/ARCHITECTURE-OF-TERRITORY-HS12_Construction-of-Territory-Singapores-Expansion-into-the-Sea.pdf

Torres, Aurora, Jodi Brandt, Kristen Lear, and Jianguo Liu. 2017. "A Looming Tragedy of the Sand Commons." *Science* 357 (6355): 970–71. https://doi.org/10.1126/science.aao0503

Toscano, Alberto. 2014. "Lineaments of the Logistical State." *Viewpoint Magazine*, September 29. https://www.viewpointmag.com/2014/09/28/lineaments-of-the-logistical-state/

U.S. House Permanent Select Committee on Intelligence. 2012. *Investigation of the Security Threat Posed by Chinese Telecommunications Companies Huawei and ZTE*. Washington, DC: Select Committee on Intelligence. https://www.hsdl.org/?view&did=722516

Valerio, Pablo. 2018. "To Comply with GDPR, Most Data Should Remain at the Edge." IoT Times. October 31. https://iot.eetimes.com/to-comply-with-gdpr-most-data-should-remain-at-the-edge/

Veel, Kristin. 2017. "Uncertain Architectures: Performing Shelter and Exposure." *Imaginations Journal* 8 (2): 30–41.

Verma, P., and S. K. Sood. 2018. "Fog Assisted-IoT Enabled Patient Health Monitoring in Smart Homes." *IEEE Internet of Things Journal* 5 (3): 1789–96. https://doi.org/10.1109/JIOT.2018.2803201

Vincent, Danny. 2019. "How Apps Power Hong Kong's Leaderless Protests." *BBC News*, June 30. https://www.bbc.com/news/technology-48802125

Vocus Communications. 2018. "Australia Singapore Cable." https://australiasingaporecable.com/

Vocus Communications. 2019. "Data and Secure Networks: Reimagining Future Revenues." Vocus Communications. October 17. https://www.vocus.com.au/news/data-and-secure-networks-reimagining-future-revenues

Wagner, Daniel. 2019. "What China's Cybersecurity Law Says about the Future." *International Policy Digest* (blog), May 13. https://intpolicydigest.org/2019/05/13/what-china-s-cybersecurity-law-says-about-the-future/

Wakefield, Jane. 2019. "Hong Kong Protesters Using Bluetooth App." *BBC News*, September 3. https://www.bbc.com/news/technology-49565587

Wang, Cunrui, Qingling Zhang, Wanquan Liu, Yu Liu, and Lixin Miao. 2019. "Facial Feature Discovery for Ethnicity Recognition." *Wiley Interdisciplinary Reviews: Data Mining and Knowledge Discovery* 9 (1): e1278. https://doi.org/10.1002/widm.1278

Wang, Zhizheng. 2012. "Systematic Government Access to Private-Sector Data in China." *International Data Privacy Law* 2 (4): 220–29. https://doi.org/10.1093/idpl/ips017

Watkins, Josh. 2017. "Australia's Irregular Migration Information Campaigns: Border Externalization, Spatial Imaginaries, and Extraterritorial Subjugation." *Territory, Politics, Governance* 5 (3): 282–303. https://doi.org/10.1080/21622671.2017.1284692

Watts, Jonathan. 2013. "Brazil Demands Explanation from US over NSA Spying." *Guardian*, July 8. https://www.theguardian.com/world/2013/jul/08/brazil-demands-explanation-nsa-spying

Weber, Leanne. 2006. "The Shifting Frontiers of Migration Control." In *Borders, Mobility and Technologies of Control*, edited by Sharon Pickering and Leanne Weber, 21–43. Dordrecht: Springer Netherlands. http://link.springer.com/10.1007/1-4020-4899-8_2

Whitted, William H., and Gerald Aigner. 2007. Modular Data Center. Patent. United States US7278273B1, filed December 30, 2003, and issued October 9, 2007. https://patents.google.com/patent/US7278273B1/en

Winseck, Dwayne. 2017. "The Geopolitical Economy of the Global Internet Infrastructure." *Journal of Information Policy* 7: 228–67. https://doi.org/10.5325/jinfopoli.7.2017.0228

Winseck, Dwayne. 2019. "Internet Infrastructure and the Persistent Myth of U.S. Hegemony." In *Information, Technology and Control in a Changing World: Understanding Power Structures in the 21st Century*, edited by Blayne Haggart, Kathryn Henne, and Natasha Tusikov, 93–120. Cham, Switzerland: Springer International Publishing. https://doi.org/10.1007/978-3-030-14540-8_5

Wong, Joon Ian. 2016. "Google and Facebook Are Doubling Down on Internet Infrastructure with a New Pacific Cable." Quartz. October 18. https://qz.com/811032/google-goog-and-facebook-fb-are-building-a-new-transpacific-submarine-cable/

Wood, Lesley J. 2014. *Crisis and Control: The Militarization of Protest Policing*. London: Pluto Press.

World Economic Forum. 2018. "Data Policy in the Fourth Industrial Revolution: Insights on Personal Data." Geneva: World Economic Forum. http://www.unapcict.org/sites/default/files/2019-03/WEF.pdf

Yang, Nicholas. 2016. "HK Well-Positioned as Data Hub." Tseung Kwan O, Hong Kong, December 8. http://www.news.gov.hk/en/record/html/2016/12/20161208_162954.shtml

Ye, Josh. 2017. "UK-Based Global Switch Opens HK$5b Data Centre in Hong Kong." *South China Morning Post*, December 13. https://www.scmp.com/business/companies/article/2124188/hong-kongs-largest-data-centre-now-live-china-telecom-global-its

Yi, Shanhe, Zhengrui Qin, and Qun Li. 2015. "Security and Privacy Issues of Fog Computing: A Survey." In *International Conference on Wireless Algorithms, Systems, and Applications*, edited by Kuai Xu and Haojin Zhu, 685–95. New York: Springer.

Yu, Elaine. 2019. "'It Would Become Like Xinjiang': Surveillance-Savvy Hong Kong Protesters Go Digitally Dark." *Hong Kong Free Press* (blog), June 14. https://www.hongkongfp.com/2019/06/14/become-like-xinjiang-surveillance-savvy-hong-kong-protesters-go-digitally-dark/

Zakaria, Fareed. 2019. "The Blacklisting of Huawei Might Be China's Sputnik Moment." *Washington Post*, May 23. https://www.washingtonpost.com/opinions/global-opinions/the-blacklisting-of-huawei-might-be-chinas-sputnik-moment/2019/05/23/9352fc66-7d99-11e9-a5b3-34f3edf1351e_story.html

Zenz, Adrian. 2019. "'Thoroughly Reforming Them towards a Healthy Heart Attitude': China's Political Re-Education Campaign in Xinjiang." *Central Asian Survey* 38 (1): 102–28. https://doi.org/10.1080/02634937.2018.1507997

Zhang, Ben, Nitesh Mor, John Kolb, Douglas S. Chan, Nikhil Goyal, Ken Lutz, Eric Allman, John Wawrzynek, Edward Lee, and John Kubiatowicz. 2015. "The Cloud Is Not Enough: Saving Iot from the Cloud." In *Proceedings of the 7th USENIX Conference on Hot Topics in Cloud Computing*, 21–28. HotCloud'15. Berkeley, CA: USENIX Association. http://dl.acm.org/citation.cfm?id=2827719.2827740

Zhang, Michael. 2019. "Hong Kong Protester Lasers Are Frying Photographers' Cameras." Petapixel. August 26. https://petapixel.com/2019/08/26/hong-kong-protester-lasers-are-frying-photographers-cameras/

Zhou, Benjamin. 2016. "DJI May Hand Over Drone Data in Hong Kong to Chinese Government." *Hong Kong Transparency Project* (blog), April 22. http://transparency.jmsc.hku.hk/?p=1940

Zuboff, Shoshana. 2015. "Big Other: Surveillance Capitalism and the Prospects of an Information Civilization." *Journal of Information Technology* 30 (1): 75–89. https://doi.org/10.1057/jit.2015.5

Zuboff, Shoshana. 2019. *The Age of Surveillance Capitalism: The Fight for a Human Future at the New Frontier of Power*. New York: PublicAffairs.

ZWF0cHVzc3k. 2019. "R/HongKong—[8.3] Clothes, Drinks and One-Way Ticket Left on Ticket Machines at Jordan MTR Station for Others to Use." *Reddit*. https://www.reddit.com/r/HongKong/comments/cln3v5/83_clothes_drinks_and_oneway_ticket_left_on/

Index

Printed and bound by CPI Group (UK) Ltd, Croydon, CR0 4YY

09/06/2025

14686110-0001